LAHORE

Topophilia of Space and Place

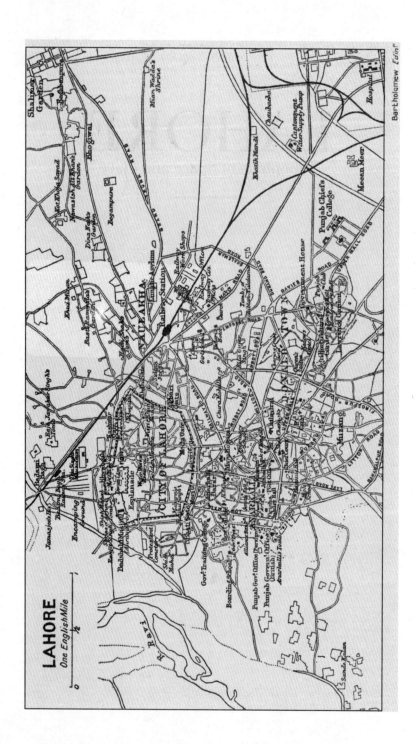

LAHORE

One English Mile

0   ½   1

Bartholomew Edin.ʳ

LAHORE

Topophilia of Space and Place

Anna Suvorova

TRANSLATED FROM RUSSIAN BY THE AUTHOR

FOREWORD BY
CARL W. ERNST

OXFORD
UNIVERSITY PRESS

OXFORD
UNIVERSITY PRESS

Oxford University Press is a department of the University of Oxford.
It furthers the University's objective of excellence in research, scholarship,
and education by publishing worldwide. Oxford is a registered trade mark of
Oxford University Press in the UK and in certain other countries

Published in Pakistan by
Oxford University Press
No. 38, Sector 15, Korangi Industrial Area,
PO Box 8214, Karachi-74900, Pakistan

ISBN 978-0-19-070645-6

Typeset in Adobe Garamond Pro
Printed on 68gsm Offset Paper

Printed by Kodwavi Printing Services, Karachi

CONTENTS

Acknowledgements   ix

Foreword by Carl W. Ernst   xi

1. On *Topophilia*   1

2. 'Lahore is Lahore'   21

3. Between Mosque and Tomb   49

4. The Name of the Garden: Shalimar and Others   77

5. The 'Immured Bride': A City Legend   105

6. 'Bread and Games!'   135

7. The City of Dreadful Night   163

8. Down the Cool Street   195

Epilogue: Lahore vs. Lucknow   219

Notes   227

Bibliography   244

Index   253

ACKNOWLEDGEMENTS

As the reader will no doubt see, this book was written under the impact of a deep affinity for Lahore. Yet, this affinity could not have arisen without the friendly participation and assistance of some people who encouraged my love for this remarkable city to deepen. They include, first and foremost, my friend and internationally renowned scholar, Professor Durre S. Ahmed, to whom this book is dedicated, and her family and friends—Shahid and Naazish Ata-Ullah, Anis and Amti Ata-Ullah, Tehmina Chaudhuri, Lubna Jehangir, and the famous sculptor Shahid Sajjad—who have made each of my stays in Lahore a celebration.

If truth be told, my interest in Lahore arose, even before my first visit to the city, at the London home of my dear friends Shakil and Farida Ahmad. Together with their children, Maham, Saadia, Asma, Ali Akbar, Tariq, and Naureen, they have become my second family and have always given me the feeling of being in Lahore even when I am in London.

I would like to express my heartfelt gratitude to the outstanding scholar Professor Carl W. Ernst, who found the time to write a wonderful foreword to this book despite his very busy schedule.

I am grateful to my friend Professor Vladimir Braginsky, who wrote the first favourable review of the Russian edition of the book in the *Bulletin of SOAS*.

I would like to thank my colleagues and friends in Russia, for their assistance at different stages of work on the book: Daniel Dynin for his help in translating the Russian text into English; Dr Ludmila Vasilyeva and Professor Natalia Chalisova for their advice on translating poetry from Urdu and Persian, respectively; and my friend and the great artist, Natalia Nesterova, for her financial support.

FOREWORD

Lahore is a city that creates loyalties. This thousand-year-old urban centre, in Pakistan's Punjab, has been an important political capital off and on for much of its history. At the same time, it has been a frequent target of invasion and conquest, typically by Central Asian nomadic empires but also by the Sikhs and the British. Despite its turbulent career, Lahore has somehow managed to be a cultural centre with a distinctive resonance and charm. I, myself, admit to having fallen under its spell long ago. Of course, scholars are supposed to claim objectivity so that they can occupy a position of lofty impartiality. In theory, such abstraction and distance is necessary to avoid charges of partisanship. Nevertheless, like many other visitors to the city, I have found that Lahore has an extraordinary charm that few other places can claim. *That* attraction is definitely worth exploring.

The book that you are holding is a remarkable investigation of attachment to place and space, which Anna Suvorova has addressed as topophilia. She has undertaken a thorough examination of the subject, with a topical organization that allows us to peruse the city of Lahore in a leisurely fashion, much like the Parisian *flâneurs* or urban wanderers that she extols as a model. Her study is richly informed with textual and architectural detail but without the oppressive detail of specialist history. While she makes a number of explicit comparisons between Lahore and other major cities, including the Muslim holy city of Mecca, the title of the second chapter ('Lahore is Lahore') makes a glancing allusion to a popular narrative about Lahore that needs to be shared here. As the story goes, an inhabitant of Lahore went to Mecca on pilgrimage, and accomplished the usual rituals with great satisfaction and delight. On completing the pilgrimage, he addressed the Almighty in prayer, saying, 'God! Your city is indeed wonderful and I am very happy to have visited but, in the end, Lahore is Lahore.' This frank and perhaps self-satisfied comment, ostensibly delivered by an unsophisticated Punjabi, states an honest truth: Lahore is the real centre of the cultural universe for its devotees. And, who are we to argue with this sentiment?

The author, Anna Suvorova, has special qualifications to undertake this study. A Russian scholar who has specialized in the study of Urdu literature, Suvorova has written about Urdu poetry (especially *masnavi*) and Sufi shrines in South Asia. She has also contributed an earlier monograph on another important Indo-Muslim city, Lucknow. This affectionate study of Lahore was originally written in Russian, and is now presented in a lucid English translation for a wider readership.

While reading through this book, I found myself returning, in spirit, to this city where I lived for a year in 1986, returning occasionally for memorable visits in later years. My family and I have experienced a remarkable culture there, spending precious time, on a daily basis, with artists, musicians, poets, diplomats, politicians, and scholars. Our landmarks were the great Sufi shrines, Mughal forts and mosques, and the old walled city and environs of Anarkali; from there, one passed from Punjab University to Lawrence Gardens (now Bagh-e Jinnah) via the Mall, and then headed out to the suburbs of Gulberg and Lahore Cantonment. We were fortunate to have an amazing friend in Maharaj Ghulam Husain (d. 2001), the great master of kathak dance, who introduced us to the full range of cultural possibilities in the city. Looked at from that perspective and memory, it has been a moving experience to read through this superb synthesis, which has brought together so many remarkable perspectives on the city of Lahore.

Suvorova rightly begins with a theoretical overview of the nature of personal attachment to place and space. Topophilia is an apt term for this deeply human sentiment, and the insights of Yi-Fu Tuan and Gaston Bachelard are indeed helpful for zooming in on the specific character of this phenomenon. The author then takes us through a multi-levelled exploration of the architecture and urban space of Lahore, which she convincingly describes as a palimpsest—a document that has been overwritten repeatedly, without erasing the comments of earlier writers. The authors she investigates include Indo-Persian poets, Mughal chroniclers, European travellers (from Elizabethan England to Czarist Russia), British colonial officials, as well as modern Urdu short story writers. The gardens and monuments of Lahore come to life for us through the words of the poet Amir Khusraw, the Emperor Jahangir, and Rudyard Kipling, all of whom had intimate links to the city. The author is not fearful of lingering over fascinating questions, such as the massive Bollywood film portrayals of the doomed romance of Anarkali and Prince Salim. She even takes the reader on a tour of the European fantasies of Lahore, in orientalist literature and opera. She vividly evokes the springtime rituals of *basant*, with its competitive kite-flying contests. She brings the reader up-to-date with dinner at Cuckoo's Den, the restaurant/ art gallery in the red light district that is now an obligatory stop for those who wish to savour a magnificent view of the city along with the fabulous cuisine of Lahore. For anyone who has spent time in the city, this richly documented essay furnishes a valuable and insightful overview of the many reasons why Lahore has many devotees.

It is all the more sobering, then, to recall recent events and see effects of the devastating acts of violence that have been inflicted upon Lahore, as they have much of the rest of Pakistan. Political opponents, foreign athletes, religious minorities, and even the great Sufi shrines have been the targets of these attacks. While the solution to such a crisis must lie outside the scope of a book like this, nevertheless, Anna Suvorova deserves our gratitude for pointing out the way in which Lahore has repeatedly survived invasion and catastrophe. What makes the topophilia of Lahore so distinctive? She persuasively argues that it is the Punjabi ethnic and cultural substratum that provides the solid character underlying the city of Lahore. I think there is truth in this observation, and I believe that Lahore will draw upon its immense cultural resources to face and overcome its current challenges—which is why one can affirm the distinctive love the city generates and that is inherent in the statement, 'Lahore is Lahore'.

CARL W. ERNST

Walled City, Lahore.

CHAPTER **ONE**

On *Topophilia*

The Cities are full of pride,
Challenging each to each—
This from her mountain-side,
That from her burthened beach.

* * *

And the men that breed from them
They traffic up and down,
But cling to their cities' hem
As a child to their mother's gown.

—RUDYARD KIPLING

In the ocean of terms used in the humanities and social sciences today, there is a word that very aptly describes the subject of this book. The word is *topophilia*. The term *topophilia*, which literally means 'love for place', is extremely rich in semantic meaning and is widely used in contemporary philosophy, psychology, sociology, and cultural studies, although it arose in the field of humanistic geography— an authoritative discipline at the junction of geography and other humanities and social sciences.

The term *topophilia* was introduced into scientific usage by the leading expert on humanistic geography Yi-Fu Tuan (born 1930), an

American scholar of Chinese origin, who proposed a new approach to studying the relationship between man and the environment in his book *Topophilia: a study of environmental perception, attitudes, and values*.[1] Yi-Fu Tuan did not invent this neologism but borrowed it from the outstanding twentieth-century Anglo-American poet W.H. Auden, turning a poetic image into a scholarly term.

According to Yi-Fu Tuan, *topophilia* can be defined widely so as to include all emotional connections between physical environment and human beings, the philosophical and psychological notion of identity, and the mental and emotional sense of belonging of an individual to a certain place, location, and space. *Topophilia*, the affective bond between people and place, is the primary theme of this book which examines environmental perceptions and values at different levels: the species, the group, and the individual. Yi-Fu Tuan holds culture and environment, and *topophilia* and environment, as distinct in order to show how they mutually contribute to the formation of values. *Topophilia* examines the search for environment in the city, suburb, countryside, and wilderness from a dialectical perspective, distinguishes different types of environmental experience, and describes their character.[2]

Europeans clearly associate the term *topophilia* with the classical concept of the *genius loci*, which refers to the unique nature, the cultural and aesthetic dimension, and the emotional perception of a certain place, be it a natural landscape or a city with its streets and buildings. Nevertheless, *topophilia* is a lot broader than *genius loci*. One reason is that *topophilia* is used in very diverse contexts from geopolitics and bioregionalism to interpersonal relations and the 'sense of home'.

More generally, *topophilia* is a palimpsest in the post-modern sense of the word—a certain 'text' that is written over other 'texts' of material and spiritual culture, which persists to show through its semantics and 'style'. Such 'overwriting' is fundamentally impossible without overlapping inter-textual meanings. In *topophilia*, just as in the palimpsest, it is impossible to separate the outer from the inner, and to differentiate between superimposed semantic nuances and autochthonous meaning, because the latter consists of the former. Understood in such a way, the 'text' gets a history and 'acquires memory'. Thus, for *topophilia*, the memory of a place and its mental reconstruction and intuitive perception are no less important than empiric experiment and rational analysis.

The philosophical basis of *topophilia*, and of the related field of humanistic geography, is considered to be the phenomenology of Edmund Husserl (1859–1938). Phenomenology was only a particular example of the general emergence of anti-scientific trends in the humanities and social sciences from the 1930s onwards. It led to an appeal to shift the focus of research to the subject, and to study man as an object and subject of consciousness—which is the core of the phenomenological method. Such an appeal was an alternative to positivism and objective knowledge, which were mostly identified with one another. The crisis of positivism led to the rapidly growing prestige of phenomenology and related 'humanistic' trends in anthropology, sociology, geography, and other disciplines.

To a considerable extent, phenomenology was created as a basis for the subsequent development of the social and natural sciences. Husserl, in his article for *Encyclopaedia Britannica* in 1927, wrote:

> 'The term "phenomenology" designates two things: a new kind of descriptive method which made a breakthrough in philosophy at the turn of the century, and an a priori science derived from it; a science which is intended to supply the basic instrument *(Organon)* for a rigorously scientific philosophy and, in its consequent application, to make possible a methodical reform of all the sciences.'[3]

Husserl's phenomenology attracted social scientists because of its fundamental approach to posing problems. One can re-read his texts repeatedly and, as one's understanding grows, find something new each time. Husserl's works stimulate scholarly research even when they are not directly connected with the reader's and scholar's field of interests. This is generally true of all classic works, including works of philosophy.

Husserl turned to a new problem: understanding reality as a holistic and continuous process of consciousness. This problem interested many people and, in particular, writers, artists, and musicians. It was particularly well-reflected in literature, especially in Marcel Proust's

In Search of Lost Time and James Joyce's *Ulysses*. Such books pointed to fundamental changes in Western consciousness. Husserl's merit lies in the fact that he perceived these changes and reoriented philosophy in a totally new direction.

Social scientists were particularly attracted to Husserl's later concept on the *Lebenswelt* (lifeworld), which is the foundation of the meaning of all human knowledge and is closely connected to the concept of *topophilia*. In contrast to the world of science, which is constructed and idealized, the *Lebenswelt* is not created artificially. One does not need a special theoretic approach to see it because every individual is clearly and directly given a *Lebenswelt*. The *Lebenswelt* is a pre-reflective given; it is the foundation on which all sciences are built. Scientific knowledge depends on a more meaningful and elevated pre-scientific (or non-scientific, to be more precise) consciousness which consists of a certain 'totality of givens'.

The *Lebenswelt* is the domain of the 'immediately obvious' that is known to all, and of the 'circle of certainties' that are treated with long-established trust. This leads to the phenomenological motto *Zu den Sachen selbst!* ('To the things themselves!'), i.e., back to living life.

An important role was also played by the fact that Husserl developed these ideas after going through a scientific period during which he tried to make philosophy a strict science. This gave humanistic trends in science greater authority, and seemed to demonstrate that the logical and general path leads from scientism to anti-scientism and humanistic approaches. This occurred in philosophy and psychology, as well as in geographic science. When the term *topophilia* arose in the 1960s, such a basis served as a powerful argument in favour of the humanistic approach.

A particularly attractive aspect of Husserl's phenomenology, which contributed to its rapid spread among the individual sciences, is the fact that it sets down a direction of work yet does not specify any details or demand that its approach be observed to the letter. Although it contains the principles of a research programme, they are not clearly defined and can be used fairly freely depending on one's scholarly values and research area. This flexibility is one of the secrets of phenomenology's success and its sustained influence on twentieth-century science.

Phenomenology has a broad and extensive area of application. The main requirement of the phenomenological method is that the study of the object be either consciousness or reality seen through the prism of consciousness. Phenomenology is irrelevant if consciousness is not taken into account. It might seem that the emphasis on human consciousness makes phenomenology a rather narrow discipline. However, if one views consciousness as a filter between subject and object, one sees that phenomenological philosophy can be used in virtually every area of scholarly study. Phenomenological philosophy is applicable anywhere that a subject and object exist.

Thus, *topophilia* studies the natural and man-made environment using the phenomenological method, i.e., through the prism of human consciousness. Nevertheless, it should be kept in mind that phenomenology examines a special type of consciousness that Husserl and other phenomenologists construct as the object of phenomenological analysis. Everyday consciousness is nothing but a starting point here.

This 'refined' consciousness is constructed through phenomenological reduction, which strips it of everything empirical. The first stage is 'eidetic reduction', which essentially puts reality in brackets. The result is pure subjectivity. During the second stage, all one's notions about consciousness and spiritual processes are also put in brackets. This allows one to attain a transcendental phenomenological level. So far, no one has managed to fully perform this procedure in the individual humanities and social sciences.

According to the principles of phenomenology, a scholar must learn to treat consciousness as an infinite stream of experiences. A particularly important notion is the 'phenomenon', through which one perceives the world. The phenomenon is an element of the stream of truth experiences. It is immediate evidence that is not the product of reflection.

The phenomenological method consists of several stages. During the first stage, trust in intuitive-contemplative cognition is restored. Then, the possibility of the intuitive apprehension of truth is clarified. Finally, the scholar turns to the phenomenon and directly enters the stream of consciousness. The phenomenological method also has other moments, such as the cultivation of the special role of 'phenomenological imagination'.

This brief foray into Husserl's phenomenology was necessary to explain the origin and presence of the word *topophilia* in the title of my book. *Topophilia* belongs to the 'circle of givens' and the *Lebenswelt*; instead of being constructed rationally, it is given to us in the phenomenological experience of consciousness. Lacking a philosophical frame of mind and the necessary qualifications, I shall not pretend that my study fully corresponds to the phenomenological discourse. Nevertheless, as a long-term admirer of Husserl's work and a devotee of literature and art that make use of ideas and images close to phenomenology, I could not deny myself the pleasure of incorporating my field of study into the 'universal horizon'[4] of the *Lebenswelt*. In other words, I would like to make the reader see an Asian city (in this case, Lahore) as a phenomenon of subjective and relativistic experience in which we are simultaneously the subjects that constitute this world in our consciousness and also objects of the *Lebenswelt*.

Returning to *topophilia*, I should say that the study of 'space and place' (the title of another well-known monograph by Yi-Fu Tuan) has become a popular theme of phenomenological research. The most influential example has been the wonderful book by the philosopher Gaston Bachelard (1884–1962), entitled *The Poetics of Space* (1958),[5] that studies the 'domesticated' space of the home, from the cellar to the attic, and its place in the outside world and in human consciousness. The objects of phenomenological analysis are doors, closets, drawers, shelves, attics, and nooks with their 'dialectics of outside and inside' and 'phenomenology of roundness'.

'I shall prove that imagination augments the values of reality,' Bachelard wrote about the aims of his book, 'a sort of attraction for images concentrates them about the house. Transcending our memories of all the houses in which we have found shelter, above and beyond all the houses we have dreamed we lived in, can we isolate an intimate, concrete essence that would be a justification of the uncommon value of our images of protected intimacy? This, then, is the main problem.'[6] He continues, 'Now my aim is clear: I must show that the house is one of the greatest powers of integration for the thoughts, memories and dreams of mankind. The binding principle in this integration is the daydream.'[7]

Bachelard's method, outlined in these citations, seems extremely attractive to me, all the more so as it was brilliantly expressed, many years earlier, in the spatial images of Bachelard's great countryman, Marcel Proust. Travelling little during his lifetime because of his ill-health, Proust kept creating literary images of cultural and geographic spaces—in particular, of cities that he wanted to visit.

Bachelard's intonation becomes very Proustian at times:

> 'When we dream of the house we were born in, in the utmost depths of reverie, we participate in this original warmth, in this well-tempered matter of the maternal paradise. This is the environment in which the protective beings live. We shall come back to the maternal features of the house. For the moment, I should like to point out the original fullness of the house's being. Our daydreams carry us back to it. And the poet well knows that the house holds childhood motionless "in its arms".'[8]

The similarity to Proust's prose, which is highly authentic in its subjectivism, convinces me that Bachelard was correct. Indeed, imagination considerably increases the value of reality and, to remain in the protective cover of this value in new circumstances, we surround the image of every new place–be it a home, street, or city—with the fences of our recollections of places where we lived before and were apparently happy. Without such phenomenological reduction, *topophilia* turns into its opposite (*topophobia*) because unfamiliar, 'unenclosed', and 'uninhabited' space taken 'in itself', without a protective structure of memories, dreams, and imagination, inevitably appears hostile to the human psyche.

Like the home, the city is opposed to the open place—the boundless, unstructured, and 'undomesticated' space that is the symbol of chaos. When founding a city, one stakes out a humanized space and breaks the seasonal, natural, and climatic cycle in which a peasant lives. The city is a place that gives the individual shelter, protection, and safety in the space of *topophobia*. The individual needs the city to overcome his horror of the void. A city is made up of walls, roofs, vaults, and towers that protect us from the onslaught of jungles and deserts. Cities are built on borders, protect borders, and always remain metaphysical *frontiers*.

The forms of organization of secular space have always been based on the respective organization of sacral space; there have always been specific means for transforming secular space into transcendent space. The act of founding a city is comparable to drawing a boundary that separates cosmos from chaos, culture from barbarity, and the 'familiar' from the 'foreign'.

Two spaces meet and intersect in the city: the chorological[9] (geographic) space and the symbolic space of consciousness. Cities are marked by semantic concentration, density of meaning, and psychological tension. A city is a place that is oversaturated with meaning, history, recollections, and signs. Etiological myths and legends about the origin of cities attach particular importance to the choice of place on which a city is built. The founders of cities are said to be deities, cultural heroes, kings, and saints.

The idea of the city, or more precisely the dream about the city, presupposes the existence of a transcendental reality (in the spirit of notions about Heavenly Jerusalem)[10] that has either always existed or was first lost and then manifested to new generations. The city is an attempt to regain lost paradise. Each city has its own mythological or quasi-historic prototype that it tries to imitate. To a certain extent, the foundation of a city is a repetition of the myth about the creation of the world. The human sacrifices that were often made when the foundations of cities, city walls, or towers were laid correspond to the original cosmogonic sacrifice.

The city re-creates the model of the world of a given culture, and reveals the hierarchic structure of the cosmos and levels of the universe. The city brings together the heavens, the earth, and the underworld. If a city is built on hills, like Rome, the image of the world mountain establishes the vertical tie between the earth and the heavens. If a city is located in the plains, this symbolic function is performed by manmade 'hills'—forts, towers, domes, and temples. The city has a 'protected' centre surrounded by walls, an inhabited periphery, and outer boundaries. These boundaries are permeable and surmountable, and every city wall has at least one gate, i.e., a breach and point of entry. For this reason, the city also represents the idea of surmounting obstacles and transgressing boundaries, both spatial and spiritual. A city gate can be compared to both the gate of heaven and the gate of hell.

The mythologem of the city is ambivalent: the city is perceived as both heaven and hell. The heavenly city is a place where gardens are laid out and palaces are built, where prayers are recited and rituals are performed—in a word, a place where culture and history are made. Such cities are guarded by patron saints and saved by righteous men.[11] The 'heavenly city' is axiologically, ideologically, and aesthetically compared to the most authoritative city model in a given culture: Moscow as the Third Rome, St. Petersburg as the Northern Palmyra, Amsterdam as the Northern Venice, etc. Lahore, the subject of this book, has most often been compared to the capital of Safavid Iran—Isfahan.

At the same time, the city harbours all the evils of the world and contains all the vices and diseases of civilization. In a city, it is difficult to resist the countless temptations and sins that lead to degradation and doom. Cities are called the 'Whore of Babylon', compared to Sodom and Gomorrah, damned by God, and doomed to destruction—for example, Tyr, Sidon, and Nineveh. Much in a city seems transitory and artificial, and thus lifeless and illusory.

In the Biblical and Christian tradition,[12] the 'infernal city' is usually compared to Babylon because Babylon is a synonym for every big city that is full of arrogance and sin. The title 'New Babylon' has been applied, at different times and for different reasons, to Rome (by the Christian apostles), Florence under the House of Medici, Paris during the Second Empire, and modern-day New York whose skyscrapers are often compared to the Tower of Babel—the symbol of human vanity and challenge to God's power. In our time, multicultural megalopolises, marked by hubbub and the mixture of tongues, have come to be inseparably associated with Babylon. This is shown, in particular, by the witty English neologism 'Babylondon'.

The image of the infernal city, the den of crime and vice, often appears in literature. It suffices to recall Eugène Sue's Paris, Dickens' London, and Dostoyevsky's St. Petersburg. As we will see below, Lahore's literary image also did not escape infernalization; Kipling called Lahore the 'city of dreadful night' in his short story of the same name.

Thus, every city lies at the boundary between different worlds and stands between heaven and hell. Not only does it soar upwards but it also totters at the edge of the abyss. It is unclear who or what prevents it from falling—a strong government or saints and righteous men. It is impossible to hide a city's vices, for it is said in the New Testament that 'a city built on a hill cannot be hidden.'[13] Every city lives out its fate and, like an individual, receives retribution for its virtues and vices.

The city is a place of free choice, risk, trial, and personal growth. In other words, it is an existential space. The city is not simply a lifestyle and a way of organizing the psychological and spiritual space of man, but also the result of man's awareness of himself as a metaphysical being. The city sets down the maximal and extreme human scale, relates human and super-human origins, and serves as an embodiment of the divine plan for man. The city bears the idea of man's escape from the chthonic power of the earth, his freedom from dependence on nature, and his breakthrough into a transcendent space.

It is no surprise that the city, as a fundamental phenomenon of civilization, has long become an object of study for many philosophical, psychological, and culturological schools and fields. Patrick Geddes and Lewis Mumford, two outstanding Anglo-American urban theorists of the early twentieth century, strove to incorporate knowledge about the city from different historic periods into a single unified system. They treated the city as an organism and uncovered organic unity behind the confusion, noise, hubbub, and disorder of city life. They viewed the city as a spatially connected entity that embodies a special kind of lifestyle with a clear spatial and social division of labour, a specific relationship to the outside world, and an evolutionary linearity (civilization and progress). These classics strove to present the city as a socio-spatial system with an inner development of its own.

Nevertheless, urban studies also have a different and later tradition that is marked by the attempt to capture the unsystematic banality of everyday city life in its many dimensions. For the philosopher Henri Lefebvre, author of the *Critique of Everyday Life* (1947), the city 'incorporates "daily life", defined as recurrent human and material practices, the "everyday" as an existential or phenomenological condition, and "everydayness" understood as a kind of immanent life force running through everything, a single and boundless space-time for "living", flowing through time and space.'[14]

This new urbanism—the urbanism of daily life—is founded on the desire to grasp a phenomenality that cannot be understood through theory or consciousness alone. The urbanism of daily life must penetrate into the mixture of flesh and stone, human and inorganic, emotions and actions. To understand a city, which cannot be grasped through one's consciousness, one must have the courage to delve into the domain of the instinctive and the unconscious.

These are the aims of *psychogeography*—a radical field created by an 'extreme left' group of French intellectuals (the so-called Lettrists) in the mid-1950s. Guy Debord, a member of the group, defined *psychogeography* as follows:

> 'Psychogeography sets for itself the study of the precise laws and specific effects of the geographical environment, whether consciously organized or not, on the emotions and behavior of individuals. The charmingly vague adjective psychogeographical can be applied to the findings arrived at by this type of investigation, to their influence on human feelings, and more generally to any situation or conduct that seems to reflect the same spirit of discovery.'[15]

As *psychogeography* also traces its origins to phenomenology, its method combines, by definition, subjective and objective approaches to its object of study—the urban environment.

Psychogeography is a critical discipline that studies the impact of the urban environment (streets, boulevards, courtyards, squares, roads, and architectural structures) on the emotions, mood, and behaviour of individuals and social groups living in this environment. The discipline emerged in 1953 when several young members of the artistic bohemian set decided to study Paris, to uncover new and 'revolutionary' possibilities that were present 'here and now'. Thus, *psychogeography* was not an academic discipline from the start.

Subsequently, in the 1960s, *psychogeography* was developed by the leftist intellectual and political group, the 'Situationists', as a critique of capitalist urbanism. At the same time, *psychogeography*, as an immediate and daily practice, emerged sporadically and flourished here and there in the anarchic, countercultural, and radical democratic milieu of the Western bohemians and those at the political margins. For the Situationists and their followers, *psychogeography* was an alternative and experimental way of creatively spending time, or a game for cultivating revolutionary attitudes among individuals. *Psychogeography* emphasizes that awareness of the ideological pressure of the social milieu is an essential condition for a productive and consistent critique of modern society.

The main method of *psychogeography* is the *dérive* (or *drift* in English), which means to stroll 'aimlessly' through a city in order to perceive and capture the feelings and ideas evoked by concrete urban landscapes. Merlin Coverley in his book 'Psychogeography' (2006) writes, 'At the very heart of Psychogeography is a contradiction: the dérive. The aimless wandering, the fact that there is no direction, you follow your own impulse; you follow your feet basically, and where they take you. The difficulty is trying to staple that onto a preordained set of ideas.'[16]

Yet one needs creative reflection and risk to draw up imaginary psychogeographic 'mental maps' of a city that could contribute to the revolutionary transformation of society. 'Mental mapping' is an extremely interesting form of cultural activity that brings *psychogeography* together with conceptual art, 'hypergraphics', and graffiti: it is no accident that artists predominated among early psychogeographers. As *psychogeography*, like conceptual art, contains a lot of play and irony, 'mental maps' were often drawn on a landscape in the shape of the nude female body (one of Guy Debord's best-known topographic collages is called *The Naked City*). The stroller's path was marked by thick red arrows, as on military maps.

A 'mental map' shows a city as it *should* be; as if the psychogeographer was describing the city for the first time. In 1957, Guy Debord presented 'an example of mapping of atmospheric unities of a city on the basis of ideas of the international Lettrist and Situationist movement. The map of Paris has been cut up in different areas that are experienced by some people as distinct unities (neighbourhoods). The mentally felt distance between these areas are visualized by spreading out the pieces of the cut up map. By wandering, letting oneself float or drift (dérive is the French word used) each person can discover his or her own ambient unities of a specific city. The red arrows indicate the most frequent used crossings between the islands of the urban archipel (separated by flows of motorized traffic).'[17]

'Mental mapping' continues to be quite popular today, including in Great Britain. The well-known, ironical, and sensational 'mental map', *Babylondon*, is a map of the London Underground superimposed on a physical map of Iraq. It resembles a respectable tourist guide that selects special routes and describes their histories in an entertaining fashion to make the city attractive to visitors. Such a method of constructing a subjective landscape of London, based on drift and personal fancies for certain places, is used by serious authors such as the writer Peter Ackroyd and the poet Iain Sinclair.

Today, *psychogeography* has essentially become part of the art of performance. The work of Iain Sinclair has led many readers and spectators to take an interest in *psychogeography* without any knowledge of the revolutionary activities of the French Lettrists and Situationists. Sinclair, convincingly, showed the value of the observations of a drifter, who roams about the streets of a big city, discovering new features in the familiar landscape every time. Moreover, he connected *psychogeography* and drift with a certain tradition of world literature and the work of Edgar Allan Poe (the title of his short story, 'The Man of the Crowd', has become a psychogeographic term), William Blake, Charles Baudelaire, Thomas De Quincey, and other classic writers who have used the romantic, symbolic, and expressionistic perceptions of a city to describe and artistically transform its image.

It should be said that, in addition to the literary tradition, *psychogeography* has made use of the experiences of the 'physiological sketch'—a genre of documentary prose in the nineteenth century. This genre includes works such as Balzac's cycle *Disappearing Paris*, Dickens' *Sketches by Boz*, and Gilyarovsky's *Moscow and the Muscovites*. The physiological sketch demonstrated the city's seamy side and social evils, as well as curious incidents of city life. This genre was borrowed by literature from the visual arts, particularly from the prints of

Jacques Callot, William Hogarth, and Honoré Daumier who created a gallery of the most colourful types of citizens and street scenes.

'Mental mapping' has also been fruitfully employed by Peter Ackroyd, author of the book *London: The Biography* (2000).[18] Ackroyd draws his London map up along a number of principal lines on which lie special 'protected' places that neither time nor natural disaster nor human activities can affect. Such places preserve memories of themselves and the social groups inhabiting them, exerting an impact on the personalities and lifestyles of the city dwellers of later generations. This inner inertia of the city, that lives according to its own laws, can be seen from the history of a single crossing in the centre of London (the former St. Giles Parish)—where a leper house was located in the twelfth century, gallows and a prison in the fifteenth century, and the Great Plague of London began in the seventeenth century. William Hogarth depicted this area in his series of engravings *Gin Lane* and *A Harlot's Progress*. In the nineteenth century, this cursed place turned into the terrible slum, Rookeries. Attempts by the city government to improve the district were fruitless.

The fact that *psychogeography* can also serve as an excellent tool for creating the image of an Asian city was brilliantly demonstrated by the book *Istanbul: Memories and the City* by the Nobel laureate Orhan Pamuk.[19] Pamuk himself has said on numerous occasions that his image of Istanbul took shape during his youth, when he wanted to become an artist and roamed about the city looking for models, i.e., engaged in a drift of sorts. A true product of *topophilia*, Pamuk's book is simultaneously a biography of the city and an autobiography of the author. In his interviews, Pamuk has repeatedly referred to the German culturologist Walter Benjamin, a cult figure of the psychogeographic community, who said that there were two kinds of books on cities: one written by people who have lived in a city all their lives, experienced it from the inside and, as a result, create a book of memoirs; the other is written by travellers who focus on the city's outer appearance, historic facts, and exotic aspects. Naturally, Pamuk, who has lived in Istanbul all his life, wrote a book of memoirs. Pamuk views Istanbul retrospectively, from the standpoint of a Turkish boy who passionately wanted to be an artist yet changed his mind and became a Nobel laureate in literature.

Pamuk's book has a pronounced psychogeographic foundation: he poses questions about the beauty of the urban landscape, why certain parts of the city seem beautiful to us while others do not, and why the city strikes us as beautiful, time and again, as we walk down its streets. In the mid-nineteenth century, the famous French writers Gustav Flaubert, Gerard de Nerval, and Théophile Gautier visited Istanbul and created an image of the city for Europeans. Their descriptions of Istanbul influenced the next generation of Turkish writers. Pamuk incorporated his personal experiences and childhood memories into this literary tradition of city image-making. The immediate and everyday perception of Istanbul, by the subject, constitutes the phenomenological experience of the city as an object; at the same time, the city itself has an influence on the spiritual growth of the subject—the man, the city dweller, and the author. While Pamuk's book has a lot of merit, including its literary virtue, it became internationally famous because of its powerful *topophilic* effect, thanks to which a reader who has never visited Istanbul becomes incorporated into its unique cultural and geographic space.

According to Pamuk, the beauty of the Istanbul landscape derives from a feeling of melancholy that stems from a certain existential loss. In the Turkish historic context, Pamuk is referring to the loss of status of the capital of the Ottoman Empire (and, earlier, of the Byzantine Empire). The cultural and geographic space of past imperial capitals, such as Rome, Delhi, and Vienna, have a particularly deep semantic layer in which relics of power and glory, and an explosive mixture of pride and nostalgia, have coexisted for centuries, making up the 'complex of an imperial capital'. Still, this is true only if, after the collapse of the empire, its capital remains a capital, be it of a new state. Otherwise, after a city ceases to be a capital, it is marked more by nostalgia than pride, and also develops a complex of provincial 'inferiority'.

This characterizes, among others, the *topophilia* of the Indian city of Lucknow, formerly the flourishing capital of the powerful Muslim principality of Awadh and now the capital of the state of Uttar Pradesh. In the eighteenth and nineteenth centuries, the image of Lucknow was marked by the *Lakhnawiyat* or 'Grand Style' to which all aspects of city life (architecture, court etiquette, art, literature, pastimes, and amusements) were subordinated. The same style led Lucknow's citizens to treat the city as an object and subject of exclusive value. The Grand Style shaped the city's most socially and aesthetically important, and 'marked', places (streets, buildings, and fragments of the urban landscape) and gave society, as a whole, a sense of belonging to these places, i.e., constituted Lucknow's *topophilia*.

However, the city's lifestyle and social and religious makeup were greatly transformed in the twentieth century, and the nature of the city's *topophilia* changed along with it. Although it continues to be a capital, present-day Lucknow bears the marks of 'second-rate' provincialism; its nostalgic spirit, which is the subject of my earlier book *Nostalgia for Lucknow*,[20] stems primarily from the feelings caused by the loss of the city's former power and splendour, i.e., from the onerous 'complex of a former capital'.

Lahore, just like St. Petersburg and Isfahan, has a very special status. Formerly the capital of two empires, and today simply the capital of the Pakistani Punjab province, it nevertheless remains a cultural capital and, most importantly, the pride of all of Pakistan.

Books about Lahore and its history, architecture, gardens, and cultural objects would fill an entire library. Lahore was mentioned by the historians of the Delhi Sultanate and the Mughal Empire although, in keeping with the laws of the genre of medieval chronicles, they wrote more about the court's place of residence than about city life. As is the case with Istanbul, the image of Lahore as a distinctive cultural and geographic space was first created by European travellers and Romantic writers (for example, Thomas Moore in his poem *Lalla Rookh*). In keeping with Walter Benjamin's classification, their accounts focused on the fanciful architecture (from the Western standpoint), the bustling and colourful crowds, and the exotic customs. A holistic and vivid artistic image of the city was undoubtedly first created by Rudyard Kipling, who lived in Lahore for many years and knew it just as well as the natives. In the twentieth century, Kipling's work was continued, first by Indian and then by Pakistani authors writing in Urdu; Lahore became the setting and object of description of an array of Urdu literature. The work of Muhammad Iqbal, Faiz Ahmed Faiz, Saadat Hasan Manto, Intizar Hussain, and many other well-known Urdu writers is inseparably tied to Lahore.

The first serious historical and cultural studies of Lahore began to appear in the late nineteenth century. The most important of them, vis-à-vis the number of facts and abundance of cited written sources, is still Syad Muhammad Latif's book *Lahore: Its History, Architectural Remains, and Antiquities* (1892).[21]

After the partition of India, and the establishment of Pakistan, in 1947 many intellectuals—Hindus, Sikhs, and Englishmen—were compelled to leave Lahore. In their recollections, Lahore eternally remains a lost paradise and the city of one's dreams. Some of these memoirs appear in the best book on Lahore of the past decade—the collection of essays, articles, narrative prose, and poetry edited by the well-known Pakistani writer Bapsi Sidhwa and entitled *Beloved City: Writings on Lahore*.[22] Thanks to its variety of themes, approaches, and genres, this book creates a stereoscopic image of city life.

Unlike Athens, Jerusalem, and Benares, Lahore does not rank among the world's oldest cities. Nevertheless, its written history goes back approximately ten centuries to the time when Lahore became the capital of the Ghaznavid Empire in the eleventh century. Moreover, it is believed that Lahore was mentioned by Ptolemy, as *Labokla*, as far back as the second century. Clearly, such a long history makes it difficult to write an exhaustive historical description of the city, which is not my aim in any case. I believe that it would be unproductive to subordinate this book to chronology because, in such an old yet living and constantly growing city as Lahore, time is not linear or, more precisely, many forms of time coexist: some city neighbourhoods belong to our century, others remain in the Middle Ages, while still others dream of the colonial era or straddle the boundary between different epochs. Similarly, the lifestyles of the different social groups also belong to different historical periods—the director of a major company who speaks English with a Harvard accent, the university professor with a refined command of Urdu, and the street seller who knows only Punjabi—meeting in space but not in time.

Lahore's cultural and chorological space is extremely vast and full of cultural artefacts,[23] symbols, and signs of the past and present. One cannot grasp it in its entirety but only live it as a phenomenological experience and enter it as a *Lebenswelt* that consists of the givens of history, art, daily life, and imagination.

...The characters of our favourite books keep walking down the streets of big cities. The nameless hero of Hamsun's *Hunger* wearily walks in circles around Kristiania in search of food. Leopold Blum (in *Ulysses*) feverishly errs in Dublin's labyrinths, constantly thinking about his wife's infidelity. Marcel, Proust's alter ego, wanders about the Faubourg ('Suburb') Saint-Germain in the hopes of meeting the Duchess. Kipling's Kim, participating in the 'Great Game', creeps along Lahore's stuffy and crowded bazaars. Constant motion, erring, and going around in circles is a phenomenological process of getting to know space that is primordially hostile or indifferent to the individual, domesticating it, and consolidating one's power over it, i.e., transforming *topophobia* into *topophilia*.

When we visit Oslo, Dublin, Paris, or Lahore it is difficult, at first, to separate the living images of the new places from the 'mental maps' that we have drawn up in the footsteps, and along the routes, of literary characters. Our experience gives us a feeling of reality only when it is supported by cultural memory and mediated on by it. If a person has no foothold in consciousness that confirms reality, he often reacts to new and even powerful impressions in a banal way: he simply says that he is dumbstruck. It is *topophilia* that overcomes our eternal fear of space and emotional dumbness and gives us a living feeling of belonging to a place—the sense of city.

Akbari gate, Lahore fort.

CHAPTER TWO

'Lahore is Lahore'

People have always been proud of the unique features of their cities, giving rise to popular sayings such as 'All roads lead to Rome', 'See Naples and die', and 'Paris is worth a Mass'.

Lahore, too, has received its share of florid compliments. According to the Punjabi saying, 'He who hasn't yet seen Lahore hasn't been born'. I have already mentioned that the ideal city for the South Asian Muslims was Iranian Isfahan. Yet, Lahoris doubt the well-known Persian saying 'Isfahan is half the world' and extol their own city saying, 'Isfahan would be half the world if Lahore were not there' (*agar lahur nabud isfahan nesf-i jahan bud*). Lahore's residents go further in asserting the superiority of their city, over the ideal of Isfahan, by claiming that 'Isfahan and Shiraz together wouldn't equal half of Lahore'.

Still, the most popular saying is 'Lahore is Lahore' (*lahaur lahaur hai*). Locals utter it every time they hear another city being praised: yes, New York is enormous, London is convenient, but Lahore is Lahore—it is unlike anything else, and this needs no proof.

The well-known Pakistani satirist, Patras Bukhari (1898–1958), wrote ironically about the blusterous Lahori patriotism in his humorous short story 'Geography of Lahore' (*Lahaur ka Jughrafia*):

> 'By way of introduction, I wish to submit that it is now many years since Lahore was discovered, thus there is no need to prove its existence through argument and

21

demonstration. Nor should it be necessary that the globe should be set in motion from the left till the country called India comes to a stop before your eyes, and on which you should start searching for the intersecting point of the longitude and latitude where Lahore is to be found. Suffice it to say that wherever you spot Lahore that exactly is where Lahore is. This research has been briefly but comprehensively summed up by our elders who state that 'Lahore is Lahore'. If you are unable to find Lahore where it is supposed to be, then your education is below par and your intelligence is of a lower order.'[1]

Indeed, a comparison of Lahore with other South Asian cities shows that it is quite unlike Delhi, Agra, Lucknow, Hyderabad, and the other former capitals of the Muslim states in the Indian Subcontinent. Despite its inevitable architectural similarity to the Mughal cities of Delhi and Agra, Lahore stands out thanks to its unique preserved urban nucleus—the Inner or Walled City (*Anderoon Shehr*).

The Walled City is the second belt of urban development around the historical centre of the fort (*Shahi Qila*), as in many other old cities in the world. In Lahore, as in Delhi and Agra, the fortress' walls still stand today, while the walls of the Inner City survived until the nineteenth century before being destroyed soon after the British annexation of the Punjab in 1849. The walls were initially replaced by a ring of parks, and then by the Circular Road.

The names of the historical parts of many of the world's cities, such as Innere Stadt in Vienna, Ichan Qala in Khiva, and Icheri Sheher in Baku, mean 'inner city'. These areas of the cities formerly housed the ruler's residence and administrative buildings, along with the related infrastructure; in our day, they are home to the principal historical monuments and other tourist sites. 'Inner cities' usually have small populations: the *Anderoon Shehr* of Lahore has less than 500,000 inhabitants, in comparison to its total population of about nine million. In some European and American cities, such as London, New York, and Toronto, the term 'inner city' has a well-defined meaning: it is the oldest part of town in which the poorest social strata and non-white emigrants live, while the well-off inhabitants reside in the fashionable suburbs that they moved to during the 'white flight'.

The inhabitants of the Walled City of Lahore, too, are not rich: unskilled and semiskilled labourers, petty vendors, craftsmen, and some members of the artistic intelligentsia that use the old buildings as ateliers. The narrow medieval streets in this part of town house no banks, luxury hotels, offices, or other places where money circulates. The traditional bazaar is the Walled City's main economic entity, determining the work patterns of the local inhabitants. The Walled City's state of sanitation is also quite medieval: frequent power outages, a poor sewage system, and a water supply that is unfit for consumption. In spite of its around-the-clock din and commotion, the *Anderoon Shehr* is slowly but surely dying.

The Walled City is essentially a relic of the pre-industrial era that must try to survive in the post-industrial world and society.

> 'The city consumes a host of post-industrial goods and services—from transistor radios to World Bank projects— but it must pay for them with pre-industrial commodities. In this exchange, it is caught in a predicament comparable to a man who gets the iron lung he needs to survive, but has to pedal it going'.[2]

Satellite television has been available in Lahore for a long time now, yet television sets are still delivered to the Walled City on carts drawn by pairs of oxen.

On the whole, the Walled City still retains the medieval 'zoned' trading system that is identified by the compact settlement of groups of tradesmen and craftsmen, and by specialized bazaars connected to these groups. Modern supermarkets, in which different types of goods are sold under a single roof, are only found in the fashionable modern suburbs, such as Model Town, Gulberg, or Defence. The inhabitants of the Walled City buy kitchen utensils at Bhanda Bazaar near Shahalami Gate, woollen shawls at Kashmiri Bazaar near Kashmiri Gate, second-hand clothing at Landa Bazaar, bamboo ladders at Bansawala Bazaar, paper at Kaghazi Bazaar, etc.[3]

Muhammad Qadeer, the modern scholar of Lahore wrote about the city's traditional structure,

'Lahore is a city that perhaps can be described more appropriately as a federation of neighbourhoods, markets and special districts, each highly individual in character. Functionally as well as architecturally, these neighbourhoods reflect consecutive historical stages of the city's growth.... Cities were divided into quarters or districts, each inhabited by a tribe or clan or a guild fraternity under the patronage of a noble family. These neighbourhoods were villages of a kind wherein rich and poor were knit together through customary obligations and privileges. There were also commercial districts and market bazaar specializing in commodities such as jewels and spices. Lahore was also organized along these lines. Within the walls of Lahore there were, originally, nine such quarters and, according to an estimate, 27 quarters of varying sizes constituted suburbs towards the east-southeast of the city'.[4]

Some time ago, the well-known architectural historian Kamil Khan Mumtaz published the Lahore Urban Development and Traffic Study (LUDTS, 1980). It has served as the basis for a conservation and restoration project that is being implemented with the support of the World Bank. The project's aim is to give new life to the Walled City, and modernize its structure while preserving its traditional appearance. It calls for reorganizing the energy, sewage, and transport infrastructure, and for providing a new 'filling' for dilapidated old buildings so making them fit for practical use and, most importantly, create new jobs.

Kamil Khan Mumtaz' group selected the most densely built-up districts of the Walled City as a pilot project for the conservation and renovation. Particular importance has been assigned to widening the narrow streets by moving exposed drainage channels, opening sewage conduits (which are often blocked up with waste) underground, and paving the streets. Over time, these efforts should allow the introduction of public transportation into the Walled City, replacing the current modes of transportation—noisy scooters and rattling antediluvian carts.

An even more difficult task is to make *Anderoon Shehr* a special city district of national importance, or a 'living protected area', by assuring a fairly high standard of living for its inhabitants and an improved quality of the surrounding milieu. This can be achieved only by changing the social infrastructure—in particular, by attracting people with average and above-average income levels to the Walled City. Many old Lahori families living in the fashionable suburbs own hereditary real estate in the Walled City. But, as these dilapidated houses are located in 'unattractive' streets, they generate no income for their owners and remain abandoned. The Walled City conservation project calls for the granting of loans, and providing of technical assistance, to the owners of houses of historical significance who choose to participate in the conservation and restoration programme.

Seen on a map, *Anderoon Shehr* resembles an irregular trapezoid, with the fort *Shahi Qila* at its upper (north-western) corner. The city was surrounded by residential suburbs. In its architecture, role in the urban space, and even trapezoidal form, the Walled City resembles the *shahristan* of medieval Central Asian cities. The Ravi River— the smallest of the five rivers of the Punjab and called the Irāvatī in ancient India—skirts the city in a semicircular arc in the northwest. Until the mid-seventeenth century, the Ravi flowed directly under the walls of the fort. In 1662, the Mughal emperor, Aurangzeb 'Alamgir, ordered the construction of a stone embankment (*band-i 'Alamgiri*) that changed the Ravi's course once and for all and made it shallow.

Patras Bukhari, in his geographic parody, wrote:

> 'Lahore is situated in the Punjab but Punjab no longer is the Land of Five Rivers (from *punj* 'five' and *ab* 'water, river'—A.S.), since only four and a half of them actually flow. The half river is no longer capable of flowing, which is why it is commonly referred to as the Old Ravi. This river may be accessed under two bridges—railway and pedestrian—where the riverbed sinks in the sand. The course of the river stopped flowing quite some time ago. This makes it somewhat difficult to say if the city is located on the river's left or its right bank.'[5]

The Walled City of Lahore is built on an alluvial plateau that is traversed by a range of hills in the north, in the area of the fort. As a result, the Walled City is considerably higher than Lahore's other districts which are completely flat. Thus, *Anderoon Shehr* is located on a hill at Lahore's highest point, as befits the city. Lahore was built on a site surrounded and defended by natural barriers, not only out of metaphysical considerations and the rules of urban planning but also on account of the city's geopolitical situation, which largely determined its historical fate: Lahore was the first and biggest trophy on the path of all the conquerors who invaded the Indian Subcontinent from the northwest.

'Several routes lead to Lahore, but two of them are very famous: one from Peshawar and the other from Delhi,' noted Patras Bukhari in his ironic geography. 'Central Asian invaders come by the Peshawar route and invaders from the United Province via Delhi. The former are called the People of Sword and they carry the nom de plume of Ghaznavi or Ghuri. The latter were called the People of Speech and they also skilfully used pseudonyms.'[6] By the People of Speech (*ahl-e zaban*), who used the nom de plume assumed by poets (*takhallus*), Patras Bukhari meant the numerous Urdu writers, who had moved to Lahore from the Indian state of Uttar-Pradesh after 1947, comparing them to conquerors.

Those who came to Lahore through Peshawar were famous rulers and warriors. First, Mahmud Ghaznavi captured the half-ruined city after seventeen raids against the Punjab. Shahabuddin Ghuri, founder of the Delhi Sultanate, later used cunning to seize Lahore. Genghis Khan's armies plundered Lahore and its surroundings. Timur conquered Lahore, yet spared its inhabitants and buildings. Babur used Lahore as a foothold for establishing his great Mughal empire. Sher Shah Suri regretted not having razed Lahore to the ground, for 'such a large city should not exist on the very road of an invader, who, immediately after capturing it on his arrival, could collect his supplies and organize his resources there'.[7] The Iranian Nadir Shah and the Afghan Ahmad Shah Durrani occupied Lahore, imposing a heavy tax on its inhabitants.

Other conquerors—Marathas, Sikhs, and Englishmen—came to Lahore by other routes, yet all of them confirmed the truth of the saying that they who possess Lahore possess India. At the same time, some of them paid for it with their lives, as shown by the famous verse ascribed to the Mughal empress Nur Jahan:

> *lāhūr rā jān barābar kharīda-īm*
> *jān dāda-īm va jannat-i dīgar kharīda-īm*
>
> I bought Lahore at the price of my life
> And giving up my soul attained a second paradise.

Despite its attractiveness to conquerors, Lahore was never particularly comfortable. In particular, it had a heavy climate and poor ecology. Nevertheless, the historical accounts of Western travellers are often contradictory. This was always the case with Europeans in the Indian Subcontinent: some were thrilled by local cities, while others found them terrible.

In the mid-seventeenth century, the British traveller Thomas Herbert expressed his delight at Lahore's sanitary state:

> 'Lahore, a city both great and famous, is competitor for the title of metropolis with Agra.... The air for eight months is very pure and restorative; the streets graceful, and well paved; most of them being cleaned and served by the river Ravi which from the Punjab and the Kashmirian mountains streams pleasantly near the city.'[8]

Jean Baptista Tavernier (1605–1689), the eminent French jewel merchant who came to India on numerous occasions in the seventeenth century, was not so enthusiastic about Lahore's climate and cleanliness of its streets:

> 'Lahore is the capital of a kingdom, and is built on one of the five rivers which descend from the mountains of the north to go to swell the Indus and give the name of Panjab to all the region which they water. The river flows at a quarter of a league distant from the town, being liable to change its bed, and the neighbouring fields often sustain much damage from its overflows. The town is large...but the greater part of its houses, which are higher

than those of Agra and Delhi, are falling into ruins, the
excessive rains having overthrown a large number.'[9]

Alas, the contradictory nature of these descriptions cannot simply
be explained away by differences in national character—of the
Englishman Herbert and the Frenchman Tavernier—as water was a
problem in seventeenth-century Lahore as it continues to be today.
Shortly before these Europeans came to Lahore, Shah Jahan's court
official known as the 'organizer of the water supply' (*Nizam Saqqa*)
invented a complicated system of supplying water to the most
populous city neighbourhoods along channels. However, this system
had already begun to malfunction in Aurangzeb's time and then ceased
to work altogether.

As Patras Bukhari's 'Geography of Lahore' shows, the situation has
changed little in modern times:

> 'The inhabitants of Lahore recently expressed the desire
> to have the climate as other cities have…. Unfortunately,
> the municipality does not have a sufficient air supply,
> and inhabitants are urged not to waste air. Instead,
> dust and, in certain cases, smoke is used in Lahore. The
> municipality has set up numerous dust and smoke supply
> that provide these elements free of charge. Water and
> air (a play on words: *ab* 'water' and *hawa* 'air' constitute
> the word *ab-o-hawa* 'climate'—A.S.) are supplied using
> a system that had been discussed by the municipality for
> a very long time. This system has existed since Nizam
> Saqqa's day. Nevertheless, most plans elaborated by
> Nizam have been destroyed, while others are difficult to
> decipher and implement. The principle of the current
> water supply system is not to let rainwater be absorbed
> by the ground.'[10]

The first historical description of Lahore is found in the anonymous
Persian treatise, *The Regions of the World* (*Hudud al-'alam*), that dates
from 982. This treatise was discovered by A. Tumansky in Bukhara
in 1893, and a facsimile was published by V. Barthold in 1930.
Nevertheless, it became widely known only after a commented English
translation was published by V. Minorsky. The treatise describes

Lahore as a city with 'impressive temples, large markets and huge orchards'. It refers to 'two major markets around which dwellings exist', and mentions 'the mud walls that enclose these two dwellings to make it one'.[11]

The author of the *Regions of the World* was clearly referring to the 'mud fort' (*kaccha kot*) with which the history of the Walled City started. The large-scale construction of the fort began in the early eleventh century after Lahore became part of the Ghaznavid Empire in 1002, and its capital a decade later, as a result of the conquests of the Turkic military commander Sabuktigin (942–997) and his son Mahmud (967–1030). Mahmud Ghaznavi entrusted Lahore to his favourite slave, Malik Ayaz, who became the first of a long line of Muslim governors of the city. Ayaz repopulated Lahore, which had become desolate after the Ghaznavid attacks and prolonged siege, and built a new fort on the ruins of the former stronghold along with a wall around the city in 1037–1040.

Malik Ayaz was a popular character in traditional Muslim poetry (with the opposition 'Mahmud-Ayaz' of Persian and Urdu *ghazal*),[12] tales, and folklore and it is no surprise that a city legend recounts how divine forces magically helped him build the city walls overnight. Ayaz lived in Lahore until his death, when he was buried in the Rang Mahal *mohalla* of the Walled City, next to the Old Mint.

The very name *kaccha kot* has Indian, or more precisely, Rajput roots: the Rajputs used the word *kot* to denote a fortress or stronghold. As with many other world cities, Lahore was known by different names at different times. These names (and changes of name) tell us a lot about the city's cultural role and place. Lahore's oldest name in the Indian tradition is *Loh-kot* or *Lav-kot* (Stronghold of Loh, or Lava). Lava, considered to be the city's mythical founder, was a son of Rama, the god-head and epic hero; Lava's twin brother, Kuśa, is credited with founding the neighbouring city of Kasur.

The *Ramayana* relates that the first performers of this epic poem were Princes Lava and Kuśa, who had heard it from the wizard Valmiki. According to a tradition that did not make its way into the *Ramayana*, Kuśa inherited Rama's kingdom of Ayodhya and continued the Raghu royal dynasty, from whom the Rajputs traced their descent, while Lava, going further west on a campaign, founded

Lavkot-Lahore.[13] Thus, Lahore's eponym is an epic hero and the son of a deity—the ideal etiological legend about a city's origins.

Historians, in turn, believe that Lahore's 'mud fort' was established by the Bhatis, a Rajput tribe that came from West India and subsequently founded the ruling dynasty of Jaisalmer. Traces of this connection persist in the name of Lahore's oldest gate Bhati Darwaza. When the Muslim conquest of India began, Lahore was ruled by the Chauhans, a well-known Rajput clan from Ajmer.

Lahore was apparently known outside India in ancient times. I have mentioned, in Chapter 1, that Claudius Ptolemy referred to Lahore as *Labokla*. More precisely, Ptolemy wrote about the city of Labokla, situated between the Indus River and Patalibothra (Patna) on the route to a country called Kasperia (Kashmir) that extended along the rivers Hydraotes (Ravi) and Hydaspes (Jhelum). These coordinates led later commentators of Ptolemy to identify Labokla as Lahore.[14]

At the same time, geographers were puzzled by the fact that no city that could be identified as Lahore was mentioned by the historians of Alexander the Great. In the nineteenth century, the British anthropologist, Alexander Burnes, conjectured that Lahore was the city of Sanghala which had been destroyed by Alexander and mentioned by Arrian in his *Indica*. During his Indian campaign, Alexander conquered the Punjab and then attacked two more unfortified cities situated between the Acesines (Chenab) and Hydraotes (Ravi) rivers, i.e., in the region of present-day Lahore. Nevertheless, Burnes produced no convincing evidence for his hypothesis.[15] The Chinese traveller, Xuanzang (600–664), does not mention any city that could be identified as Lahore in his *The Great Tang Records on the Western Regions* either, in spite of the fact that he spent several years in the Punjab.

By contrast, early Arabian geographers and travellers frequently mentioned Lahore under different names. Most of them, including al-Biruni in his *Book of India* (*Kitab al-Hind*), spoke of *Alahwar* or *Lohawar*. Abul Hasan 'Ali al-Hujwiri (died 1076), a famous Muslim mystic and Sufi *sheikh*, visited Lahore in the eleventh century; he was destined to become the city's principal patron saint, known as Data Ganj Bakhsh. In his celebrated work, *Revelation of the Veiled* (*Kashf al-mahjub*), he related, 'I myself had become a captive among uncongenial folk in the district of Lahawur, which is a dependency of Multan.'[16]

Lahawur and *Lohawar* of the Muslim writers is essentially the same as the Rajput *Loh-kot* because the word *awar* (from the Sanskrit *āwarana*) is a synonym of the word *kot*, and also means 'stronghold' or 'fort'. It is part of many South Asian toponyms (e.g., Peshawar, Sonawar, Kathiawar, etc.).

At the end of the Ghaznavid period, Lahore was called *Mahmudpur*, in honour of Sultan Mahmud Ghaznavi, for a short period of time. Yet, during the Delhi Sultanate in the thirteenth century, the great Indian poet Amir Khusrau Dehlavi wrote a poem called '*Meeting of the Two Fortunate Planets*' (*Qiran al-sa'dain*) in which he returned to a version of the old name—*Lahanur* (*nur* is a distorted form of the Indian *nagar* 'city'):

> *az had-i sāmāniya tā lahānūr*
> *hīch 'imārat nīst magar dār-i qasūr*

> From the boundaries of the Samanids to Lahanur
> There is no building except Kasur.[17]

In the early fourteenth century, Rashid al-Din, author of the famous historical work *Compendium of Chronicles* (*Jami' al-tawarikh*), spoke of *Lohur* or *Rahwar*. The latter name derives from the city's location on the imperial road (*rah*) connecting Kabul and Peshawar with Delhi and Agra. This key transportation artery of the Indian Subcontinent was subsequently called the Grand Trunk Road; Lahore's position on this highway has given it great strategic importance during all periods of history down to the present day. Indian rulers (first Muslim and later English) travelled along the Grand Trunk Road while moving about their capitals, going hunting in Kashmir, or setting forth to fight in Kandahar and Kabul; they inevitably passed through Lahore on their way.

'And truly the Grand Trunk Road is a wonderful spectacle', wrote Kipling. 'It runs straight, bearing without crowding India's traffic for fifteen hundred miles—such a river of life as nowhere else exists in the world. They looked at the green-arched, shade-flecked length of it, the white breadth speckled with slow-pacing folk.'[18]

The early accounts of European travellers to Lahore, stemming from the early seventeenth century, describe the city's wealth and prosperity during the reigns of Akbar, Jahangir, and Shah Jahan. For example, the Spanish monk Fray Sebastian Manrique, who visited the Punjab in 1641, wrote

> 'The city of Lahore is beautifully situated, commanding agreeable views, having on one side a river with crystal waters which descends from the mountains of Kashmir, and continues its course, moistening and fertilizing the ground, till it arrives at the city of Multan, where it pays its tribute to the famous Indus. Lahore, the second city of the Moghal Empire (as well on account of riches as its size) is ornamented with fine palaces and gardens, also tanks and fountains. As to the abundance of provisions, it would be unnecessary here to describe it. The riches of the principal street (known as the Bazar Del Choco [which may be transcribed as Bazaar Dilkusha]), if shown to advantage, would equal the richest European mart.'[19]

This was the time of Lahore's heyday, when it became a cultural and chorological image in European and, in particular, English literature. It has been mentioned by John Milton (1608–1674) in *Paradise Lost* (1667) as one of the great cities of the world that Adam sees from Paradise:

> His eye might there command wherever stood
> City of old or modern fame, the seat
> Of mightiest empire, from the destined walls
> Of Cambalu, seat of Cathaian Can,
> And Samarchand by Oxus, Temir's throne,
> To Pacquin, of Sinæan kings, and thence
> To Agra and Lahor of Great Mogul...[20]

Our discussion of the names that were applied to Lahore, throughout history, shows that the city was founded by Rajput tribes around the late first or early second millennium AD (Ptolemy's *Labokla*). During the first Arab expedition to Northwest India, led by the Baghdad caliph's military commander Muhammad bin Qasim in 711–712, the largest city of the Punjab was Multan while Lahore was still the small Rajput fort of *Lavkot*. However, at the time of Sabuktigin's campaigns in the tenth century, Lahore was already the rich and powerful capital of a Hindu principality ruled by King Jaypala of the Hindushahi dynasty; the city was able to resist military attack and afford a ransom of a million dirhams. In the eleventh century, Lohawar became a fortified capital surrounded by walls, which were still made of mud at the time.

As the legendary phoenix, Lahore rose from its ashes on numerous occasions during its long history, going through periods of destruction and revival, burning and reconstruction. For this reason, it has an inter-textual and multi-layered spatial structure, providing a graphic example of the principle of the palimpsest. In addition to frequently being reconstructed after military invasions, buildings were often demolished during peace-time for their bricks. Historical sources show that only the Great Mughals truly knew how to build; their extensive building experience and love of architecture were derived from their celebrated Timurid traditions. All the other rulers of Lahore—in particular the Sikhs and the British—used what lay at hand, razing dozens of architectural masterpieces simply to obtain their bricks and other building materials, or stripped the precious marble from the buildings' façades.

The marble removed from Lahori buildings, and especially from the tombs, was used to build the main Sikh shrines, including the famous Golden Temple in Amritsar, and the mausoleums (*samadhi*) of Guru Arjun Dev and Ranjit Singh. The British, to some extent, continued the Sikh practice by defacing and destroying old buildings for their new civil structures—the National Museum, the Government College, and the Punjab University are examples of this. Thus, the architectural history of Lahore consists of several centuries of glory and several centuries of barefaced barbarity.

After Malik Ayaz, the city was partially rebuilt by the Delhi sultans from the Ghulam Dynasty, Qutbuddin Aybak and Iltutmish. They greatly embellished the city and, in the words of the early thirteenth-century medieval chronicler and author of *Crown of Glorious Deeds* (*Taj al-ma'asir*, 1205) Hasan Nizami,

'*Lohur* was among the mothers of the countries of religion
and among the chiefs of the provinces of Islam, the abode
and repose of the excellent and pious, which, for some
days, on account of a number of calamities and changes of
governors and the sedition of rebels, had been distracted
by the flames of turbulence and opposition, but had now
been again reduced to order.'[21]

Qutub-ud-Din Aibak made Lahore his capital, and was buried here
in 1210. In the mid-thirteenth century, the city was sacked by the
Mongols; Sultan Ghiyasuddin Balban restored it, as described by
the historian Ziauddin Barani in his famous *Chronicle of Firuz Shah*
(*Tarikh-i Firuzshahi*): 'The sultan re-peopled the towns and villages
of Lahore, which had been devastated by the Moghals, and appointed
architects and superintendents to restore them.'[22]

The radical reconstruction of the Walled City, including the large
scale construction of palaces and administrative buildings within the
fort and the erection of new brick city walls, dates from the rule of the
Great Mughal, Akbar, who made Lahore his capital in 1584–1598. At
the same time, thirteen city gates were built—the most characteristic
historical feature of old Lahore. These gates have been mentioned by
both the local chroniclers and foreign travellers in their accounts of the
Walled City.

The following is an account by the British indigo merchant, William
Finch, who visited Lahore in 1611 at the very beginning of Jahangir's reign:

'Lahore is one of the greatest cities of the east, being
near twenty-four coss (about 48 miles—*A.S.*) in circuit,
round which a great ditch is now digging, the king having
commanded the whole city to be surrounded by a strong
wall. In the time of the Patan empire of Delhi (Delhi
Sultanate—*A.S.*), Lahore was only a village, Mooltan
being then a flourishing city, till Humaion thought proper
to enlarge Lahore, which now, including its suburbs,
is about six coss in extent. The castle or royal town is
surrounded by a brick wall, which is entered by twelve[23]
handsome gates, three of which open to the banks of the
river, and the other nine towards the land.'[24]

The walls and gates gradually became dilapidated. So, in 1812 Ranjit Singh, the founder of an independent Sikh state with Lahore as its capital, ordered that they should be reconstructed out of old bricks. This is mentioned by, among others, the English veterinary surgeon William Moorcroft who visited Lahore during Ranjit Singh's reign in 1820: 'The wall of the city was still under repair, and 3000 men are said to be on work on it and upon the moat which the Raja was about to add to the defences. The place, however, could oppose no effectual resistance to European assailants.'[25]

The walls and gates were rebuilt for the last time by the English, who annexed the Punjab in 1848. Eternally concerned about the lack of fresh air in the overpopulated cities of the Indian Subcontinent, the English razed half the walls of the Inner City 'for sanitary reasons', filled in the moat, and demolished some of the gates. In actual fact, they simply destroyed the city's fortifications.

Naturally, gates existed in the Walled City even before Akbar's time and were essential elements of the system of fortifications. The historian Hasan Nizami referred to the Bhati and Lahori Gates, which subsequently preserved their names. Nevertheless, gates began to play a key role in Lahore's social infrastructure during the Mughal period.

The history of city gates, as a cultural phenomenon, is inextricably linked with the history of urban civilization. 'There is no city without a gate' (*shahr bi darwaza nist*), goes a Persian saying. I mentioned in Chapter 1 that the gate was a metaphysical breach and a phenomenological and architectural symbol of the transition from one condition or state to another. This explains why the gate was a symbol of duality in ancient mythology (the god of gates in Ancient Rome was the double-faced Janus). Passing through a gate symbolized initiation and purification from sin and evil among the Etruscans, Romans, and other ancient peoples (the same meaning exists in medieval Christian and Muslim urban culture).

Entering a city through a gate also symbolized military triumph, which led to the tradition of building triumphal arches in honour of victors. The gate pillars symbolized the world tree, while the vault and arches referred to the celestial sphere. People sacralized gates to such an extent that they even made sacrifices to them. The locations, orientations, and even names of city gates refer to cultural values and thus, according to Yi-Fu Tuan's theory mentioned above, determine a culture's *topophilia*.

The very word used for 'gate', in the different languages, signifies might and power, both in the Bible[26] as well as in historical practice—for instance, the mighty Ottoman court was also known as 'Sublime Porte'. The Seven Gates of Thebes in Ancient Greece, the Phoenician pillars of Melqart, the sacred gates of Babylon (lit. 'Gateway of god') glorifying Marduk and Ishtar, and the Golden Gate through which the Saviour entered Jerusalem, are all extremely meaningful mythologems and cultural and geographic images. In the Muslim tradition, the word for gate (*bab*) has a supplementary mystical connotation, figuring in the titles of saints and religious figures who serve as the 'gates' through which God expresses his will. Bab (1819–1847), the founder of *Babism*, a religious movement in Iran, is the best-known example of such a title.

In medieval cities, not only were gates a means of defence but they also had various social functions. In particular, they were outposts for the city's trade—bazaars, tax collection points, and money exchange offices were often located in or around the gates. This was also the place where court cases were heard, administrative decrees promulgated, and day labourers and artisans hired. The gates were the noisiest place in town. Here, visitors met local inhabitants for the first time and learnt the local news and prices, as well as the metric standards used in the city.

In Lahore, as in other old Muslim cities, the city gates (*darwaza*) were monumental arched structures with high portals (*pishtaq*[27]) on their façades. The portals were key elements of the city landscape, shaping the city's image no less than its minarets, arcades, and mosque domes. The portals were decorated with ceramic tiles, calligraphic and floral ornaments, and other permitted images (lions, birds, etc.), making each city unique. The corridor-like inner spaces of the gates contained covered shops and a passageway through which elephants with burdens or passengers could easily walk. Small cell-like domed rooms, for the watchmen and tax collectors, were built along the walls of the corridors.

Galleries were situated above the gates; guardhouses (*naubat-khana*), in which drummers struck the hours, were located there. Gates sometimes also housed prisons where convicts awaited punishment. Ceremonial and military processions (*sawari*) occasionally passed through the gates. Hence, the gates were brightly illuminated at night, as compared to the residential neighbourhoods. Some city gates were open around the clock while others were closed at night. This is reflected in the toponymy of cities in different countries, including Pakistan—for example, Darband or Derbend ('closed gates'). It was the general rule in India, and other Asian countries, that the more ornamental and majestic the city gate or building's entrance, the greater the reputation and standing of the city and its ruler or the building and its owner.

As trade caravans stopped next to the gates, caravanserais were built in their vicinity and rooms inside the gates were rented out. Kipling described the appearance and function of the city gate, Kashmiri Darwaza, as follows:

> 'Half pushed, half towed, he arrived at the high gate of the Kashmir Serai: that huge open square…surrounded with arched cloisters, where the camel and horse caravans put up on their return from Central Asia. Here were all manner of Northern folk…taking on new grooms; swearing, shouting, arguing, and chaffering in the packed square. The cloisters, reached by three or four masonry steps, made a haven of refuge around this turbulent sea. Most of them were rented to traders, as we rent the arches of a viaduct; the space between pillar and pillar being bricked or boarded off into rooms, which were guarded by heavy wooden doors and cumbrous native padlocks.'[28]

Only six of Lahore's thirteen city gates, built during the Mughal era, still survive; only Roshnai Gate has escaped large-scale reconstruction since the sixteenth century. The other gates continue to be architectural symbols of the city, yet bear the marks of later reconstruction. The names of the gates, as with other historical toponyms in Lahore, tell us a lot about the people and events of the past. Drawings and old photographs in the Lahore Museum show that direct access to the gates was blocked from the outside: high semicircular or rectangular barriers were erected in front of the gates to impede attack.

The city was considered particularly well fortified in the north, where the mountain range and river served as natural barriers against invaders.

Four city gates faced in this direction. Roshnai Gate, next to the main mosque—Badshahi Masjid, was the main entrance to the Walled City from the side of the fort, and was used by the nobility. Rich court processions moved through this gate, which was brightly illuminated at night (thus its name—'Gate of Light' or 'Gate of Splendour'). In 1673, Aurangzeb constructed the Abdar-khana Square, next to Roshnai Gate, before the main entrance to the Badshahi Masjid. A century later, Ranjit Singh turned the square and gate into a regular park, Hazuri Bagh, which now unites the fort and mosque in a single architectural ensemble.

Roshnai Gate is linked to a dramatic incident during the Sikh period of Lahore's history. After Ranjit Singh's death in 1839, the throne was inherited by his elder son, Kharak Singh, who died after ruling for only one year. He was succeeded by the young Nau Nihal Singh. When the latter was hurrying to his own coronation, from his father's funeral, a fragment of the gate fell on his head, killing him. Before his death, Nau Nihal Singh had ordered that certain structures be demolished for their bricks, including the mausoleum of the revered Muslim saint, Muhammad Ghaus. The city's Muslims considered the Sikh crown prince's fatal accident to be divine punishment for blasphemy.

Kashmiri Gate, which faces in the direction of Kashmir, is also located to the north. The gate housed the large Kashmiri Bazaar, and the caravanserai described by Kipling. Masti Gate, of which only ruins remain, stood immediately behind the fort, near Kashmiri Gate. The gate was named after the adjoining mosque—its name stemming from the Punjabi pronunciation of *masjid* or 'mosque'. The masjid, the oldest in the city, was built by Emperor Jahangir's mother, Empress Mariam Zamani. The district around Masti Gate is always noisy: it has the largest shoe bazaar in Lahore, and leatherworkers and shoemakers traditionally settle here.

Khizri Gate, to the north of the city, opens directly onto the river. It was named in honour of the legendary Muslim saint, Khwaja Khizr (al-Khadir), who was said to have become immortal after drinking from the Water of Life (whence his name *Zinda Pir* or 'Eternal Old Man' in popular Islam). Commentators of the Qu'ran assert that the *sura* 'The Cave' refers to Khizr, as the teacher and companion who reveals the secret mystical truth to Prophet Musa (Moses). While the Sufis considered Khizr to be the spirit of Muslim gnosis, he was considered the spirit of the rivers, springs, and water streams in popular Islam. Saint Khizr is also identified with Prophet Ilyas (Biblical Elijah), who connotes water in all Abrahamic religions. The Punjabis worshipped Khizr as the patron saint of the professions connected to the water and navigation—sailors, boatmen, and ferrymen. The ferry across the Ravi was located in front of the Khizri Darwaza, giving rise to the gate's initial name. After Ranjit Singh ordered that two cages, with lions in them, should be placed next to the gate as a symbolic warning to potential enemies (the cages were subsequently replaced by stone effigies of lions), the gate came to be known as Lion's Gate (Sheranwala Darwaza, from *sher* or 'lion').

The eastern gate, Yakki Darwaza, was named in remembrance of the numerous Mongol attacks; the name of one of the oldest districts of the city, Mughalpura, has the same origin. *Yakki* is a distorted form of the Arabic word *zaki* ('pure, virtuous'). Zaki was the name of a legendary martyr for the faith (*ghazi*) who defended the city, from Genghis Khan's army. According to legend, although his head was chopped off in battle, his body continued to fight for some time. Subsequently, a gate was built on the site of his death, and two tombs were situated inside: one contained his head, and the other his body.[29] No traces of Yakki Gate remain.

Further along the eastern periphery stands the massive Delhi Gate, through which rulers and troops passed *en route* to the main imperial highway leading to Delhi. In the seventeenth century, the district of the Walled City around Delhi Gate belonged to Prince Dara Shikoh and bore his name (*chowk-i dara*). The prince's residence, the palaces of his harem and courtiers, and the famous horse market (Nakhkhas Mandi) were located here. The gate's strategic importance saved it from destruction. The English razed the high Mughal portal and rebuilt the gate in the Victorian style with a façade resembling Marble Arch in London. Behind the façade was a deep domed passageway (*deorhi*), with the magistrate's office and police headquarters (*kotvali*) on either side. The Wazir Khan Mosque, one of Lahore's most important architectural monuments, is located next to Delhi Gate.

Beyond Delhi Gate stood Akbari Gate (no longer extant), named in honour of Padishah Muhammad Jalaluddin Akbar, the founder and

builder of Mughal Lahore. Next to it stood the noisy bazaar Akbari
Mandi. The English razed Akbari Darwaza, in order to destroy the
city's fortification, and promised to rebuild it as a 'civil structure'. But
the promise was never kept; we can only appreciate Akbari Gate via
its old photographs and watercolours.

To the south, *Anderoon Shehr* borders upon Lahore itself and
further upon other districts of the Punjab. The city has grown steadily,
in this southerly direction, in modern times. In the '*Geography of
Lahore*', Patras Bukhari has written, 'It is said that Lahore formerly
had four boundaries. However, to make it easier for students studying
Geography, the municipality abolished them, and now there are no
boundaries in the south of Lahore. Certain experts believe that, ten or
twenty years from now, Lahore will become a province with Punjab
as its capital.'[30]

Thus, the most strategically important entryway to the south
is Lahori Gate, which faces Lahore, just as Delhi Gate faces Delhi
and Kashmiri Gate opens onto the Kashmir Mountains. Caravans
from Multan and the cities of Sindh passed through Lahori Gate.
The aforementioned *kaccha kot* was located directly behind Lahori
Gate, and the boundaries of the Ghaznavid capital (during Malik
Ayaz' time) passed through it. Next to the Lahori Gate stands the
mausoleum of Sultan Qutub-ud-Din Aibak (died 1210), founder of
the Delhi Sultanate, who died after falling from a horse during a game
of polo. Between Akbari Gate and Lahori Gate lay the stone-paved
Royal Trail (*shahi guzar-gah*), down which court processions moved.
Today, the government of the province of Punjab is restoring it with
the help of the World Bank.

In 1799, the keeper of the Lahori Gate, Mohkam Din Choudhri,
opened the city to Ranjit Singh and his troops—who entered Lahore
and became its ruler (*sirkar*) for forty years.[31] Both the Sikhs and the
English took good care of Lahori Gate, preserving its initial appearance
during reconstruction in view of its great importance for transport
between Lahore and the Punjab. Lahori Gate had another phonetically
similar name—Lohari Darwaza, from the word *lohar* 'smith'—on
account of the smithies' and jewellers' shops located nearby.

The three other gates along the southern periphery of the Walled
City were destroyed long ago. Mochi Gate's name implies that

craftsmen of the Mochi caste, i.e., leatherworkers, cobblers, and saddle makers, lived in its vicinity. However, some historians of Lahore believe that *mochi* is a garbled form of *moti* or 'pearl'. Others say that the gatekeeper in Akbar's day was a certain Moti Ram, after whom the gate was named.[32] In the noisy bazaar around Mochi Gate, one can buy dried fruits as well as kites and fireworks—demand for the latter is particularly high in early spring when Lahoris celebrate their favourite holiday, *Basant*. Immediately behind the gate lies the garden Mochi Bagh—a place of public gatherings, meetings, and poetic symposia (*mushaira*), where many leading Pakistani political figures and poets have spoken. Here Muhammad Iqbal first read his poem 'Response to the Complaint' (*Jawab-e shikwa*).[33] Immense crowds gathered in Mochi Bagh to celebrate the Muslim League's signing of the Lahore Resolution (1940) which has been largely interpreted as a demand for a separate Muslim state, Pakistan.

Mori Gate was not a gate as such but a passageway or opening in the city walls through which refuse and waste materials were taken out of the city. The word *mori* signifies 'underground water sewer, canal, passageway'. There were similar sanitary exits in all other fortified cities of the world, such as the Dung (Mugrabi) Gate in Jerusalem. When the English built a modern refuse removal system in Lahore, they razed Mori Gate.

During Partition in 1947, the southern Shahalami Gate was completely destroyed by fire. It was called Sheep Gate (Bherwala Darwaza) in Akbar's time as it led to pastures. For Christians, this name will bring to mind Sheep Gate in Jerusalem, next to which Jesus performed the miracle of healing the sick man (John 5: 2–8). In the eighteenth century, Bherwala Darwaza was renamed in honour of Shah 'Alam Bahadur Shah I, Aurangzeb's son and successor, who became ruler of the Punjab in 1694. He was held in great esteem by the Lahoris although he was a Shia (the overwhelming majority of Punjabi Muslims were Sunnites) and often behaved in an eccentric manner. He began by ordering that Sikhs should shave off their beards, which is strictly forbidden by their religion. When this decree had no effect, he ordered that all dogs in the city should be killed (for an unknown reason). Consequently, the inhabitants hid their dogs in the city during the daytime and sent them across the Ravi early in the morning.[34] Perhaps it was the Emperor's eccentricities that made him so memorable for the city's dwellers, leading them to change the name of Sheep Gate to Shahalami Gate after his death in 1712.

The very old Bhati Gate still stands in the south-western part of the city. It was named in honour of the city's prehistoric founders—the Rajputs of the Bhati tribe. During the Ghaznavid period, the Bhati Gate was the principal entrance to the city. After Akbar expanded Lahore to the east, and divided it into nine districts (*guzars*), the gate and adjoining bazaar became the boundary between the city's eastern and western parts (*guzar mubarak-khan* and *guzar talvara*). Bhati Gate is often mentioned in memoirs and historical works because of the nearby *Data Darbar*, the shrine of Saint Data Ganj Bakhsh. This revered tomb puts Lahore on the list of Sufi holy cities (*Sharif*), along with Konya, Bukhara, Shiraz, and others.

Taxali Darwaza, the only gate leading to the Walled City from the west, was named after the nearby mint (*taxal*). Before this mint was built by the Mughals (Lahore had an older mint, dating from Malik Ayaz' time), the gate was called *Lakhi* after the numerical unit *lakh* (one hundred thousand); places where large amounts of money circulated—such as the quarters where the rich merchants, money lenders, and exchangers lived—were often named Lakhi. Taxali Gate was connected to Delhi Gate by a road that crossed the Walled City from west to east. Although Taxali Gate was demolished by the English, it is still visible in detail in William Simpson's watercolour, *View of Taxali Gate* (1865),[35] which shows the heavily fortified approach to the gate.

This digression into the history of Lahori gates shows how traditional consciousness determines the landmarks of city space and turns geographic coordinates into chorological representations. The centre of Lahore was not only the Fort—the symbol of power and the place where it was concentrated—but also the city. The latter included the inner *Anderoon Shehr* as well as the constantly expanding 'outer city' beyond the city walls. The city was spatially organized around the gates—the symbols of society. Government and society were connected by the 'passageway' through which power manifested itself—Roshnai Darwaza, the Gate of Light.

The main economic activities and personal interactions in society took place around the gates, i.e., in the adjoining bazaars, caravanserais, exchange offices, and craftsmen's shops. In the Fort, contacts were determined by class subordination and court etiquette, i.e., by non-economic factors. The names of certain gates (*Mochi, Lohari, Khizri, Taxali,* and *Mori*) stemmed from the traditional settlement patterns of the castes/occupational groups (leatherworkers, smiths, jewellers, etc.) while others bore elements of the urban infrastructure (ferry, mint, and place of waste removal) pointing to socioeconomic ties.

A city is a spatial structure lying on the axis of time. Unlike extraordinary events, such as wars and natural disasters, the normal passage of time does not bring about major changes in the historical appearance of a city. In every street and quarter, buildings, landscape and architectural forms, and urban planning models stemming from different periods lie on top of each other, layer by layer. In Lahore, this simultaneity of city images is seen in the chronological 'variety' found in the names of the gates—*Bhati, Akbari, Shahalami,* and *Sheranwala*—which refer to the city's Rajput founders, its chief builder Akbar, its keeper Shah 'Alam, and rebuilder Ranjit Singh, respectively.

Every traditional city is built on spiritual foundations. Its gates—key meeting points of the human and the divine, the finite and the infinite—serve as spatial and temporal channels through which the sublime spirit of the world order is transformed into the human energy of city building. In Lahore, the names of the gates *Masti* (from *masjidi*) and *Yakki* (from *zaki*) point to this aspect of city structure.

The mosque of Mariam Zamani (the 'second Mariam'), and the tomb of the martyr for the faith Zaki, are crucial buildings for Muslims and the gates here mark the places (*topoi*) with a high spiritual intensity. The areas around Delhi Gate, Roshnai Gate, and Bhati Gate contain Lahore's main religious sites: the Wazir Khan Mosque, Badshahi Masjid, and Data Darbar, respectively. The mosques and the saints' tombs are Lahore's key spatial values that determine its *topophilia*.

I have mentioned, on several occasions, that a city gate is a spatial breach and a 'passage' through which the city flows out into the surrounding world with which it constitutes a dualistic whole, somewhat like the Catholic *Urbi et Orbi*. The names of the

Kashmiri, Delhi, and Lahori Gates express chorological notions about the position of the city with respect to the cardinal directions, and thus about its place in the geography of the inhabited world. It is interesting to note that the gates, judging from their names, mark only 'friendly' directions that are relatively safe for the city.

Kashmiri Gate points to the north—the direction of the insurmountable Himalayas that reliably protect the Indian Subcontinent, and of the Kashmir Valley—a 'green paradise', studded with flowering gardens and cool lakes, a place of rest and tranquillity with traditionally positive connotations in South Asian culture.

Delhi Gate faces east or, more precisely, south-east in the direction of India's other capitals of Delhi, Agra, and during British rule, Calcutta. In the public awareness, these cities and their associated cultural and geographic images formed a whole with Lahore, though in different ways. Delhi and Lahore were ancient Rajput cities controlled by the Chauhan clan, and historic capitals of the Delhi Sultanate. Lahore, Agra, and Delhi were strongholds of the Great Mughal Empire. Finally, Delhi, Lahore, and Calcutta were united by British rule (*Raj*) and, as such, were opposed—in the colonial mentality—to arbitrary lordship in independent principalities and dangerous chaos in tribal territories.

Finally, the southerly direction and Lahori Gate were associated with local ethnic unity within the Punjab. This direction led, in particular, to Multan and Ucch—cities that pre-dated Lahore, and had been more powerful than Lahore before they lost their pre-eminence during the Great Mughals. Through Lahori Gate, the city asserts itself in the 'friendly' space of its neighbours, i.e., in the space of *topophilia*.

The three gates named after toponyms, therefore, determine Lahore's position as an integral part of bigger or smaller spaces united by certain principles in the Subcontinent, state, or ethnic group.

Lahore has no gates to the north-west: the constant danger that threatened Lahore from this direction was expressed in the city plan. The north-western direction is the space of *topophobia*; the city erected walls and closed all gates and passages before it. As the double name of a single western gate (*Taxali/Lakhi*) shows, it topologically stressed Lahore's wealth and economic and political independence, as minting coins was the prerogative of independent cities and states.

The role played by gates in Lahore's chorological structure makes it resemble the topological model of Jerusalem. In their present-day state, Jerusalem's gates also mark the cardinal directions (Jaffa, Damascus, and Zion Gates), refer to city infrastructure (Dung Gate), and preserve the memory of city builders (Herod's Gate and Lions' Gate named after lions placed there by Sultan Baibars) and saints (Lions' Gate was also known as St. Stephen's Gate, in honour of one of the first Christian martyrs).

Nevertheless, there are many more differences than similarities between Jerusalem and Lahore. One reason, of course, is that Jerusalem is an ancient city and has a more complex and multi-layered cultural and geographic image than any other city in the world. At the same time, the centre of Jerusalem has always been a holy shrine, even though it was a different one for the three Abrahamic religions, and it is no surprise that the Golden Gate is considered to be the place of the Messiah's future coming by Jews and the gate of theophany by Christians. In contrast, Lahore's main gate—Roshnai Darwaza—was meant to demonstrate the shine of temporal power.

Two city models—Jerusalem and Rome—are particularly important for the history of Western civilization. Jerusalem is seen as the model of the ideal utopian city that lives simultaneously in the past, present, and future. It is a *chronopolitical*, rather than a *geopolitical*, city. When a new city is created, be it Rio de Janeiro, Islamabad, or Chandigarh, its founders always aim to create an ideal city that would resemble the lost or 'other' paradise.

The second city model, which is particularly pertinent for modern civilization, is Rome. The entire modern system of public utilities, management, civil norms, and trade is patterned after the Roman model. Rome was an incessantly growing city, bulging with monuments and wealthy villas, subordinating the landscape to its utilitarian needs. Most importantly, Rome was a megalopolis and a centre of imperial power and administrative control that lived off conquered riches. In contrast to *chronopolitical* Jerusalem, Rome was the model of a *geopolitical* city.

Thus, the two ideal city models that determined the urbanism of European civilization were the City of God and simply the City, as Rome, the international centre of power, was often called.

In Islam, the ideal chorological prototypes were the City of God and the City of the Prophet—the holy cities of Mecca and Medina. The urbanistic model itself was theocratic in nature. In the Qu'ran, Mecca is called the 'mother of cities' (6:92), which emphasizes its primordial role in the development of city culture. As Islam spread, its entire territory, from Mecca on, acquired an unbroken spiritual significance. No matter where they stand, Muslim mosques always face Mecca. Thus, for Muslims, the entire world space is organized around a single religious centre.

In addition, Muslim city dwellers did not try to isolate themselves from their natural surroundings. City quarters usually had exits leading directly to the steppe or desert outside. This led to the application of 'frontier' connotations to the areas around city gates in Islamic urban culture: the gates separated the city, inhabited by Muslims, from the territory of the infidels. The notion of nature as an extra-urban environment that is alien and dangerous to man is not found in Islam: all space belongs to the sphere of human activity.

Such chorological perception led Muslims to use all conquered territory actively. A city was not just a chaotically built-up, and growing uncontrollably, living space but also a frontier of the spread of faith and civilization. According to tradition, Mecca was consecutively settled by different tribes and included the Upper and Lower Cities. A bazaar was located in the centre, to the south of al-Ka'ba. Residential quarters consisted of large walled land plots with dwellings belonging to related families. A separate quarter was allocated for each tribe and social group. Thus, the city brought all the people together around the faith.

As the city that was built on by people who had converted to Islam, and had already developed their own pre-Islamic urban culture, Lahore brings together all the aforementioned city models. It turns to Mecca during prayer, preserves the memory of its imperial past, and considers itself to be a megalopolis similar to Rome. As a city that was founded by the son of a deity and built by a hero of poetry and legend, Lahore lives in several temporal dimensions simultaneously, like Jerusalem. It is both timeless—existing in the space of medieval hagiography—and modern, living on the 'mental maps' of *psychogeography*.

Wazir Khan Mosque, Lahore.

CHAPTER THREE

Between Mosque and Tomb

Lahore's social and economic space was organized around its city gates, yet its spiritual chorology extended between the mosque and the tomb—the two fundamental architectural symbols of the Islamic world. Nevertheless, the mosque and the tomb have opposing functions in Islam. For example, the Shari'a looks down upon the ornamentation of tombs and speaks out against building anything over tombs, such as stones with images of the dead, or rich family vaults, sepulchres, and mausoleums which run against Islamic egalitarianism, as they can demean poor Muslims or evoke jealousy. Furthermore, the Shari'a strictly forbids using tombs as places of prayer. This explains the Shari'a decree that monuments to the dead should not resemble mosques.

Nevertheless, the interdiction notwithstanding, along with the mosque the mausoleum (*maqbara*) became the most widespread form of Islamic monumental architecture. During their lifetimes, the rulers, nobility, and wealthy built lavish mausoleums that surpassed many mosques in their architectural beauty and interior decoration, while the tombs of Sufi saints and righteous people (*mazars*) have always been places of pilgrimage and prayer. The very word *mazar* means a 'place that people visit'.

The Shari'a categorically forbids the visiting of tombs for the purpose of asking the dead for something or in seeking their assistance in worldly matters. In Islam, this is a great sin called *shirk*—associating

49

partners to Allah, worshipping other than Allah, i.e., violating the dogma of monotheism. Despite this prohibition, *ziyarat*, or visiting the tombs of saints, righteous people, and spiritual mentors is a very popular practice in the whole Islamic world; its aim is to ask for spiritual intercession or even for help in more concrete 'worldly' affairs (recovery from disease, birth of heir, auspicious marriage, success in affairs, etc.).

In India and Pakistan, tombs and mosques are frequently situated side by side: every major ritual complex (*dargah*) has a mosque next to the saint's tomb. Mosques were also built alongside the mausoleums of temporal rulers and aristocrats. Visitors were supposed to perform rituals around the saint's tomb (reciting prayers for the dead, offering and consecrating gifts, etc.) yet pray at the nearby mosque. Such architectural solutions, used at Lahore's major ritual sites including Data Darbar, Mian Mir's tomb, and Madho Lal Husain's shrine, were meant to reconcile the contradiction between the mosque and the tomb. Still, visitors have tended to pray at a saint's tomb rather than at the nearby mosque.

The earliest examples of ritual architecture in Pakistan are found in Multan and Ucch, and date from the Delhi Sultanate. The domed multi-storey octagonal citadel-like mausoleum arose here and subsequently influenced funerary buildings in other parts of the country. The overwhelming majority of extant mosques and mausoleums in Lahore were built during the reign of the Great Mughals and therefore bear the typical marks of Mughal architecture.

The Great Mughals were gifted and prolific architects, and their buildings served the same goals as their intricate and extensive administrative apparatus: the affirmation of the eternal grandeur of imperial rule and the constant reminder of its all-pervasive presence and control over the lives of its subjects. The architectural means for expressing these goals were monumentality, grandeur, lavishness, and the coexistence of a multiplicity of building techniques, materials, and ornamentation that were beyond comparison with Central Asian and Iranian architecture.

'The real strength of the Mughals, however, lay in their self-reliance and confidence in themselves', wrote Kamil Khan Mumtaz, a well-known specialist on Pakistani architecture. 'They believed that they were the architects of a new world, and that theirs was a golden age of which they themselves were the fountainhead. This faith enabled them to experiment with impunity and inventiveness. Even their eclecticism was not an awe-inspired submission to a glorified past, but rather a magnanimous acceptance of tributes and new ideas which could be exploited to advantage in the service of the court.'[1]

Despite stylistic variations stemming from different times and clients' tastes, all buildings constructed under the patronage of the Great Mughals belong to a continuously developing yet unified architectural tradition that should be evaluated as a single whole. For example, early forts in Attock and Lahore, built at the start of Akbar's rule, consist of small buildings with abundant reliefs on red sandstone that give them a certain mass and volume. This is the earliest example of the transition from the Hindu architectural and sculptural style to the new architectural conception.

Jahangir's tomb in Lahore should be studied together with I'timad-ud-Daula's earlier tomb in Agra, in order to grasp the transition from the 'relics' of the architectural and sculptural style of Akbar's age to the delicate refinement of Shah Jahan's buildings. In both of these tombs, the fine geometric incrustation of white marble in dark sandstone marks the transition from a monochromatic stone surface to a polychromatic decorative treatment of the surfaces. As for the floral ornaments of the *pietre dure*[2] that were used by the builders of both mausoleums, they anticipate the lustrous precious texture of the Taj Mahal and of the Naulakha Pavilion in the Lahore Fort. Another borrowing from the past is the positioning of the tombs at the intersection of the axes of a regular park, in accordance with the Persian model that was first used by the Mughals in Humayun's Tomb in Delhi.

Mughal architects never copied their models blindly, including 'kindred' Timurid models. The Mughals borrowed their decorative system of vegetal and geometric ornament from India, where it was already used during the Delhi Sultanate. Yet, whereas early Muslim architecture employed strictly abstract forms, the Mughal architects and artists took a new interest in nature and representation and introduced a unique naturalism into this system, creating ornaments of 'real' flowers, plants, and animals that corresponded to their botanic and zoological prototypes.

Still, what sets the architecture of the Great Mughals apart is the generally recognized monumentality that is found in their buildings of all sizes. In most cases, Mughal buildings stun the viewer, not because of their size but due to their magnificence and rich ornamentation. Even Lahore's biggest architectural complexes, such as the Badshahi Masjid, the tombs of Jahangir and his relatives in Shahdara, and the Shalimar Gardens, impress us not with their grandeur but with their perfection, clarity of proportions and layout, harmony of the different parts, and the architectural saturation of the surrounding space. The polyphony of the different elements—masses, volumes, materials, forms, and ornaments—constitute a grand and powerful orchestra.

Scholars of Mughal history and architecture often note that buildings constructed by different dynasty members reflect not only their own tastes but also their personalities. Although Babur's edifices in India have not survived, most were gardens which the dynastic founder used to consolidate his conquered territory. Humayun spent much of his rule in exile in Iran. So, his rare buildings, such as the mosque in Thatta, greatly resemble Persian architecture. The 'grand style' of the Great Mughals emerged under Akbar, and his large-scale monumental projects (the capital of Fatehpur-Sikri, Humayun's Tomb, and Sikandariya) were strongly influenced by Hindu building techniques and architectural forms, i.e., they bore the mark of programmatic religious tolerance and eclecticism, characterizing the ideological and political views of this emperor.

Emperor Jahangir, who preferred painting to architecture and private life to state activities, gave a lot of importance to the interior decoration of buildings. It was fashionable, during his rule, to decorate interiors with frescos depicting plants and animals. Jahangir's passion resulted in the unique 'Picture Wall' (*taswirat ki diwar*) that frames the Shah Burj Gate, and stretches along the northern wall of Lahore Fort. Commenced in 1624–25 (and completed by Shah Jahan in 1631–32), this wall is divided into rectangular and arched panels, filled-in with coloured glazed-tile mosaics showing detailed naturalistic images of animals, people, dragons, winged angels, and *peris* (fairies).

Some mosaics have detailed depictions of court amusements, such as elephant, camel, and bull fights, hunting, and playing *chaugan* (polo).[3]

Power and architecture were synonyms for Shah Jahan, and it is no coincidence that the three main Mughal citadels in Delhi, Lahore, and Agra took their final shape during his reign. The architecture of Shah Jahan's time was marked by a degree of elegance and refinement that had not been seen up to then. The widespread use of white marble as the main building material, instead of sandstone, created an overall impression of luxury, which was enhanced by the filigree handling of the material, creating the effect of luminosity, transparency, and 'preciousness'. In addition to the world-famous Taj Mahal, all the most artistically valuable buildings in Lahore—the Naulakha Pavilion, the Moti Masjid, the Shish Mahal in Lahore Fort, and the Shalimar Gardens—were built under Shah Jahan's patronage in accordance with the new architectural trends.

Finally, Emperor Aurangzeb's rigour and religious asceticism was reflected in the architecture of his time. The giant 'Alamgiri Gate, which became the main entrance to Lahore Fort, creates an impression of monumentality because of its size and mass. In terms of its height and volume and its lack of ornament, it is disproportionate to the buildings within the Fort. Aurangzeb's main building project in Lahore was the imperial mosque—the Badshahi Masjid—which is also marked by asceticism and very sparse external decoration. Despite the mosque's perfect proportions, from the outside it has the effect of a colossus that overwhelms the individual—the embodied metaphor of the predominance of government and religion. Still, this effect is purely external: the mosque looks totally different inside, marked by the soaring, permeable, and spiritually liberating space of faith.

Badshahi Masjid is the best place to begin our account of Lahore mosques. It is the second biggest mosque in Pakistan (after the modern Faisal Mosque in Islamabad), accommodating up to 60,000 worshippers. Although mosques abound in each of the many administrative districts of present-day Lahore,[4] extant historical mosques are rare and Badshahi Masjid is rightly considered to be foremost among them. It was built on the emperor's order in 1674, as the Persian inscription on the marble plaque over the arch of the main entrance states: 'The mosque of the victorious (*Abu zafar*) warrior for the faith, Emperor Muhyuddin Muhammad 'Alamgir. Completed under the supervision of the humblest court servant Fidai Khan Koka in A.H. 1084 (= 1673/74).' Fidai Khan Koka was the emperor's foster brother, and was mentioned on several occasions by Bernier as the Master of Ordnance at the Mughal court.[5]

Certain historical sources point out that the marble and red sandstone used to build the mosque had previously been acquired by Dara Shikoh to build a shrine for his beloved saint and spiritual mentor, Mian Mir. However, Dara was killed before he could finish his pious project, and the precious building materials were confiscated by his victorious brother and used for another religious purpose: to build the grandiose Badshahi Masjid. It is no surprise that the orthodox Sunni Aurangzeb, and the mystically oriented Dara, had different understandings of religious duty.

In addition to its primary ritual function, Badshahi Masjid was one of the richest reliquaries in South Asia, housing unique Islamic relics. In a room closed to visitors, glass cases contained the green turban, coat, sandals, and quilt of the Prophet; his white banner with verses of the Qu'ran; and his footprint (*qadam Rasul*) in a sand-coloured stone. Other cases contained Caliph 'Ali's turban and amulet (*ta'wiz*) and the surah *Yasin* transcribed by his hand; Fatimah's embroidered veil and prayer rug; Imam Husain's golden turban and banner, as well as a handkerchief with stains of his blood; the turban and prayer rug of the great saint 'Abdul Qadir Jilani (*Ghaus al-'Azam*); and a number of other relics ascribed to the Prophet's family members and associates.

According to various sources, these relics were seized by Timur when he conquered the city of Damascus (1401), and were subsequently handed down, from generation to generation, in the Timurid dynasty until Babur brought them to India in the sixteenth century. The Great Mughals had possession of the relics for two centuries until the death of Emperor Muhammad Shah (1748). His widow, Malika az-Zamani, whose position at the court of Emperor 'Alamgir II in Delhi had become precarious,[6] took the relics away to her native city of Jammu and, experiencing financial difficulties, sold them there to the local Muslim aristocracy. The relics changed hands several times until they were finally seized by Sardar Maha Singh, Maharaja Ranjit Singh's father, who brought them to Lahore.

Although the Sikh rulers of Lahore recognized the relics' material value, they did not treat them as religious objects and stored them in the official royal residence, Shish Mahal. Only after the British annexation of the Punjab were the relics returned to the Muslim community and placed in the Badshahi Masjid.[7]

The stylistic model for the Badshahi Mosque was the Jama' Masjid in Delhi. Built by Shah Jahan in 1648, the Jama' Masjid was also marked by the predominance of rationalism over ornamentalism. Both mosques stand on high platforms, reached by staircases, giving them dominating positions in their cities. In the Lahore mosque, staircases with twenty-two steps are located on three sides, forming a pyramid.

One enters the Delhi and Lahore mosques through monumental arched two-storey gates with minarets at the four corners. In the Badshahi Masjid, the gate's projecting *pishtaq* is flanked, on both sides, by thin columns with white marble spheres on top. A serrate balustrade runs, between the columns, over the central arch; it is shaped like an arcade, and each arch is topped by a small marble cupola (*gunbadi*). An open kiosk (*chhatri*), with a projecting canopy (*chhajja*)[8] and a marble dome, is located between the balustrade and the corner minaret on each side. This architectural solution recalls the famous gate, the Buland Darwaza (1602), situated in front of the entrance to the mosque in Fatehpur-Sikri. There, as with the Badshahi Mosque, the harmony of the gate's façade is emphasized by a crowning openwork gallery with miniature domes.

The structural module used in the gate is repeated in the mosque's courtyard and in the exterior design of the prayer hall. It consists of a combination of minarets, columns, and spires (i.e., vertical structures) of different heights and shapes (rectangular and octagonal cross-sections) made of red sandstone, with domes and spheres of different sizes and volumes carved out of white marble. The combination of these constantly repeating and varying basic elements gives the entire mosque complex a wholeness and a dynamic 'pulsating' rhythm, illustrating the conception of the unity of large and small, vertical and horizontal, three-dimensional and flatly decorative, that marks all Mughal buildings and symbolizes the same theme of the all-pervasiveness of centralized imperial power that rules over aristocrats and the common folk (*khass-o-'am*), the rich and the poor (*amir-o-gharib*), the important and the insignificant.

The mosque's courtyard has an area of almost 85,000 square metres and is divided into two levels. The lower level, which has an area of 760 square metres and is where prayers for the dead are held, has a cistern for ritual ablutions. The courtyard is surrounded by a wall with 80 arched niches. Fifty-four-metre-high minarets, with rectangular cross-sections, stand at the four corners of the outer wall. The prayer hall, with an area of about 7,000 square metres, is situated at the rear of the courtyard. It has three marble domes on cylindrical drums. The domes are crowned by golden spires that seem to grow out of upside-down lotuses. The octagonal minarets at the four corners of the prayer hall are crowned with domed kiosks with projecting canopies. They are considerably lower than the courtyard minarets. The façade of the prayer hall is decorated similarly to the gate's façade, yet has many marble incrustations in which the *islimi*[9] ornamention predominates.

As with other masterpieces of Mughal architecture, the Badshahi Mosque suffered greatly at the hands of the Sikhs and the British. Ranjit Singh turned the mosque into army stables. Prohibited from entering the building, Muslims could only pray in the courtyard. During the civil war over 'Sikh heritage', that began after Ranjit Singh's death, the minarets were the most affected. The upper parts of some of the minarets collapsed during the earthquake of 1840. In 1841, the ruler of Lahore, Sher Singh, ordered that cannons be mounted on the tops of the minarets, from where he bombarded the Fort when it was besieged by supporters of Maharani Chand Kaur. Several years later, this barbaric act was repeated by Vizier Hira Singh,[10] whose soldiers opened fire on the Fort, from the mosque's minarets, using *zamburah* guns with which they had fought in the Kashmir mountains.[11]

Although the English showed respect for Hindu and Muslim shrines, they continued to employ Badshahi Masjid as a military warehouse and destroyed part of the walls of the courtyard to prevent it from being used as a bastion. When the mosque was finally returned to Lahori Muslims for ritual purposes, it was in a half-ruined state. Restoration work began in 1852, yet proceeded slowly as funds were lacking. The mosque regained its original appearance only in 1960.

Across from Badshahi Masjid rises the already mentioned 'Alamgiri Darwaza, the main gate of Lahore Fort, built in 1674. It is marked by the same monumental yet ascetic style as the mosque. The gate's *pishtaq* is flanked by 'bloated' massive semicircular fluted towers crowned by high pavilions resembling watchtowers. The gate's façade has corner cylindrical columns (*guldasta*) on both sides. On the whole, the 'Alamgiri Gate resembles a well-fortified defensive structure, which is entirely in keeping with the personality of its builder. Together, the Badshahi Mosque and the 'Alamgiri Gate constitute a unified architectural ensemble embodying the dual nature of the power of the Great Mughals—a power that was based on both military superiority and religious zeal.

The severely graphic architecture of Badshahi Masjid is more the exception than the rule in Lahore. In other Mughal mosques and secular buildings, the clarity of architectural forms dissolves in rich and intricately intertwined vegetal ornamentation, elegant calligraphic contours, bright colours and iridescent hues of polished marble encrusted with multicoloured stones, gilding, and curved stonework that blends with the fancy shapes of elaborate cusped arches and ledges.

In contrast to Central Asian and Iranian architecture, Mughal ritual buildings were rarely decorated with coloured ceramic tiles or mosaics. Jahangir's 'Picture Wall' in the Fort is unique in this regard. Nevertheless, these techniques—called *kashikari*—are widely used in quite a few buildings outside the Fort in Lahore. According to Kamil Khan Mumtaz,

> 'The use of glazed faience tiles, rare in Mughal buildings, was restricted mainly to the Punjab and Sind.... The restriction of this decorative technique to a small area in the empire as well as the architectural character of these buildings places them clearly outside the mainstream of Mughal court architecture. Indeed, there appears to have co-existed in 17th century Lahore a distinctly independent local tradition which derived its inspiration equally from Safevid Persia and Delhi. It is perhaps significant that only those buildings commissioned by the emperors themselves are in the imperial style of Delhi and Agra with a prominent use of stone and plastered external surfaces,

while those built by lesser nobility or local lords and ladies
have the provincial characteristic brick structures with
glazed tile mosaics on the outer walls.'[12]

These 'provincial features', that Kamil Khan Mumtaz calls the 'Lahore
school' of architecture, are found in many historical seventeenth
century Lahore buildings: the mosque of Dai Anga (1635), the rich
and influential wet nurse of Shah Jahan; Chauburji (1646), the
entrance gate to the garden of Princess Zebunnisa; the gateway to
the no longer extant garden Gulabi Bagh (1655) that had belonged
to Mirza Sultan Beg, a relative of Shah Jahan; and the mosque of
Muhammad Saleh Kanbuh (1660s), Shah Jahan's court chronicler. All
these buildings were richly decorated with tiles, mosaics, and frescos.

Still, the best building of the 'Lahore school' is Wazir Khan Mosque,
the most beautiful city mosque that chroniclers poetically called the
'splendid mole on Lahore's cheek.'[13] Its builder was Hakim 'Ilmuddin
Ansari, commonly known as Wazir Khan, who had a brilliant career at
Shah Jahan's court. He became a court physician and close attendant
of the emperor while the latter was still Prince Khurram; he was
entrusted, in particular, with accompanying the body of Empress
Mumtaz Mahal from Burhanpur to Agra (where she was subsequently
buried, in the Taj Mahal). In 1620, Wazir Khan was awarded the title
(*mansab*) of 'Commander of 5,000' (*panch-hazari*)[14] and charged with
overseeing the emperor's private apartments at the Lahore Fort. Soon
afterwards, he was made governor (*subedar*) of the Punjab.

In his description of the Padishah's arrival in Lahore in 1628, the
court chronicler Saleh Kanbuh mentioned Wazir Khan's role:

> 'The Padishah's camp arrived at the capital on the seventh
> day of Ramadan. At some distance from the city, the
> Shelter of the World (the Padishah—*A.S.*) was met with
> a lot of pomp by Wazir Khan, who presented him with
> a thousand *ashrafi* in the form of a *nazr*,[15] and by all
> the aristocratic and noble inhabitants of Lahore. The
> Padishah entered the palace after the first day watch. On
> the ninth day of Ramadan, Wazir Khan gave the High
> Lord precious stones, gold and silver tableware, carpets,

horses, and camels worth four *lakhs* rupees that he had
amassed while ruler of the Punjab.'[16]

The principal reason for building the Wazir Khan Mosque was the
lack of a congregational mosque (*Jama' Masjid*) in the Fort in the first
half of the seventeenth century. The palace mosque of Moti Masjid
('Pearl Mosque', 1630), like two other mosques of the same name
located in the forts of Agra (1637) and Delhi (1659), is a miniature
snow-white building. It is an architectural metaphor, of a real pearl,
that was intended for a select group—the women of the imperial
harem. In general, the palace 'chamber' mosques of the Great Mughals
often bore the names of precious stones: Mina Masjid (from *mina*,
'blue stone, lapis lazuli') and Nagina Masjid (from *nagin*, 'precious
stone') in Agra Fort, Lal Masjid (from *lal*, 'ruby') in Aurangabad, etc.
All were small in size and lacked a prayer courtyard.

Lahore's oldest mosque (1614) was built by Jahangir's mother,
Empress Mariam Zamani, and bears her name. It is located in the
immediate vicinity of the Fort, next to Masti Gate. It is fairly large in
size, yet lacks a prayer courtyard that could have accommodated all
the members of the congregation (which was an essential element of
the congregational mosque). For this reason, the Wazir Khan Mosque
served as the city's congregational mosque until the Badshahi Masjid
was built: every week, a lavish court cavalcade went there from the
Fort, through Masti Gate to Delhi Gate for the Friday prayer.

In our day, visitors to the Wazir Khan Mosque pass through Delhi
Gate and slowly make their way through the narrow and crowded
Kashmiri Bazaar until they get to the square Chowk-e Wazir Khan.
This vast territory formerly belonged to Wazir Khan, who turned it
into a *waqf* (inalienable property whose profits are used for religious or
charitable purposes) that became the mosque's main source of income.
The Chowk, which may be considered to be the mosque's forecourt,
used to play an important role in the Walled City: all the principal
arteries leading to the main bazaars converged here.

The mosque's arched gateway, with a deep covered passageway
forming an inner courtyard (*deorhi*), opens onto the Chowk. From
north to south, along the octagonal forecourt, stretches a *riwaq*—a
covered gallery with double rows of arcaded chambers, resembling

bazaar-like corridors or galleries. Like the mosque, the gateway is made of brick. The form of brickwork is indicated on the gate's surface with numerous white lines; this technique of imitating brick was called *tazakari*. The first thing that impresses the visitor is the gateway's colour, which is quite unusual for Mughal architecture. Both the gateway and the mosque itself have a vibrant purple terracotta hue, which differs from the soft colour of red sandstone. This effect of vibrant luminescent colour was attained by covering the brick with moist plaster (*chunam*) that was painted with water-based 'Indian red' pigment while wet; like all genuine fresco techniques (*buono fresco*), this creates a sensation of transparency and colour vibration.

John Lockwood Kipling (1837–1911), an authority on both Eastern and Western art, called the Wazir Khan Mosque a 'school of design', and wrote about its paintings:

> 'In the mosque itself are some very good specimens of Perso-Indian arabesque painting on the smooth *chunam* walls. This work, which is very freely painted and good in style, is true fresco painting, the *buono fresco* of the Italians, and, like the inlaid ceramic work, is now no longer practiced, modern native decoration being usually *fresco secco* or mere distemper painting. The reason of this is that there has been no demand for this kind of work for many years.'[17]

In view of the uniqueness of the frescos and mosaics of the Wazir Khan Mosque in Pakistani architecture, it was obligatory for all students at the Mayo School of Arts (now the National College of Arts)—founded by J.L. Kipling—to study and copy them.

The purple surface of the walls of the gateway and mosque was covered with vertical and horizontal panels that were slightly sunk into the surface. In each panel, plaques of multicoloured ceramic mosaics (*kashi*) form an arch. The mosaic ornament is quite diverse, including traditional calligraphic inscriptions and arabesques, as well as *islimi*, *band-i rumi*, and *girih* ornaments.[18] The ornamental motif of cypress, which subsequently became widespread in Lahore architecture, appeared here for the first time. The gaps between the wall and the sunken panels were covered with gilding and painted with vegetal ornaments. The combination of purple walls, white lines, blue mosaic decoration, gilding, and polychromatic ornamentation creates a highly decorative effect, a colourful elegance, and even gaudiness that are very untypical for Mughal architecture as a whole. Coloured ceramic mosaics cover not only the mosque's walls but also the *muqarnas*—the stalactites, alveolar vaults, and cornices of the entrance arches.

The mosque's interior is divided into five naves, with several low 'flattened' domes that are typical of the early architecture of the Delhi Sultanate. Octagonal minarets crowned by high kiosks are located at the four corners of the mosque; the kiosks rest on massive projecting platforms. Neither the shape of the domes, nor the minarets with their 'heavy' tops, correspond to the usual building practices of the Great Mughals. Just as with the abundant use of coloured tile mosaic, these are traits of the 'provincial' architectural style of the Lahore school. Similar minarets, crowned by massive projecting platforms, are found at the Dai Anga Mosque and in Chauburji.

The *kashi* technique was also used to create the Persian inscriptions on the gateway inside the mosque, which contains a chronogram of the date of construction. In accordance with the tradition of comparing the entrance of a religious building or shrine with the Gate of Paradise, one of the inscriptions states:

> *dihqān diravad ba hashr ay nīksirisht*
> *dar mazra'-i ākhirat har ān chīz ki kisht*
> *dar bāb-i 'amal banā-yi khayrī biguzār*
> *k-ākhar hama rā rah ast z-īn dar ba bihisht*

> O virtuous, the farmer gathers the harvest [on the field]
> Of the Day of Judgment
> From all that he has sown on the field of the end of the world.
> Leave a good foundation under the gate of action,
> For all have to pave their way to paradise through this gateway.[19]

Every new religious building in South Asian countries—whether a mosque or a saint's tomb—was built, as a rule, on the site of a previous shrine that had a 'history' of religious worship or sacralization. The

Wazir Khan Mosque was no exception: it was built over the tomb of
the Persian mystic Sayyid Ishaq Gazeruni, known as Miran Badshah,
who came to India during the Tughluq dynasty. The tomb is preserved
in the mosque's basement and attracts pilgrims to this day.

In the mosque's courtyard, one can see the white dome of another
shrine—the tomb of the saint, Syad Suf, who was a contemporary of
Miran Badshah. This is one of the rare saints' tombs that was built
during the colonial era with the permission and participation of the
British Administration, as the Persian inscription states:

> 'At the suggestion of Sahib possessing high dignity, Major
> George Macgregor, Deputy Commissioner of Lahore
> District, this sacred mausoleum of His Holiness Syad
> Suf was built by Sheikh Sultan, the Contractor of the
> Honourable the East India Company (May their dignity
> last for ever) in the year A.D. 1852, corresponding to 1908
> Samvat, and 1268 Hijri.'[20]

Its architectural uniqueness and originality notwithstanding, the
Wazir Khan Mosque is an example of a 'place that preserves its own
memory', as described in Chapter 1. During the Tughluq dynasty in
the fourteenth century, during the Mughal Empire in the seventeenth
century, and during English rule in the nineteenth century, this place
continued to be a topos of high spiritual concentration. Even the
bazaar adjoining the mosque (a space with different functions, it
would seem) is organically incorporated into its architectural complex,
with its arched cells (*hujra*) that resemble the layout of *madrasa*
and other educational institutions that have always existed around
mosques.

Such topoi, that transmit their functions and cultural and
geographic images over the centuries, make up the specific character
of Lahore's *topophilia*: the city keeps presenting new objects and
landscape contours that are not frightening in their novelty but
continue old and well-known chorological images that have long
become part of the historic memory of society and are perceived by
our consciousness as pre-given and self-evident elements of *Lebenswelt*.

By the Later Mughals' era, in the mid-eighteenth century, ritual
architecture in Lahore totally abandoned its former traditions of

monumentality and stylistic purity. Architects did not want, or were unable, to create ensembles and adapt the size of buildings to their surroundings; they also began to use simpler and less refined ornamentation, anticipating the vulgarization of the principles of Mughal architecture that took place during the Sikh period in general, and in the mausoleums (*samadhi*) of Guru Arjun Dev and Ranjit Singh in particular. An example of such far-reaching deterioration is the Golden (or, more precisely, Gilded) Mosque (*Sonehri Masjid*) that was built in 1753 by Nawab Bhikari Khan, son of the vice-governor of Lahore during the reign of 'Alamgir II.

Bhikari Khan, whose position in society was fairly modest, unexpectedly rose through the ranks thanks to his good looks. He became a favourite of Murad Begum, widow of Mir Mannu—the powerful ruler of the Punjab who had managed to tergiversate for a long time between the Mughal emperor in Delhi and the Afghan Ahmad Shah Durrani, who invaded the Punjab three times. After Mir Mannu's death in 1752, Murad Begum declared herself the ruler of the Punjab—a unique event for Muslim society at the time. When Bhikari Khan became Murad Begum's favourite, he was allowed to dispense treasury funds freely and could commission buildings. The Sonehri Masjid was the result. It should be added that this love story had an unhappy ending: for some reason, Bhikari Khan evoked the wrath of his powerful mistress and she ordered her servants to beat him to death with slippers. Murad Begum's rule was shortlived. In 1755, Vizier 'Imadulmulk captured Lahore and arrested Murad Begum as a usurper, sending her to Delhi to face trial at the imperial court. In her despair and wrath, she cursed the Delhi rulers and predicted the fall of the Great Mughal dynasty and the destruction of its capital, which soon took place.[21]

The location of the Golden Mosque was ill-chosen from the start: the mosque stands at the end of the long and narrow Kashmiri Bazaar, surrounded by shops and residential buildings on all sides, and seems stifled by the lack of space and perspective. The mosque's name stems from its three copper-fluted domes covered with polished gilding, whose bright lustre is visible from afar. Similar gilded domes crown the corner minarets. Whereas classic Mughal architecture makes use of bulbous domes, the Golden Mosque's cupolas are somewhat grotesque, resembling a turnip that is wider at the base. The pinnacles, that form the 'tips' of these 'turnips' are framed by thin hanging leaf-shaped plaques. The mosque itself is not big; the cupolas, which stand out because of their shape and lustre, dominate the building and make it look low-built.

A balustrade with an open arcade crowned with small replicas of the domes of the prayer hall stretches over the *pishtaq* entrance, as in the Badshahi Masjid and other Lahore mosques. The only difference is that the traditional serrations of the balustrade have the form of the *naga* (swollen snake hoods) ornament—a decorative element that is totally foreign to the aesthetics of Mughal architecture; similarly so for the lower part of the columns, which are shaped like a lotus growing out of its bulb.

The non-traditional elements in the architecture and decoration of the Golden Mosque apparently attracted the attention of non-Muslims because, as soon as Maharaja Ranjit Singh came to power, the military Sikh order—*Akali*—seized this particular mosque, consecrating it in their own peculiar way by spreading cow dung over the floor and installing their holy book—the *Guru Granth*—in it. Muslims repeatedly beseeched Ranjit Singh to return the mosque but their petitions were successful only after the intercession of a water carrier named *Gullu Mashki* who was a confident of Maharani Jindan, the wife of the ruler. In return for the Golden Mosque, the Muslims handed over the proceeds from the rental payments for the adjoining bazaar, and promised to read the *azan* (call to prayer) more quietly.[22] It is curious that a water carrier, a member of the low *mashki* caste, could help to solve matters related to communal disputes and the confiscation and return of property in seventeenth century India.

Although mosques have always played the dominating role in Lahore's chorology, most early European visitors to Lahore were primarily struck by the countless mausoleums, tombs, and sepulchres. Lahore's tombs fall into two categories: the mausoleums (*maqbara*) of the rulers and aristocrats, which are interesting from a historic and architectural standpoint; and the ritual complexes (*dargah*) and shrines (*mazar*) of the saints and Sufi teachers that are mass pilgrimage sites despite their often very modest size, and so are topoi of a timeless and spiritual value.

The oldest tomb, in the first category, is the mausoleum of Qutub-ud-Din Aibak, founder of the Ghulam dynasty and one of the creators of the Delhi Sultanate, who died in 1210 as a result of an accident during a game of polo. The mausoleum was completely restored in the 1970s, on the order of Zulfikar 'Ali Bhutto, and is today a unique architectural relic of its kind from the pre-Mughal era.

Another mausoleum of this type is the tomb of 'Ali Mardan Khan, which is now without its original marble facing. 'Ali Mardan Khan, who died in 1657, was one of Shah Jahan's principal associates, *subedar* of the Punjab, and *mansabdar* 'of seven thousand' (*hafthazari*). He is known in history as the builder of the two major canals in Delhi and Lahore, as well as the irrigation system in Kashmir. Similarly, the following mausoleums have survived, mostly without decoration: the domed tombs of Khan-i Khanan (Zafar Jung Kokaltash), Dai Anga, and Saleh Kanbuh (the chronicler is buried alongside his brother Sheikh 'Inayatulla Kanbuh, author of the classic Persian narrative '*Bahar-i Danish*'); the pyramidal mausoleum of Princess Zebunnisa; the plain two-storied pavilion with the tomb of Nadira Begum, widow of Dara Shikoh; the tower of the Cypress Tomb of Sharafunnisa Begum; and other half-destroyed tombs of Mughal aristocrats. Most of them are situated in the former suburbs of Mughalpura and Begumpura.

A prominent example of such half-destroyed buildings is the ruins of the massive domed edifice known as *Buddhu-ka-ava* (Buddhu's brick-kiln). This building, which was apparently a tomb (judging from its architecture), was supposedly built during the reign of Shah Jahan by Buddhu, the court potter. He owned several similar kilns on the outskirts of Lahore and produced burnt bricks for the needs of the court. A legend recounts that, one cold winter day, a disciple of Saint Mian Mir came to the *Buddhu-ka-ava* to warm himself by the kiln. However, Buddhu's servants and apprentices drove the dervish away. In his wrath, he cursed the potter and his kiln, causing the fire to be extinguished forever.[23] The building was, supposedly, abandoned afterwards until it was seized by the Sikhs. A dervish's curse cannot be annulled, that is why the Sikhs experienced a constant shortage of bricks and expropriated them wherever they could find them.

The most valuable ritual buildings, from the historical and architectural standpoints, make up the complex on the banks of the Ravi river, in the suburb of Shahdara, containing the tombs of Padishah Jahangir and his brother-in-law Asaf Khan and the mausoleum of Empress Nur Jahan and Ladli Begum (her daughter from her first marriage). The Shahdara ensemble is considered a masterpiece of Mughal architecture, and art historians rank Jahangir's mausoleum second only to the Taj Mahal.

The Shahdara ensemble consists of three connected rectangular courtyards situated on a single axis. The central courtyard of Akbari Serai was formerly a caravanserai for travellers. Here, in a continuous row of small arched cellular chambers, lived the guardians, gardeners, caretakers, and other personnel. The Akbari Serai was surrounded by a wall with two pairs of gates: the southern gate is the main entrance, from the side of the river; the eastern gate leads to the courtyard of Jahangir's tomb; the western gate is the *mihrab* of the mosque, beyond which stands the mausoleum of Asaf Khan at the end of the third courtyard; and the northern gate is purely decorative, built for the purposes of symmetry. The tomb of Nur Jahan is situated somewhat at a distance, outside the walls of the complex. The fact that Jahangir and his favourite wife were buried apart was a reflection of the life-long enmity between the empress and her stepson Shah Jahan.

Jahangir died in 1627 in Kashmir; he willed that he be buried in Lahore, in the garden of Dilkusha. The court chronicler, Saleh Kanbuh, ascribes the construction of Jahangir's mausoleum to Shah Jahan. He wrote, 'The Refuge of the World expressed his desire to be buried in the garden of Dilkusha on the other side of the Ravi. Inspired by the precepts of Sunnite faith and the example of his brilliant predecessor Babur, he ordered his tomb to be built in the open so that rain and dew could freely fall on it. Respecting his will, his son and successor Padishah Shah Jahan built an elegant mausoleum out of red sandstone around the tomb of his father, while the tomb itself stands on a raised open platform and is made of white marble inlaid with precious stones and decorated with exquisite carvings. Despite the building's modest size, it took a decade to build and cost ten lakhs.'[24]

At the same time, Kipling and Thornton wrote, on the basis of other sources, that 'Nurjehan, his lovely and accomplished wife, devoted herself to the task of raising a monument to his memory.

The tomb was raised by her piety and devotion at her own expenses.'[25] Kamil Khan Mumtaz also wrote that the mausoleum was built on the order of Nur Jahan, who 'designed his tomb taking as her model of the tomb of I'timad-ud-Daula, her parents' burial place at Agra'.[26]

The mausoleum itself is a single storey rectangular building made of red sandstone. It stands on a platform and has eleven arches pierced in its façade. The mausoleum's walls are richly decorated with ornamental elements, made out of white marble, in the *pietre dure* technique—in particular, the motifs of the *aftaba* (ewer), *qab* (fruit dish), and *ghulab pash* (rose water sprinkler). The four-corner minarets are crowned with white marble cupolas and rise, in four stages, nearly 30 metres above the ground. The tomb's interior is decorated with frescos and mosaic panels in the *kashikari* technique.

In the centre of the hall, there is a white marble cenotaph—a vertical plate resembling a cut-off multi-level pyramid standing on a wide base. Such cenotaphs are found in many Mughal tombs, including the Taj Mahal. The entire cenotaph was inlaid with floral and calligraphic ornament. Ninety nine 'beautiful names' (*asma' al-husna*) of God are inscribed on its sides, the Fatiha (the opening surah of the Qu'ran) on its top and, on its back, the Persian inscription 'The illuminating resting place of His Majesty, the asylum of mercy, Nuruddin Muhammad Jahangir Badshah in 1037 Hijra [= 1627]' (*marqad-i munawwar-i 'ala hazrat-i ghafrān-panāh-i Nūr al-dīn Muhammad Jahāngīr bādshāh fī sanat 1037*).[27]

Nevertheless, the most attractive aspect of Jahangir's tomb is its location—its situation in the surrounding regular garden. The mausoleum opens itself up to the visitor gradually, as he walks through the park. The building is 'hidden' in the far section of the garden and appears, from time to time, in the distance at the end of canals and walk-paths and behind fountains and trees. This architectural idea, remindful of the frailty of world fame and the insignificance of the great of this earth before God's greatness, permeates the whole ensemble with its *memento mori* mood, characteristic of certain genres of classic Muslim poetry.

Most of the mausoleums of the rulers and aristocrats have not been reconstructed and preserve the original traits of Mughal architecture, or of the provincial 'Lahore school', even if in a deformed or half-ruined form. In contrast, the tombs of the saints, as objects of ongoing worship, have constantly been rebuilt, expanded, and renovated. This explains their peculiar eclecticism, violating all architectural canons. *Mazars* are characterized by excessively sumptuous and even garish interior decoration—a profusion of gilding, crystal chandeliers, brocade, and velour; or, in more modest tombs, mirrors, mica, and bright coloured tinsel. In a nutshell, this type of architecture can be described by the pithy word *desi*, which means 'local', 'native', and 'provincial' in contrast to 'universal', 'mainstream', and 'metropolitan'.

A simple list of Lahore *mazars* would take up too much space and time, as one can note from the information posted on the website '150 Lahore Buzurg'.[28] Without a doubt, the main such tomb is *Data Darbar*—an extensive ritual complex (*dargah*) of the city's patron saint, Abul Hasan 'Ali al-Hujwiri (died between 1072 and 1076), who is better known in popular Islam as Data Ganj Bakhsh (from the Sanskrit *data* 'giver', 'generous', and the Persian *ganjbakhsh* 'generous', 'prodigal'). I have described *Data Darbar* and the life of the saint himself in detail elsewhere,[29] and so will only make a few comments here on the role of this tomb in Lahore's *topophilia*.

Over the centuries, *Data Darbar* has played the singular role of a spiritual 'entrance' or 'passageway' to the Indian Subcontinent, which is most likely linked to a long-established practice that Dara Shikoh wrote about in his time: 'He (al-Hujwiri—A.S.) surpasses all other Indian saints, and no new saint can step on this land without first asking for his spiritual permission.'[30] Indeed, the route taken by the Sufis, from Afghanistan and Central Asia to India, usually passed through Lahore; no pious mystic ever passed through the city without paying his respects at the tomb of the patriarch of Indian saints, as hagiographic literature has often recounted. Many saints and mystics have gone to Lahore, over the ages, to be blessed and for spiritual enlightenment: Mu'inuddin Chishti, Baba Farid, Bahauddin Zakariya Multani, Lal Shahbaz Qalandar, Mian Mir, Shah Husain, Bulleh Shah, Sultan Bahu, etc.

Khwaja Mu'inuddin Chishti (1142–1236) spent forty days in *Data Darbar*, after which he embarked upon his great mission: spreading Sufism in the traditional Hindu regions of India, such as Ajmer.

According to Sufi sources, he was the first to give the saint the title *Ganj Bakhsh* ('lavishing treasures'):

ganjbakhsh-i fayz-i 'ālam mazhar-i nūr-ī khudā
kāmilān rā pīr-i kāmil nākasān rā rahnumā

Lavishing the treasures of worldly goods,
Manifestation of Divine Light,
For the perfect, [he] is the perfect mentor,
for the imperfect [he] is a guide.[31]

The outstanding poet and popular saint, Shah Husain (1539–1593), lived and served at *Data Darbar* for twelve years, while he was an itinerant dervish. Spiritual insight and revelations have also occurred at *Data Darbar* in modern times. According to tradition, it was here that Muhammad Iqbal conceived the idea of a separate Muslim state—Pakistan.[32] Finally, *Data Darbar* continues to be an 'entrance' for those seeking recognition, including political leaders. In 2007, when the former prime minister of Pakistan, and present leader of the opposition, Nawaz Sharif returned to his homeland after many years abroad, he first appeared in public at *Data Darbar*. In other words, in the *topophilia* of Lahore, *Data Darbar* plays the chorological role of a place where spiritual pursuits, new ideas, and political missions become manifest.

The *dargah* of Mian Mir (1550–1635) may have a lesser spiritual authority than *Data Darbar*, and may be visited by pilgrims less frequently, yet it is also an extremely important cultural and geographic image of Lahore. In 1852, the British turned the city neighbourhood in which Mian Mir's tomb stands into a military station (cantonment) for the Lahore Division and named it after the tomb. This was common practice in colonial India: naming city districts after their most prominent monuments or buildings. *Anarkali*, the first British military station in Lahore, was named after another historic tomb that will be described below.

As with his predecessor, Data Sahib, Mian Mir is considered to be Lahore's patron saint, whose tomb protects the city from destruction and other calamities. This has been referred to by medieval hagiographers, in particular Dara Shikoh, who described the saint's life in his *Abode of Saints* or *Sakinat al-awliya*, as well as by modern writers, including Muhammad Iqbal. In his poem, *The Secrets of the Self* (*Asrar-i khudi*), Iqbal wrote,

> The holy Sheikh Miyan Mir Wali
> By the light of whose soul every hidden thing was revealed,
> His feet were firmly planted on the path of Mohammed,
> He was a flute for the impassioned music of love.
> His tomb keeps our city safe from harm
> And causes the beams of true religion to shine on us.
> Heaven stooped his brow to his threshold.[33]

Mian Mir is one of the rare saints who are equally venerated by different confessional groups—the Muslims and the Sikhs, in this case.[34] Descriptions of Mian Mir and his teachings are found in Muslim and Sikh hagiography as well as in historical sources—such as Jahangir's memoirs, *Tuzuk-i Jahangiri;* 'Abdul Hamid Lahori's chronicle *Badshah Namah;* and Muhammad Saleh Kanbuh's *Shah Jahan Namah*. Taken together, these sources show that Mian Mir was not only an extraordinary spiritual figure but was also prone to taking very courageous civil stands. Although he was the favourite of several Mughal emperors, and the spiritual mentor of the crown prince, he did not hesitate to support disfavoured Sikh Gurus who openly opposed the Mughals.

Mian Mir was born in Iranian Sistan, and traced his spiritual genealogy to Caliph 'Umar. As a youth, he joined the Sufi brotherhood Qadiriyya—which was named after 'Abdul Qadir Jilani—and was sent as a missionary to India. He spent some time in Sirhind, where he fell ill. Hagiographic works recount that Mian Mir was cured by 'Abdul Qadir himself, who appeared to him in a dream and told him to go to Lahore, which was the capital of the Great Mughal Empire at the time. There, the saint settled in the Khafipura Quarter where he led an ascetic and secluded life. Nevertheless, his solitude was often disturbed by court messengers inviting him to the palace or informing him of the emperor's impending visit.

The Mughal emperors Jahangir and Shah Jahan held the saint in high esteem. After meeting Mian Mir in Agra, the former wrote,

'He is truly God's beloved. He is without peer today in his holiness and purity of soul. This humble one (the emperor—*A.S.*) visited the dervish on several occasions, and the latter explained to him many details of his doctrine. I felt the urge to make him a monetary offering, yet, as he was above worldly cares, I did not dare give him money and simply presented him with an antelope hide that he could use as a prayer rug. Thereupon he left for Lahore.'[35]

'Abdul Hamid Lahori relates a similar story about Shah Jahan's visit to the saint in 1628: 'The High Lord, who held fakirs in great esteem, visited the saint Mian Mir. The latter was indifferent to worldly matters and spoke little. As the Padishah knew that the saint did not accept worldly wealth, he gave him prayer beads and a white cloth turban and got his blessing in return.'[36] Mian Mir was apparently categorical in his refusal of money; the same source recounts that, the following day, Shah Jahan visited another Lahore dervish, Sheikh Bilawal, who accepted the emperor's gift of two thousand rupees. At the same time, hagiographic descriptions of Mian Mir's meetings with emperors contradict the accounts of the historical sources: they emphasize the saint's reluctance to deal with the authorities in any way and cite his ironic and insolent replies to the rulers.[37] These descriptions are sometimes anecdotal in nature.[38]

Sikh hagiography describes Mian Mir as a close friend, and even an associate, of Guru Arjun Dev (1562–1606), the fifth Sikh guru who compiled the sacred book, the *Guru Granth Saheb*. According to tradition, Guru Arjun Dev invited Mian Mir, in 1588, to come to the sacred pond Amritsar—after which the city was named—to take part in the laying of the cornerstone of the Golden Temple, the most important Sikh shrine. After the foundation ceremony, which the saint attended wearing a robe made of coarse wool (*khirqa*) and a pointed hat adorned with a rose, Guru Arjun Dev and Mian Mir embraced and paid their respects to one another.[39]

When Guru Arjun Dev was accused of supporting the rebellious prince Khosrow, and imprisoned in Lahore Fort where he was cruelly tortured, Mian Mir supposedly visited him in prison and proposed interceding with the emperor, Jahangir, on his behalf.[40] Guru Arjun Dev refused assistance, saying that mortals should not interfere in divine providence. After Guru Arjun's martyrdom—or miraculous disappearance, according to the Sikhs—Mian Mir continued to support his successor, Guru Har Gobind (1595–1644), in whose time the Sikhs established their own army. Muslim and Sikh hagiographies clearly contradict each other. Given the social conventions and customs of the age, it is difficult to imagine that Mian Mir could have been on friendly terms with Guru Arjun Dev and his successors while at the same time remaining in favour with the Great Mughals.

Mian Mir died from dysentery in 1635. His death was accompanied by prophetic dreams and miracles, as recounted by Dara Shikoh. In particular, the latter gave a detailed description of his spiritual experience on the eve of the saint's death:

> 'By sheer bad luck and because of the difficulties at that time with many evil days I, the poor one, was not present at the time of the death of the master, but I was in Agra. One day, it was three hours before the end of the day, I saw in a dream that I was present with Hazrat Mian Jiw. He gave some advice and then said to me: "You have to say the prayer of the dead for me!" As I could not understand this type of order, I became quite excited and declined to do it, but the master says it with a strong emphasis and at that very moment I see that he clearly dies, and I say the prayer of the dead as he had ordered me to do. I awoke in a confused and sad state, and the marks of sadness and tears were quite visible. This event made me very astonished and I had to think often about it. Several days later the horrible message arrived from Lahore that at the same day and at the exact same time as I had seen all of this, the terrible event took place.'[41]

In contrast to *Data Darbar*, which all the rulers of Lahore strove to embellish and expand, Mian Mir's tomb virtually escaped reconstruction; therefore, it is a priceless example of Mughal mortuary architecture in its original form. This laconic cubic building rests on a marble platform, has greatly projecting eaves (*chhajja*), and an umbrella-shaped white dome on a low drum. Dara Shikoh built the lower part of the tomb out of marble. The upper part was finished by the thrifty Aurangzeb in brick. The tomb's walls were decorated with frescos, and the windows covered with wide green carved screens (*jali*), so giving the building a white-green colour.

As with many other ritual complexes in Lahore, Mian Mir's *dargah* was surrounded by a wall, with a central gate made of pink sandstone leading to a spacious courtyard paved with red sandstone. The combination of pink and red stone, and the white marble and green window screens, gave the entire complex an elegant and refined appearance. The upper level of the gate was covered with ceramic panels, with a chronogram of the saint's death that was written by his disciple Mullah Fathulla Shah:

> *miyān mīr sardaftar-i 'ārifān*
> *ki khāk-i dar-ash rashk-i iksīr shud*
> *safar jānib-i shahr-i jāvīd kard*
> *az īn mihnat-ābād dilgīr shud*
> *khirad bahr-i sāl-i vafāt-ash nivisht*
> *ba firdaus-i vālā miyān mīr shud*

> Mian Mir, who is the opening of the book of the enlightened,
> The dust of whose door evokes the envy of elixir.
> He just travelled on to the eternal city.
> Here, in the valley of tears, he was suffering.
> The reason wrote down the date of his death: '*Mian Mir went towards the Highest Paradise.*'[42]

The last line '*Mian Mir went towards the Highest Paradise*' indicates the date of the saint's death in the *abjad* system: 1043 Hijra or AD 1635.

In addition to its large ritual complexes, such as the *Data Darbar*, Mian Mar's *dargah*, as well as the tombs of Shah (Madho Lal) Husain, Miran Husain Zanjani, Pir Makki, Shah 'Abdul Ghani, Muhammad Ghaus, Bibi Pakdaman, and Baba Shah Jamal, Lahore also has many small tombs of local saints or, one could say, *desi* saints. Only Lahoris know these tombs, hidden in labyrinths of narrow streets that tourists do not visit; their devotees often live in the same neighbourhoods.

One such shrine is the tomb of Ghore Shah (Patron of Horses), which does not even have a building of its own. The hereditary saint—a descendant of the famous Ucch-Bukhari dynasty of mystics and spiritual mentors—is buried under a simple canopy in a small garden surrounded by a wall with a high gate. Ghore Shah became famous because of his love for horses and horseback riding. He worked miracles for everyone who presented him with a real, or toy, horse. Ghore Shah's father was angered that the boy revealed his secret gift, of working miracles, in exchange for toys and pronounced a curse upon him. As a result, Ghore Shah died at a young age in 1594. Yet, as befits a saint, he continued to work miracles even after his death. The site around the tomb, as well as its wall, is covered with small clay figures of horses that the pilgrims bring to this touching saint.

Another local shrine was the *Chhajju Bhagat-da-chaubara*. The *chaubara* (a one-storey house) formerly belonged to a Hindu moneylender called Chhajju, whose life changed completely after he met Mian Mir. Under the saint's influence, Chhajju abandoned all worldly affairs and became an ascetic. Instead of converting to Islam, he became a *bhakt (bhagat)*, a preacher of the doctrine of *Dadu-panthi*, and a follower of the *sant* (poet-mystic) Dadu Dayal (1544–1603). People of all faiths went to Chhajju Bhagat's cloister, giving the place the reputation of exceptional holiness—which is reflected in the popular Punjabi saying (*akhaan*): *jo sukh chhajjū de chaubāre na balkh na bukhāre* 'which, literally, means that the pleasure which you find at this place, you don't find either at Balkh or at Bukhara (holy places for Muslims); and, allegorically, it would mean that the pleasure which you find at home, you don't find anywhere else.'[43]

Although the saying has a banal meaning, it keeps the memory of Chhajju, and his cloister, alive among present-day Lahoris. Ranjit Singh rebuilt and expanded the *chaubara*, constructing a marble mausoleum above the saint's relics, a shrine, and a *dharmaśala* (inn for pilgrims). None of these buildings have survived; the saint's memory was preserved only by a well that he supposedly filled with water from the far-away Ganges, through the force of his prayers, so that poor Hindus would be able to bathe in the sacred waters without leaving their city. Nevertheless, the *Chhajju Bhagat-da-chaubara* continued to be a site of pilgrimage, even in its destroyed state. This confirms that a city's *topophilia* is shaped not only by places, but also by the memory of places, and by the possibility of reconstructing the meaning and values that they formerly possessed.

Thus, I have tried to show that the cultural and chorological image that characterizes the spiritual and emotional ties between the physical environment, and human beings, in Muslim Lahore took shape between the mosque and the tomb. The Lahoris' notion of identity and belonging to the city and, more generally, the province, the state, and the Islamic world as a whole is directly tied to places of ritual and religion. These places—mosques and saints' tombs—gather the great integrative power of the thoughts, feelings, and hopes of worshippers and the powerful concentrative energy of the faith and prayer. This explains why mosques and tombs are fundamental or 'power' points on the city's 'mental map'. Moreover, the semantics of the dual object 'mosque-tomb' has a universal component—canonic symbolism of the mosque, classical traditions of Mughal architecture, and the Arabic-Persian bilinguism of the inscriptions—as well as a local or *desi* component—specific features of Punjabi saints' cults, the provincial Lahore architectural school, and the epigraphic of Farsi-Urdu-Punjabi—leading to the overlapping of inter-textual meanings that is typical of *topophilia*.

Shalimar Gardens, Lahore.

CHAPTER **FOUR**

The Name of the Garden:
Shalimar and Others

The Mughal history of Lahore literally began in a garden. In July 1540, Emperor Humayun entered the city that he had just captured from Sher Shah Suri and pitched camp in the garden of a certain Khwaja Dost Munshi which, according to a chronicler, was 'the most charming spot in Lahore'.[1] While spending the night in the garden, he had a dream foretelling the birth of a long-awaited heir who would become the powerful ruler of all Hindustan. The dream came true two years later: Humayun's son, the future emperor Akbar, was born in 1542. It was Akbar who turned Lahore into a flourishing capital city. Subsequently, it became customary for Mughal emperors, on their arrival in Lahore, to spend the night in one of the city's numerous gardens and parks, of which there were fifty according to the historians.[2]

Along with architecture and miniature painting, landscaping and garden design became a favourite form of cultural patronage for the Timurids, including the Great Mughals. Timur himself was interested in gardens; several gardens were built in the suburbs of his capital, Samarqand during his reign, the water being drawn from the Zarafshan River. The famous Timurid garden 'World-adorning'— *Jahanara*—was known far beyond Central Asia.

77

The first Great Mughal 'landscape designer' was the dynasty's founder, Babur, who built gardens along the principal points of his long path of conquest: Kabul, Delhi, Agra, Devalpur, Lahore, and other cities in the Indian Subcontinent. We know from the *Babur-namah* that Babur built a large garden, called the *Kabul-bakht*, to mark his victory at Panipat in 1526; it was apparently his first garden in India.[3] Babur was the first to grow Central Asian melons and certain varieties of grapes in his gardens—still known as 'grapes of Samarqand' (*angur-i samarqandi*) in India and Pakistan—while many Mughal gardens are known as 'grape gardens' (*Anguri Bagh*).

According to historians, Babur's love for gardens had a political motivation: they were a metaphorical expression of his territorial expansion, his control of conquered Indian territories, and the establishment of a new Muslim 'aesthetic order'. James Wescoat, a well-known American scholar of Mughal gardens, has called Babur's gardens 'the gardens of conquest and transformation'.[4] Nevertheless, Babur's landscape activities may have also had a personal motivation: the longing for flowing water, shade, and a respite from the heat— pleasures that only a garden can offer.

In 1530, Babur died in Agra, where he had built several gardens; he was initially buried in his garden, *Ram Bagh*. According to his daughter and biographer, Gulbadan Begum, he said before his death, 'I cherished the thought for a long time to give up my crown to Humayun Mirza and to retire to the Garden Scattering Gold (*Bagh-i zarafshan*)'.[5] His love for gardens persisted, even after his death: according to his will, he was buried in Kabul, in 'Babur's Garden' (*Bagh-i Babur*). Following his example, Babur's descendants surrounded their tombs with magnificent gardens; the indissoluble tie between state power and garden design accompanied these rulers to the ends of their lives.

Mughal chroniclers meticulously noted the names of new gardens and parks, and their dates of construction, as matters of state importance. As a result, we have a fairly good idea of the chronology of Mughal garden and park design. Looking ahead, one can say that the tradition of garden and park design did not cease, even after the decline of the Mughal Empire, in Lahore. Several parks, such as *Hazuri Bagh* in the city centre, date from the Sikh period of Lahore's history. Other gardens, such as Mayo Gardens and Lawrence Gardens, were built by the English who took great pains to plant trees in their residential neighbourhoods. In particular, the Mall—the main street of colonial Lahore and now called Shahrah-e Quaid-i-Azam—was popularly known as *Thandi Sarak* (Cool Street) on account of the cool and shade created by the trees planted along its sides.[6]

But, let us return to the Great Mughals. For them, as for all Muslims, earthly gardens brought the Islamic Paradise (*jannat*) to mind. As the earthly representation of Paradise, a garden embodies the entire world, both visible and invisible. The space of the garden, whether in a natural setting or enclosed in a book, symbolically includes the human heart. For the mystical Sufi consciousness, the garden is a place where the seeker can come to know the Divine Essence; therefore, gardening serves as an allegory for perfecting one's inner world. Muslim gardens existed in material as well as spiritual reality, as a notion of the ideal state of the real world, literary text, or human soul. The garden became a model and paradigm of the universe and of society and, embodying the principles of proportionality and harmony of all its elements, had strict geometric forms.

As the *loci communes* of Islamic art, gardens were a popular subject of miniature painting and an essential element of descriptive narratives. Every correctly structured and stylistically embellished literary text resembles a garden; the most immaculate literary works are often called the 'gardens of poetry'. The titles of many Muslim books, irrespective of their genre or content, often contain the word 'garden' or 'flower garden': from *Gulistan* (Rose Garden) and *Bustan* (Orchard) by Sa'di, a classic Persian poet of the thirteenth century, to *Bagh-o-Bahar* (Garden and Spring) by Mir Amman, a nineteenth-century Urdu prose-writer. The word 'flower garden' (*gulshan, gulzar*) figures in the titles of works of very diverse genres, including the Sufi treatise *The Mystic Rose Garden* (*Gulshan-i raz*) by Mahmud Shabistari, the historical chronicle *The Flower Garden of Ibrahim* (*Gulshan-i ibrahimi*) by Firishta, the saints' hagiography *The Flower Garden of the Righteous* (*Gulzar-i abrar*) by Muhammad Ghausi Shattari, the romance *The Flower Garden of Nasim* (*Gulzar-e nasim*) by Dayashankar Nasim, etc. In all these works, 'garden' or 'flower garden' have no direct relation to the book's content; they have a purely symbolical meaning or serve as a chronogram of the date of composition.

The tradition of comparing literary texts to gardens, and their inevitable mutual correlation, stems from *Gulistan*. At the beginning of the poem (Chapter: Cause for Composing the *Gulistan*), Sa'di recounts how he and a friend once had to spend the night in a beautiful garden. In the morning, his friend began to gather fragrant roses and hyacinths, to take the fragrances of the flowering garden with him. Sa'di stopped him, saying that live flowers wither quickly and that their flowering season is brief—in short, a garden is transient and perishable. When his friend asked him about what one could do, Sa'di replied, 'I may compose for the amusement of those who look and for the instruction of those who are present a book of a Rose Garden, a *Gulistan*, whose leaves cannot be touched by the tyranny of autumnal blasts and the delight of whose spring the vicissitudes of time will be unable to change into the inconstancy of autumn.'[7] Thus, according to Sa'di, not only do books, poetry, and literature resemble gardens and can serve as substitutes for them, but they surpass the natural gardens thanks to the longevity and imperishability of the images that are created by the poets and writers.

Comparison between a garden and a book is a common phenomenon in world culture. In many different traditions, literary works and compositions are called 'gardens' or 'enclosed gardens' (*hortus conclusus*). Given that a text resembles a garden, a garden, in turn, can be composed, read, and understood as a text. A garden-text can be read on two semantic levels. The first level consists of different allegories and symbols of various notions, events, and people, as well as the purely verbal expression of meaning in inscriptions and legends on buildings in the garden. The second semantic level is the general relationship of elements of landscape architecture to a certain conceptual and stylistic order.

Both in the East and in the West, gardens and parks are always multifunctional and closely linked to the lifestyle of a given society. We can learn about the function of Muslim gardens from historical works, literature, and the fine arts (miniature painting). Mughal gardens were designed for court celebrations, official ceremonies (in particular, for the reception of foreign ambassadors), judicial proceedings, and large musical gatherings with song and dance. Cages and menageries, housing rare animals were built in the gardens to astound guests.

At the same time, gardens were places for meditation, solitary thought, prayer, and pious conversation. Mughal miniatures often depict emperors (Akbar, Jahangir, or Aurangzeb) talking, with a Sufi teacher or an itinerant dervish, in a garden. Finally, gardens were also a refuge for lovers and a place for trysts and lovemaking: there are countless miniatures depicting lovers embracing in a garden. In a tropical climate, gardens were, generally speaking, the most comfortable place to be during the hot season. The Mughal gardens that have survived have special residential buildings where the ruler and his harem could spend the night (*khwabgah*, *aramgah*).

Legend credits King Cyrus the Great, the founder of the Persian Achaemenid Empire (late seventh—fourth centuries BC), with the invention of the traditional layout of a Muslim garden—the *char-bagh* or 'four gardens'. However, the *char-bagh* concept actually took shape during the Timurid period, after the fourteenth century. Gardens of this type were always surrounded by a high wall, suggesting that they were as protected and hard to reach as the Garden of Eden. This orderly, closed, and decorated space is opposed to the chaotic, perishable, and woebegone vale of human suffering. It is in this sense that the *char-bagh* resembles the European *hortus conclusus*—which symbolizes the 'hidden' space of Paradise, separated from this world, as well as the sin-free state of mankind before Adam's banishment from Eden.

In Christianity, the enclosed garden—a garden separated from sin by a wall—is the symbol of the Virgin Mary. The source of this image is the Biblical *Song of Songs*: 'A garden enclosed is my sister, my spouse, a spring shut up, a fountain sealed. Your plants *are* an orchard of pomegranates with pleasant fruits, fragrant henna with spikenard, spikenard and saffron, calamus and cinnamon, with all trees of frankincense, myrrh and aloes, with all the chief spices' (Song 4:12–15).[8] Numerous works of medieval European literature and fine art[9] attest to the popularity of the theme of the 'enclosed garden', which is connected with Marian symbolism and the notion of the 'Mary's Garden' (*Mariengarten*).

The layout and symbolism of the *char-bagh* derives from descriptions of paradisiacal gardens (*jannat*) in the Qu'ran, where water (numerous sources, canals, and ponds) plays a primordial role: 'A parable of the garden which those guarding (against evil) are promised: Therein are rivers of water that does not alter, and rivers of milk the taste whereof does not change, and rivers of drink delicious to those who drink' (47:15).[10] Further on:

> 'And for him who fears to stand before his Lord are two gardens […] Having in them various kinds […] In both of them are two fountains flowing […] And besides these two are two (other) gardens […] Both inclining to blackness […] In both of them are two springs gushing forth […] In both are fruits and palms and pomegranates' (55:46–68).

This is essentially a description of the structure of the *char-bagh*: four gardens separated by four canals with water flowing and gushing (fountains).

The pond Al-Kausar (108:1) plays a special role among the bodies of water of Paradise. Commentators describe it as a river or pond into which all the rivers of Paradise flow. The Qu'ran describes Paradise as having several gates and several levels (*darajat*) for different categories of the righteous. Among the numerous paradisiacal pleasures, coolness and tranquillity play a special role. The righteous live 'amid thornless lote-trees, and banana-trees (with fruits), one above another. And extended shade, and water flowing constantly, and abundant fruit' (56:28–32). As we will see below, these basic features of Muslim Paradise are symbolically embodied in the layout and atmosphere of the *char-bagh*.

The Indian *char-bagh*, in a form close to its Timurid prototype, exists only in Kashmir, which is mountainous (like Herat and Central Asia) and has fairly cold winters. 'The basic fact was that the gardens of Herat and Samarqand could not be transferred to the Indian plains,' wrote Donald Wilber, a specialist on Muslim gardens. 'The climate was not suitable for orchards and vineyards, which require a cold season to establish a dormant state in the plants and trees. In the mountainous regions the fine gardens had been the outgrowth of the bustan, or orchard, and the concept of the gulistan, or flower garden, matured at a later date. Lacking the possibility of producing dense, productive orchards, the Indian gardens developed towards great open spaces and wide expanses of water.'[11]

Timurid gardens of Central Asia, and Mughal gardens in Kashmir, were laid out on slopes, down which water flowed with the force of gravity alone. This natural relief was imitated by artificial terraces (*kursi*), with numerous chutes (*abshar*) through which water ran, on the flat plains of Uttar Pradesh and the Punjab. The surface of the chutes was inlaid with undulate mosaics or carved in a fish-scale pattern to augment the effect of flowing water. The upper terrace was usually covered with a striking living carpet of flowers and plants, while the lower terrace gave 'extended shade' and the cherished coolness. The terraced Mughal garden symbolically reproduced the two aforementioned levels of the Garden of Paradise.

Facing the four corners of the world, surrounded by a high wall with two or four gates and partitioned by four paved walkways (*khayaban*) and canals (*nala*) that create the geometric structure of the 'four gardens', the Mughal garden corresponds to the descriptions of Paradise in the Qu'ran. The famous verse attributed to Amir Khusrau Dehlavi, and written on the ceiling of the Hall of Private Audience (Diwan-i khass, built in 1648) in the Red Fort of Delhi, makes this comparison explicit: 'If there is Paradise on the earth, it is here, it is here, it is here' (*gar firdaus bar ru-yi zamin ast hamin ast-u hamin ast-u hamin ast*).

The four sections (*chaman*) into which the garden is partitioned by its transverse axes can be further divided into any number of parts, along the same principle insofar as the garden's overall area allows. Water is present in the garden, not only in the canals but also in the decorative pools (*hauz*) and the artificial cascades (*chadar*) and fountains (*fawwara*) that fill the air with a moist mist of droplets and coolness. The upper terrace contains the main pool, that draws in all the garden's water resources and serves as a metaphor for the paradisiacal al-Kausar.

In the climatic conditions of South Asia, water plays a more important role than earth in the structure of the Mughal garden. As a moving and dynamic substance, water brings the different levels of the garden together and changes the spatial arrangement of its parts; water droplets, scattered in the air, form a mist or veil of sorts that visually soften the strict geometric layout and alleviate the impression of heaviness of the stone buildings that, in the absence of water, would look too harsh and dominating under the scorching sun. Generally speaking, Mughal gardens resemble European Baroque gardens from the aesthetic standpoint in their use of different levels, terraces, water 'artifices' in cascades and fountains, and the play of reflection and light patches that strive to make an expressive impact on all human senses through colour, smell, and the noise of rushing water.

Unfortunately, the current state of the Mughal gardens does not correspond to their historic appearances, as the modern system of irrigation in Indian and Pakistani gardens is an anachronism that was introduced by Lord Curzon, Viceroy of India (1899–1905), who ordered that the derelict gardens be restored along the model of English lawns and squares. None of the Mughal gardens have been preserved, as per their historical appearances, with the exception of the Taj Mahal gardens and the *Shalimar* and *Dilkusha* in Lahore.

Most Mughal gardens were laid out along riverbanks. In contrast to the classical *char-bagh* layout, buildings were located not in the garden's centre but at its end, next to the wall of the upper terrace with their rear façades facing the river. This location offered the most impressive view over the garden and fort. Scholars call such gardens 'waterfront' or 'riverfront' gardens.[12] The palace gardens of the three major Mughal forts in Delhi, Agra, and Lahore were built according to this principle of providing a panorama of the upper terrace (*suffa-i 'ali*) from the river below or from the opposite bank.[13]

Water from the river was raised to the walls of the upper terrace with a waterwheel. From there, it flowed down an aqueduct to the garden, and further along the top of the wall through a system of terracotta pipes. This system supplied the fountains with water at the required pressure. Over the centuries, the rivers on whose banks the gardens stood changed their courses (in particular, the Jamna and the Ravi), the aqueducts stopped functioning, and the gardens became derelict. Some of the gardens were restored by the English, who tried to adapt those using modern horticulture and irrigation practices, changing their original appearance in the process.

According to the classification adopted by scholars, Mughal gardens belong to four categories: (1) residential gardens around palaces and mansions (*haweli*); (2) funerary gardens surrounding mausoleums and tombs; (3) journey gardens where rulers stayed over night during voyages; and (4) pleasure gardens for rest and recreation.[14]

The first category included the imperial gardens in the fort—in particular, the garden of the so-called Jahangir's Quadrangle in the Shahi Qila. Special gardens were built for the royal ladies outside the fort; one example is *Chauburji Bagh*, the garden of Zebunnisa (Aurangzeb's daughter), of which only the monumental gate survives.

The British indigo merchant William Finch, who visited Lahore in the early seventeenth century, described a typical residential garden:

> 'On the east side of the castle, hard without the wall, is the garden of Asoph Khan [Asaf Khan, Emperor Jahangir's brother-in-law and governor of the Punjab—*A.S.*], small, neat, with walkes (planted with cypress trees), divers tanks and jounters, as you enter, a fair devoncan supported with stone pillars, with faire tank in the midst, and in the midst of that, on four stone pillars, a jounter for coolness. Beyond are other galleries and walkes, divers lodgings for his women neatly contrived, and behind, a small garden and a garden house…. In the midst of the garden is a very stately jounter with fair buildings overhead, and a tank in the centre with large and goodly galleries alongst the four sides thereof, supported with high stone pillars. Adjoining to this is a garden of a king, in which are very good apples, but small, toot (mulberry) white and red, almonds, peaches, figges, grapes, quinces, oranges, lemons, pomegranates, roses, stock yellow flowers, marigolds, wall flowers, iris, pinks white and red, with divers sorts of Indian flowers.'[15]

As we see, this 'small' residential garden was not all that little as it had room for different buildings, tanks, galleries, pavilions (jounter), halls (devoncan), an orchard, and a flower garden.

The second garden type—the funerary garden—refers to the image of the Muslim Paradise in its eschatological dimension as the place of eternal rest of its owner. Many gardens, including Humayun's tomb garden in Delhi, the Taj Mahal gardens in Agra, and *Sikandra Bagh* and *Dilkusha* (gardens around Akbar's and Jahangir's tombs, respectively), were intentionally built as funerary gardens for the ruler. Funerary gardens were located outside the city walls, in the suburbs, and were walled territories with a square or octagonal building at the intersection of the axes in the centre. The building had a large central cupola, and often four smaller cupolas at the four corners. It stood on a low platform from which wide walkways radiated in the four directions, ending in monumental gates. Marble-faced canals, with fountains in them, were built along the walkways.

During the ruler's lifetime, the building could be used as a *baradari*—a summer country pavilion for rest, receptions, and celebrations. The *baradari* (from *barah* 'twelve' and *dar* 'door') had twelve doors, three in each façade. The doors could be turned into windows by installing carved stone or marble screens (*jali*) that let in air and light yet softened the sun's rays. The *jali* cast an ornamental shadow on the floor or opposite wall; this constant play of shadows in the interior constituted a single whole with the play of water and light outside in the garden.

After the ruler's death, the functions of the building and garden changed completely. The ruler was buried below the central cupola; over time, his wives and close relatives were buried next to him or under the corner cupolas. In this way, the building became a dynastic or family mausoleum. Such family mausoleums, surrounded by gardens, were formerly found on the outskirts of many cities of the Indian Subcontinent. They dotted the landscape in the suburbs of Delhi and Agra, and between the Ravi River and the Grand Trunk Road in Lahore. Ruins of funerary gardens are also found in Lucknow, Allahabad, and Aurangabad. Medieval historical sources, which are prone to exaggeration, speak of 777 gardens in Kashmir, many of which were funerary.[16] After the owner's burial, a garden could no longer be used for receptions and celebrations; the English practice of holding 'garden parties' and 'light and music shows' at the Taj Mahal, *Dilkusha*, and other funerary gardens can only be explained by their ignorance of local customs.

Another type of funerary garden is found around the tombs of Muslim saints and spiritual mentors. Many rulers gave Sufi sheikhs plots of land outside the city walls where they could plant small 'pharmaceutical' gardens with medicinal plants and herbs. After the death of a sheikh who was considered to be a saint, a domed tomb was built on the site, along with a garden with lawns and trees where the numerous pilgrims and saint's disciples could gather. Among Lahore's Sufi gardens, the biggest and most visited was the garden around the tomb of Mian Mir (1550–1635), the beloved spiritual mentor of many members of the ruling dynasty from Jahangir to Dara Shikoh. The mausoleum of the Punjabi folk saint Shah Husain (1539–1593) adjoins the *Shalimar* gardens. Sufi gardens had no pools, canals, fountains, or other amusements.

It would be incorrect to assert that every Mughal garden became a funerary garden over time. Pleasure gardens, the most common type of garden, turned into funerary gardens only if their central building became a tomb. Nevertheless, such gardens could preserve their original function as places of rest and recreation through the ages, such as the Kashmir royal gardens or *Shalimar* in Lahore.

As a capital city with an excellent geopolitical location, Lahore attracted many; however, land and buildings were very expensive in the Walled City. Thus, the court nobility from the different provinces, as well as rich merchants from Afghanistan, Iran, and Central Asia, preferred to buy plots of land on the city's outskirts, along the major roads that linked Lahore with Delhi to the south-east, Multan to the east, and along the Grand Trunk Road to the west. They turned these plots of land into gardens, and used them as residences when they visited Lahore. The rest of the time, these suburban plots served as 'journey' gardens where rulers, courtiers, military commanders, and sometimes less illustrious travellers stopped—at their final stop before reaching the city or their first halt after leaving the city.

The Great Mughals travelled a lot: Akbar journeyed throughout his empire monitoring his administrative system; Jahangir went hunting and in search of other pleasures; Shah Jahan looked for new places to build palaces and engineering structures; and Aurangzeb constantly moved his troops about. Medieval historical works often mention the names of gardens where emperors pitched camp. For example, the *Akbar-nama* recounts that Akbar stopped in the *Dilamiz* garden on numerous occasions on leaving Lahore; in 1597, he was accompanied by Father Xavier, the Portuguese Jesuit missionary from Goa, who left behind a brief description of the 'journey' garden.[17] In his memoirs, Jahangir made various references to his stops in the garden of Mirza Kamran, the brother of Jahangir's grandfather Humayun. In the second year of his rule (1606), he judged the rebellious prince Khosrow in this garden. A year later, Jahangir made a four-day halt there on his way to Kabul. In 1620, upon his return from Kashmir, he spent several days in the garden of Mu'min 'Ishaqbaz; after this halt, he triumphantly entered Lahore Fort seated on an elephant.

'Abdul Hamid Lahori wrote, in his historical chronicle *Badshahnama*, that Emperor Shah Jahan, who built the *Shalimar* Gardens in 1641, often stopped there on his way to Agra, Kashmir, and Kabul. Aurangzeb also stopped there, in particular in 1658 when chasing his brother Dara Shikoh who had fled to Multan from Lahore. At different times, Aurangzeb gave receptions and welcomed official visitors at the *Dilkusha*, which was the funerary garden of his grandfather Jahangir. In 1674–1675, during the Afghan War, he spent a year-and-a-half in Wah Bagh Gardens in the town of Hasan Abdal, 195 miles from Lahore, from where he directed military operations.[18] Hence, pleasure, funerary, and residential gardens (the latter adjoined private residences or *hawelis*) could serve as 'journey' gardens on certain occasions.

At the same time, journey gardens, in the strict sense of the term, seem to have also existed along the Grand Trunk Road and next to caravanserais. The need for such gardens stemmed from the difficulties in travelling along the treeless plains of the Punjab, especially during the hot season, when a stop on the way allowed travellers to replenish their water supplies or rest in the cool shade. Lahore's oldest garden suburb, *Shahdara* (literally 'main entrance', which was the name given to the gardens in front of the rulers' palaces and to settlements on the riverbanks) arose in Akbar's time along the road to Kashmir and Kabul. It was a frequent place of imperial halts: rulers and courtiers made their first stop there after crossing the Ravi on their way to rest in Kashmir or to hunt in Sheikhupura. In the garden suburbs lived the people who took care of the numerous city gardens—gardeners, diggers, craftsmen, overseers, etc. One of these suburbs, Baghbanpura (from *baghban* 'gardener'), still has the word for garden in its name.

As we see, different types of Mughal gardens were found in Lahore. The gardens were named either after their owners—*Bagh-i Mirza Kamran, Bagh-i Nur Jahan, Bagh-i 'Ali Mardan Khan, Bagh-i Asaf Jah*, etc.—or had names of their own. These names were sometimes connected to the building that the garden adjoined—*Chauburji Bagh* and *Hiran Minar Bagh*—and sometimes to the crops grown in the garden—*Anguri Bagh* (grape garden), *Anar Bagh* (pomegranate garden), *Badami Bagh* (almond garden), and *Gulabi Bagh* (rose garden). Mostly, the name was an epithet expressed by a qualitative adjective reflecting the garden's beauty and great merits—*Dilaram* (Heart-easing), *Dilkusha* (Heart-expanding), *Dilafroz* (Heart-enlightening), *Dilazar* (Heart-tormenting), etc. In literary language, all these epithets have a common meaning—'charming, captivating'— and are used in poetry to refer to the beloved (*ma'shuq*). In other words, a garden was not only an image of Paradise but was also referred to as an ideal imaginary beloved. The latter is a highly polysemantic concept that symbolizes the Absolute in its mystic meaning. A further form of garden name is an epithet that would usually refer to government, its institutions, and its representatives: *Jahanara* (World-adorning), *Jahan-numa* (World-exhibiting), *Faizbakhsh* (Bestowing favours), *Farhatbakhsh* (Imparting happiness), etc.

Nevertheless, the name of Lahore's main garden, *Shalimar* (or *sh-ālāmār*, to be more precise), remains a mystery. It is usually translated as 'Abode of Light' or 'Moonlight', without any grammatical or lexical explanations.[19] Several Mughal gardens bear the name *Shalimar*: the first garden of this name was built by Jahangir for his favourite wife, Empress Nur Jahan, near Srinagar in Kashmir. It is situated on four terraces, the uppermost of which was intended for the women of the harem and was the least visible from outside. Irrigated by mighty cascades and numerous fountains, and planted with trees that changed colour in spring and autumn, this garden was one of the most beautiful sights of the Indian Subcontinent.

Shalimar enticed European poets as far back as the early nineteenth century, as is apparent from Thomas Moore's poem *Lalla Rookh* (1817):

'They had now arrived at the splendid city of Lahore whose mausoleums and shrines, magnificent and

> numberless, where Death appeared to share equal honors
> with Heaven, would have powerfully affected the heart
> and imagination of Lalla Rookh, if feelings more of this
> earth had not taken entire possession of her already. She
> was here met by messengers dispatched from Cashmere
> who informed her that the King had arrived in the
> Valley and was himself superintending the sumptuous
> preparations that were then making in the Saloons of the
> Shalimar for her reception.'[20]

For educated Englishmen of the first half of the nineteenth century, the word *Shalimar* was associated with Thomas Moore's poem. Thus, when the well-known memoirist, Emily Eden, visited the Lahore gardens in 1838, she also related them to *Lalla Rookh*: 'Shalimar is the garden where Dr. D. and W. lived when they suffered so much from heat last year. We are encamped close by it. I believe it is the real Shalimar where Lalla Rookh recognized Feramorz, but we do not have a "Lalla Rookh" at hand.'[21]

Delhi, too, formerly had a *Shalimar* garden of its own, although it was not preserved. However, the best-known *Shalimar Bagh* is the garden in Lahore, which was put on the UNESCO world cultural heritage list in 1981 (and on the 'world heritage in danger' list in 2000). In the twentieth century, the word 'Shalimar' became famous, far beyond the Indian Subcontinent, thanks to the perfume of the same name created by the French perfumer Jean-Paul Guerlain in 1925. This perfume launched a worldwide fashion for 'oriental fragrances', i.e., long-lasting, complex, sweet, spicy, and sensual fragrances. Whereas Guerlain named his perfume after an Oriental garden, the garden itself may have been named after one of the large diamonds in the imperial treasury; the stones were frequently given names, such as Kohinoor (= Kuh-i nur 'Mountain of Light'), Derianoor (= Darya-yi nur 'Sea of Light'), and Taj-i mah ('Crown of the Moon').

Three etymologies have been proposed for the word *Shalimar*: Arabic, Turkic, and Sanskrit. The latter version, which is cited in modern travel guides to India, does not withstand criticism as the Sanskrit word *śālā* 'abode, house, place' always comes last rather than first in compound words—as in *dharmaśālā* ('hospice for pilgrims', 'charitable institution') and *pāthśālā* ('place of study', 'school'). From this standpoint, the etymology of *śālāmār* as the 'abode of joy', as proposed by the travel guides, runs against linguistic norms.

The Turkic etymology also evokes doubts. The alleged translation of the garden's name, proposed by popular works,[22] as 'abode of pleasure' from the Turkic *shālā* ('pleasure') and *mār* ('place') is rejected by Turkologists. A more likely etymology would derive from the Chagatai verb *shālātmaq* (a synonym of the Persian verb *ārāstan*) which means 'decorate', 'dress' as well as 'create', 'build'. In this case, *shālāmār* may be a verbal noun where *shālā* is the root, *ma* is the affix of the result of action, and *r* is the marker of transitivity. If this reconstruction is correct, the garden's name means 'decorated' or 'dressed up', which is in keeping with the traditional practice of naming Mughal gardens.

Nevertheless, given that the absolute majority of Mughal gardens, including gardens built before *Shalimar*, have names of Persian or Arabic origin, the Turkic version seems doubtful. In particular, none of the gardens of Babur, whose native language was Chagatai, have Turkic names. Therefore, the most correct etymology is Arabic or, more precisely, Arabic-Persian. This etymology has been proposed by, among others, the Brockhaus and Efron Encyclopedic Dictionary, which derives the garden's name from the Arabic expression *shāh al-'imārāt* ('master of buildings'). It should be kept in mind that the word *'imārāt* ('building', 'structure') was historically used for park architecture and gardens in general. Muslim sources often refer to gardens as 'structures' (*'imārāt*). Still, the word 'structure' can hardly be applied to a diamond, if we accept the version that the garden was named after a diamond. However, the other proposed Persian prototype of the garden's name—*shŏ'la-i māh* 'moonlight'—could well apply to a diamond, although one could ask why the commonly accepted word *māh* ('moon') turned into *mār*. In any case, no matter what *Shalimar* means, it most likely has Arabic-Persian roots.

In fact, the garden was not named *Shalimar* initially. Built between July 1641 and October 1642, the garden had several names, according to contemporary chroniclers 'Abdul Hamid Lahori and Muhammad Saleh Kanbuh: the uppermost of the three terraces was called *Farahbakhsh* ('Garden of Delight'), while the middle and lower terraces were called *Faizbakhsh* ('Garden of Bounty').[23] It is not known when or why the garden began to be called *Shalimar* (after Jahangir's garden in Kashmir). In historical works, the name *Shalimar* began to be applied to the Lahore garden in the first quarter of the eighteenth century, in Khafi Khan's chronicle *Extraction from the Core* (*Muntakhab al-lubab*), i.e., during the reign of Bahadur Shah I (Aurangzeb's son).[24]

Located along the old course of the Ravi River, *Shalimar* is a typical 'riverbank garden'. In former times, it took travellers many hours to reach it from Lahore, no matter whether they were mounted or on foot. The gardens appeared as a long-awaited oasis and a man-made wonder amid the hot, dry, and flat plains. *Shalimar* was (and, to a certain extent, remains) such a majestic and perfect work of landscape architecture that no voyager who visited Lahore, over three centuries, could avoid the temptation of capturing it in writing or painting. Poeticized, glorified through the centuries, and studied down to the last fountain, *Shalimar* stands on par with the gardens of the Alhambra and Versailles in terms of the power of its emotional and aesthetic impact on the visitor. Michael Brand wrote: 'At Shalimar a combination of aesthetic and technical ingenuity produced a garden that must have stunned early visitors: never before had a garden of such focused power been constructed on the hot plains of the Subcontinent.'[25]

The creation of the large-scale gardens, such as *Shalimar*, in arid Lahore became possible only after the construction of the *Shah Nahar* Canal, once again on the orders of Shah Jahan. In 1639, the Governor of Lahore, 'Ali Mardan Khan worked out the plan of a 160-kilometre-long canal that would bring the waters of the Ravi to Lahore, from Rajpur (today Madhpur in India) where the water rushed down from the hills to the plains. After the canal was opened in 1641, another courtier, Khalilullah Khan, was appointed superintendent for the construction of the future garden. He chose a site on the Grand Trunk Road, three kilometres away from the city.

This site belonged to a family of landed gentry (*zila'dar*) known as Mians from Baghbanpura. The family's forefather, Muhammad Hayat Madini, came to India with Muhammad bin Qasim's Arabic military expedition in the eighth century. Subsequently, members of this influential family played a prominent role in the political life of India and, later, Pakistan. Mian Muhammad Yusuf, the head of the family during Shah Jahan's reign, gave this plot of land to the Emperor as a gift, under pressure (or so it is believed) of the governor and the superintendent. In recompense, Shah Jahan gave him the hereditary title of *mian* and keeper of the imperial gardens, which the family bore for over 350 years. Only in 1962, after the Mians spoke out against the imposition of martial law by General Ayub Khan, were the *Shalimar* gardens nationalized by law.

As with all other Muslim gardens, *Shalimar* is surrounded by a high crenellated red-brick wall. On both the outside and inside, the wall has shallow arched niches of different sizes. At the corners stand towers (*burj*), crowned by octagonal kiosks made of red sandstone. As mentioned above, the gardens are situated on three terraces that descend from south to north and cover an area of 16 hectares. The gardens were accessed by a gate in the western wall at the level of the lower terrace. Guests visited the gardens and, depending on their social status, ascended to higher terraces, constantly discovering new sights as they progressed. Such a gradual ascent also corresponded to the traditional Sufi notion of the Path of the soul to the Absolute and to conceptions of the Muslim paradise.

The upper and lower terraces are typical *char-bagh*, divided by canals and decorative pools with long rows of fountains (410 in all). The middle terrace is partitioned into three sections; the central section is slightly raised and has the largest pool, with fountains, surrounded by openwork pavilions (*baradari*). The upper terrace is a living carpet of flower beds, the middle terrace is dominated by water, and the lower terrace is planted with fruit trees. According to chroniclers, all kinds of fruit grew in the *Shalimar* Gardens: apples, cherries, plums, oranges, mangoes, peaches, quinces, almonds, and mulberries. The gardens also had many different decorative trees, such as cypresses, poplars, and plane trees, as well as decorative shrubs. The predominant flowers were roses, tulips, irises, cyclamens, lilies, carnations, and jasmine. Generally speaking, the concept of the *Shalimar* Gardens included the cultivation of flowers, fruits, and plants belonging to 'different seasons and climates' that would flower and bear fruit in turn, constantly changing the gardens' appearance.

The fruit gardens of *Shalimar* are linked to a well-known episode of Punjabi hagiography. At one time, the main gardener of *Shalimar* was 'Inayat Khan, a mystic of the Qadiriyya Brotherhood. His disciple, the great Punjabi Sufi poet Bulleh Shah (1680–1758), once came from Kasur to visit him in Shalimar. To demonstrate his spiritual progress to his mentor, Bulleh Shah mentally ordered a mango to fall into his hands from a tree. In response, 'Inayat Khan pronounced a spell whereby all the mangoes in the garden fell to the ground and then returned to the trees.[26] The hagiographic meaning of this legend is clear: mystics were forbidden to boast of their spiritual aptitudes, and Bulleh Shah was taught a lesson to this effect. At the same time, the historic aspect of this legend demonstrates that gardeners had a fairly low social status, considering the fact that Bulleh Shah was so disrespectful towards his mentor.

Waters from the *Shah Nahar* Canal reach the gardens at the southern wall of the upper terrace. Flowing under the building of the 'Resting Place' (*Aramgah*), the water reappeared in the main canal, filling the central tank at the intersections of the canals and then overflowing into the side canals. From there, crossing the upper terrace, it rippled over the marble cascade (*chadar*) and discharged into the main tank of the middle terrace, which served as the storage reservoir for the irrigation of the rest of the garden. After filling the tank, the canal water split into two small cascades in the eastern and the western sides; flowing over the *Sawan Bhadon* pavilion, it passed into the lower terrace canals.[27] The three walls of the pavilion have long rows of niches that formerly housed camphor lamps. Their light shimmered through the streams of falling water, and the smell of camphor blended with the gardens' scents.

The upper terrace, which was the least accessible, housed the harem and the emperor's private residence. It had eight buildings—four at the corners of the perimeter and four in the middle of the sides. In the middle of the southern side stood the aforementioned *Aramgah*, with three arched openings in the façade. Today, it serves as an entrance to the garden, yet its walls were formerly decorated with frescoes and a fountain stood in the centre of the hall. A Persian inscription, with a chronogram of the gardens' founding date, is inlaid in mosaic above the entrance gate:

chūn shāh jahān bādshah-i hāmī-yi dīn
ārāsta shālamār ba tarz-i matīn
tārīkh-i banā-yi īn zi rizvān justam
guftā ki bigū namūna-i khuld-i barīn

When Shah Jahan, the emperor defender of the faith,
Laid out the Shalamar in a majestic style,
I asked Rizwan (the keeper of Paradise—*A.S.*) about its
foundation date.
He replied, 'Say that it is an *example of heavenly
paradise.*'

The words '*example of heavenly paradise*' are a chronogram of the date
1047 AH or AD 1637.

The *Aramgah* faced the arcade of the *Aiwan*, or Main Hall, next to
the northern wall, from which two lateral staircases led to the middle
terrace. On the eastern side stood the building of the Hall of Private
and Public Audience (*diwan-i khass-o-'am*), with a covered ceremonial
balcony (*jharoka*). In keeping with Mughal court ritual, the emperor
performed the *darshan*, i.e., appeared in all his splendour before his
courtiers and subjects, on this balcony every day. The *Naqqar-khana*
('House of drums') guardhouse was located across from the balcony, at
the corner of the eastern wall; here, the hours were struck on large drums.

Opposite the *Jharoka*, on the western side of the terrace, stood the
building of the female sleeping chambers (*Khwabgah-i Begum Sahib*),
which belonged to Shah Jahan's daughter, Jahanara. After the death of
her mother Mumtaz Mahal, Jahanara became the leading lady at the
imperial court and bore the title Begum Sahib. The sleeping chambers
of the emperor himself (*Khwabgah*) were located at the corner of the
western wall. This 'forbidden' part of the terrace (*Khasspura*) was
partitioned off with a carved marble screen and protected by guards.
Only the emperor, the women of the harem, and the eunuchs were
allowed to enter.

In the south-eastern corner of the middle terrace stood the building
of the Baths (*hammam*), which was adjoined by two small annexes:
sard-khana ('cold bath') and *rakht-khana* ('dressing room'). Water
came to the Baths, not from the canal but from a very wide and deep
well outside the gardens' walls that was called *Barah Hatta* ('Twelve

Wheels'); the water was pumped into it by twelve Persian waterwheels. *Baradari*, made of red sandstone, were situated along the pool's sides on the eastern and western sides of the middle terrace; stone platforms led from the *baradari* to the water. A large marble platform (*chabutara*) called *Mahtabi* ('of the moonlight') covered the dry part of the middle terrace; it was used for sitting out-of-doors, to enjoy the moonlight. A carved marble throne (*takht*), surrounded by an encrusted screen, was erected between the large cascade and the pool; seated on the throne, the emperor watched the dancers and musicians performing on the *Mahtabi*. The north part of the terrace had two small marble pavilions with small niches (*chini-khana*), in which golden flower vases were placed during the day and camphor wax candles at night. The candles made an endless chain of shimmering light and created colour reflections on the water-sheet in front of the niches.

There were no buildings on the southern side of the middle terrace. Here, long rows of lamps were placed along the tank's edge; their flames were reflected in the still waters of the *hauz*, creating the effect of ripples and a play of light—a sight called *Deep Mala* or 'chain of lights'. The same play of light and water figures in the name of the cascade, *Sawan Bhadon*, which stems from the two months of the Indian calendar that make up the *barsat*, or monsoon season—the most poeticized season in the Indian tradition. The figurative sense of the words *Sawan Bhadon* is 'sunlight and rain'; this is precisely the effect created by the *Shalimar* cascades, which were once described as 'waterfall of tears' by Princess Zebunnisa (died 1699) who wrote under the poetic pseudonym *Makhfi* ('Concealed'):

> *ay ābshār nauhagar az bahr-i kīstī*
> *chīn bar jabīn figanda zi andūh-i kīstī*
> *āyā chi dard būd ki chūn mā tamām-i shab*
> *sar rā ba sang mīzadī yu mīgirīstī*

> O waterfall! For whose sake art thou weeping?
> In whose sorrowful recollections hast thou wrinkled thy brows?
> What pain was it that impelled thee, like myself, the whole night,
> To strike thy head against stone and to shed tears?[28]

In addition to the aforementioned two gates, which were decorated with tiles, the lower terrace contained the arched building of the Palace for Private Audience (*daulat-khana-yi khass*). The gardens of the lower terrace have not been preserved: today, they are simply an enormous lawn planted with poplar and cypress trees; one tends to see groups of school or university students picnicing under the trees during their history class outings to the gardens. An interesting feature of the lower terrace is the huge and coarsely-hewn ramps for the mounted elephants (*hathi pa'on*). The comfort of these animals had to be provided for as they were the main means of ceremonial transport. Lahore Fort has a special Elephant Gate (*Hathi pa'on darwaza*) that is accessed by a wide staircase of massive flat steps that can bear an elephant's weight.

In the structure of the *Shalimar* Gardens, buildings, plants, and especially water have a symbolism of their own that is connected, above all, to traditional notions of power and society. For example, the garden's entire complicated hydro-technical system, that was built by the court hydrologist Mullah 'Ala ul-Mulk and that has still not been fully understood by modern scholars, is a metaphor of the hierarchical distribution of goods within the Mughal Empire. As we saw above, water first entered the royal residence on the upper terrace, from where it was gradually distributed among tanks and canals, descending to the middle and lower terraces. Likewise, the emperor was the source of all worldly goods which he distributed among courtiers and subjects, not arbitrarily but in accordance with a just law and a strict order, similar to the order of a regular garden. Just as a stream of water descends from high to low ground, moistening the earth, watering the flowers and trees, and scattering cool drops in the air on its way, royal mercy pours out on a hierarchically structured society, giving it life and prosperity.

After the decline of the Great Mughal Empire, the *Shalimar* Gardens went through many tribulations. They were completely ransacked, even before Ranjit Singh came to power during the reign of the so-called 'Sikh triumvirate' of Gujjar Singh, Lahna Singh, and Sobha Singh (1764–1773). The members of the triumvirate needed funds to fight the Afghans who invaded Lahore every year. They stripped all the precious stones from the gardens' buildings, and the copper facing from the fountains, and sold them to city jewellers and craftsmen.[29] The gardens were devastated, the flowerbeds were trampled upon, the trees were broken and uprooted, and the tanks and canals were filled with rubbish. During Ranjit Singh's reign, the gardens' vegetation was restored and the canals and *hauzes* were renovated. Yet, most of the gardens' buildings were stripped of their marble facing, which the new ruler of the Punjab sent to Amritsar for the construction of the Golden Temple. This explains why many buildings in *Shalimar* are faced with imitation marble (polished plaster-covered brick) today.

In 1842, Prince Alexy Soltykoff visited *Shalimar* and left behind a description of the garden after its restoration by Ranjit Singh:

> 'Before Lahore, we spent a whole day in the Shalimar Gardens. This is the name of a garden located four miles from the city; it means the same to Lahore as Versailles to Paris […] The characteristic features of this place are the fresh verdure of the bitter orange trees and the pools inhabited by whole flocks of ducks and geese. Countless fountains and cascades scatter ethereal water mist throughout this Eden; after you stroll for half an hour through the straight alleys of the gardens, your clothes are sure to be soaked. The kiosks and pavilions, some of which are made of marble, are not particularly beautiful yet are draped with exquisite cashmeres and surrounded with crystal-clear waters that seem adamantine.'[30]

As we have already seen above, *Shalimar* is Lahore's principal, yet far from only, garden. It is true that most city gardens have come down to us in fragments or ruins, such as *Gulabi Bagh* and *Chauburji Bagh*, of which only the entrance gates survive. Yet, they suffice; we can appreciate why Lahore has been called the 'city of gardens' over the centuries. It is easy to draw a 'mental map' of Lahore's gardens from the website of the international project, 'Gardens of the Mughal Empire'.[31]

Let us begin with the oldest city section—the *Shahi Qila*. The gardens, here, consist of an enfilade of quadrilateral courtyards that begin immediately behind the Hall for Public and Private Audience (*diwan-i 'am-o-khass*) and are connected by narrow arched passageways or long paved walkways. All of them are bounded, on one side, by the riverfront fortress walls. The most representative gardens are located before Jahangir's Chambers (*khwabgah*) and in front of the Mirror Palace (*Shish Mahal*). This is a purely architectural type of courtyard garden, devoid of vegetation and organized around a shallow tank; in form, it is either a quadrangle (the so-called Jahangir Quadrangle) or a circle inscribed in a square (the *Shish Mahal* Garden). The area around the tanks is paved with black, grey, or yellow marble slabs, while vegetative ornament in the *pietre dure* technique replace living flowers on the marble columns.

Another fort garden is the already mentioned *Hazuri Bagh*, which lies immediately beyond the *'Alamgiri* Gate and was built during the Sikh period of the city's history. It brings the Fort and the Badshahi Mosque together in a single ensemble. A large caravanserai once stood on this site. A large *baradari*-like marble pavilion stands in the centre of this garden, built on the model of the *char-bagh*, suggesting that the Sikhs had a certain respect for the landscape architecture traditions of the Great Mughals. From the functional standpoint, *Hazuri Bagh* is a funerary garden that lies in front of the mausoleum (*samadhi*) of Ranjit Singh. It also contains the mausoleum of Muhammad Iqbal, the great Muslim poet-philosopher of the Indian Subcontinent.

Standing on the fortress walls, from where an immense panorama of the megalopolis opens up today, one can see wide clearings in the dense network of streets and lanes. These are traces of the old highways (*shahrah*) that lesouth-west in the direction of Delhi, and north and north-west in the direction of Kashmir and Peshawar. The south-west highway leads from the Delhi Gate of the Walled City, through the suburb of Mian-Mir (named after the city's patron saint). Remains of milestones (*kos-minar*) can still be seen along the road today.

A former village, Mian-Mir turned into a flourishing suburb thanks to Prince Dara Shikoh who often stayed there when visiting his spiritual mentor, Mullah Shah, a disciple of the saint. Dara Shikoh had a typical funerary garden built around Mian Mir's tomb; the tomb and garden survive today. Near the saint's mausoleum stands a two-storey garden pavilion, in the centre of a tank, where Dara Shikoh's wife, Nadira Begum, is buried. Mullah Shah's tomb is also located in the garden; just as with the aforementioned tombs, it is a synthesis of a Mughal funerary garden and a Sufi garden.

The road running north-west, from Mian-Mir along the Grand Trunk Road, leads to Begumpura ('Women's Suburb'), which was founded in the mid-seventeenth century by the royal ladies and their female attendants. One of the most famous gardens of Begumpura is the funerary garden of Shah Jahan's wet nurse Sharafunnisa, better known as Dai Anga (died 1671). Dai Anga was a wealthy and pious woman who was engaged in religious charitable work. Mosques bearing her name, and built at her expense, have been found in Delhi, Agra, Lahore, and Ajmer. Dai Anga's wealth is also revealed by the fact that her funerary garden was larger than the garden around the mausoleum of the powerful courtier 'Ali Mardan Khan, and was comparable to the garden around the mausoleum of Asaf Khan, Shah Jahan's father-in-law and grand vizier.

Another female tomb is located a short distance away from Dai Anga's mausoleum—the Cypress Tomb (*Sarvwala maqbara*), named after the cypress tree ornament on its façade. This building was constructed in the eighteenth century and has the form of a low tower, which is quite rare for the residential and ritual architecture of the Indian Subcontinent.[32] I will recount the history of this tower later, and for now will only say that a large garden formerly surrounded the Cypress Tomb; a part of the wall, balustrade, and several dozen old trees are all that is left today. During the Mughal period, Begumpura was essentially a long succession of gardens, separated by walls and connected by roads. It stretched east, along the Grand Trunk Road, until it merged with Baghbanpura ('Gardeners' Suburb').

As mentioned above, Baghbanpura was initially settled by gardeners (*mali*) and other personnel of Shalimar and the other gardens in its vicinity. It should be mentioned that the work, formerly done by the residents of an entire suburb, is performed today by twenty people. The reason lies not in the use of modern methods of gardening but in the fact that the number of gardens and the amount of associated work has decreased manifold. The suburb is situated on a natural embankment formed by the Ravi and is an ideal place for building terraced gardens. Many residential and funerary gardens of aristocrats and Sufi mentors have survived, though often in a half-ruined state:

Anguri Bagh, *'Inayat Bagh*, *Bhogival* (or *Raja Bagh*), the garden around Shah 'Abdul Ghani's tomb and, finally, the garden around the tomb of Saint Shah (Madho Lal) Husain which adjoins Shalimar.

The road leading from the fort, to Kashmir and Peshawar, passes through the already-mentioned old city suburb of Shahdara. Strictly speaking, the history of Lahore's gardens began here: in 1527, a year after Babur's conquest of India, his son Mirza Kamran built the first *char-bagh* in the area. Changes in the course of the Ravi turned the garden's site into a small island that can be accessed from the bridge connecting Lahore and Shahdara. The garden was formerly famous for its fountains, cascades, and tank in the shape of an eight-pointed star, yet all that remains today is a pavilion (*baradari*) surrounded by water. Shahdara is mentioned numerous times in Mughal chronicles, from the time of Akbar's reign and onwards, in connection with its gardens in which the emperors stopped on their way to or from Kashmir and Kabul; also in the travel notes of English voyagers (William Barr, Colonel Wade, etc.) who spent some time in Mirza Kamran's garden.[33]

The gardens of Shahdara gradually ceased to be pleasure and journey gardens and turned into a vast ritual complex that includes the funerary gardens of Emperor Jahangir (*Dilkusha*), his wife Empress Nur Jahan, his stepdaughter Ladli Begum, and his brother-in-law (Nur Jahan's brother) Asaf Khan. Of all these gardens, only the garden around Jahangir's mausoleum has been preserved in its original appearance. It is a typical *char-bagh*, surrounded by a high brick wall and partitioned by canals; six waterwheels pumped water from the river into them. The garden was accessed by a high monumental gate made of red sandstone that is connected to the arched building of the *Akbari Serai*.[34]

Jahangir's mausoleum itself was described at length in the previous chapter. Here, I will simply note that *Dilkusha* is a popular place for outdoor celebrations and picnics today. This shows that the traditional functions of funerary gardens have been totally forgotten, even in a country as conservative as Pakistan.

The last point on my 'mental map' of Lahore's gardens also lies to the north-west of Lahore: it is Sheikhupura. Akbar gave it, as a gift, to Prince Salim while he was still an adolescent, which explains why it bears the prince's childhood nickname, Sheikhu. During the

Mughal period, Sheikhupura was the site of the imperial hunting grounds where deer, roe deer, antelopes, and wild fowl were bred. Only members of the imperial family could hunt here. A lover of animals and hunting, Jahangir built a 100-foot-high minaret in the reserve in 1627, in memory of his tame antelope Mansraj which was buried nearby. As a result, the minaret and the entire reserve became known as *Hiran Minar* ('Antelope's Minaret').[35] Around the minaret, Shah Jahan built an architectural complex consisting of a garden, a square tank, and an octagonal pavilion standing on a platform in the centre of the pool. The pool had small square kiosks at its four corners, and gently sloping brick descents on the four sides for the animals that came to drink at the pool.[36]

The study of Mughal landscape architecture has become a separate field of art history, in which many South Asian and Western scholars are fruitfully working at present. This field of study grew out of the pioneering work *Gardens of the Great Mughals* (1913) by the English writer and watercolourist Constance Mary Villiers-Stuart (1877–1966).[37] Constance came to India in 1908 as the wife of a colonial civil servant. She spent most of her time in Pinjore (near modern-day Chandigarh), where Emperor Aurangzeb's foster brother, Fidai Khan Koka—who also constructed the Badshahi Mosque in Lahore—built the garden *Yadavindra*.

Having an innate passion for gardening, as befits every true Englishwoman, and living in the environs of a magnificent Mughal garden, Constance became so interested in the history and practice of Indian landscape architecture that she visited all the well-known gardens of the Subcontinent in Delhi, Agra, Kashmir, Lahore, and Rajasthan (Deeg Fort), where she made watercolour sketches and gathered materials for her book. The *Gardens of the Great Mughals* made a great impression on Sir Edwin Lutyens, the architect of New Delhi. It is said that it was Constance Mary Villiers-Stuart's book that led him to take an interest in the Mughal landscape design and to build his famous Mughal gardens at the Rashtrapati Bhavan (Presidential Palace) in Delhi. All subsequent studies of Mughal gardens were based, to one degree or another, on the work of this remarkable woman.

Simultaneously images of paradise (i.e., divine metaphors) and symbols of temporal power, Mughal gardens accompanied people during their entire lives, from birth to death and burial, forming a 'garden' type of living environment and lifestyle. Literature, art, and historiography seldom speak about how people spent their time in the closed space of the palaces and mansions, yet recount, in detail, what they did in the gardens. Designed to make an impression on all the human senses, gardens were a 'synthesis' of different arts. Gardens bring together architecture, poetry, music, and miniature painting in virtually the same proportions. Poetry is read, and music is performed, in gardens; gardens, poetry, and miniatures merge with each other, treating common themes, and employing the same formal and stylistic techniques.

Finally, gardens create a powerful and vast zone of *topophilia* that encompasses virtually the entire city, from the centre to the suburbs. Apparently, it was easy and pleasant to live in Lahore, at least for the social strata that had access to 'garden' pleasures. The most widespread psychophysical type of the true Lahori of today—a bon vivant, gourmet, wit, and aesthete—may well stem from centuries of 'garden pastime'.

The Mughal garden is complex, diverse, and impossible to apprehend immediately—just like life itself. On a level terrain, it opens up new vistas and far-away perspectives to the visitor, unfurling water parterres that, like giant mirrors, reflect the world and expand space. On a terraced terrain, the garden displays the movement, turbulence, and expressiveness of water as a symbol of the transience of life. On the one hand, the garden is built according to a strict geometric plan, just as life is determined by Divine Providence. On the other, the play of reflections, light patches, colour hues, shadow, and light gives it the novelty and unpredictability that characterize an individual's fate.

In the final analysis, human life is a garden that constantly changes its seasonal appearance and eternally performs what Mirza Ghalib called:

gardish-e rang-e chaman hai māh-o-sāl-e 'andalīb

'The days and nights of the nightingale revolve around the changing hues of the garden.'

Anarkali's tomb, Lahore.

CHAPTER FIVE

The 'Immured Bride': A City Legend

> *Yet each man kills the thing he loves*
> *By each let this be heard,*
> *Some do it with a bitter look,*
> *Some with a flattering word,*
> *The coward does it with a kiss,*
> *The brave man with a sword!*
> —OSCAR WILDE, *'The Ballad of Reading Gaol'*

Virtually all old European and Asian cities have tales and legends of their own. One type is the etiological legend, which traces the origins of a city to the will of deities and other supernatural beings, the deeds of kings and heroes, or the action of natural cataclysms. An example of such a legend is the founding of Rome by Romulus, who was the grandson of Aeneas according to one version and the son of the god Mars according to another. Not only did he become the city's eponym and first king, but also the founder of its principal institutions. Another type is the toponymic legend, which explains the name of a city or its districts (neighbourhoods, streets, and squares); these usually derive their names from the bygone events of the remote past, the lives of saints, or local lore. A third type is a city legend, itself ; it is connected with the different stages of a city's development, the destruction and restoration of its various sections, reconstruction and expansion, the relationship between the centre and the suburbs, and the construction of the most important buildings (cathedrals/ churches/mosques, forts, towers, and bridges).

While city legends frequently adorn tourist guide books, they are rarely studied by scholars because of their 'unimportance'. Nevertheless, it is clear, even to the most superficial or 'touristic' observer, that different cities belonging to different historical periods and national cultures have similar city legends.

One of these common legends concerns the construction of castles, towers, and bridges, i.e., the fundamental structures of the medieval city, and has a highly macabre theme: the murder of a girl or young woman who was immured alive in the wall or foundation of a building. While the motive for the immurement may have varied, its true cause was always practical, functional, and 'purely architectural': it was held that an immured virgin strengthens a building and protects it from destruction. As we will see below, the emergence of such legends corresponded to the real architectural practice of different peoples who had mytho-poetic notions about the sacral power of innocence, the magic force of virginity, and the protective field of female purity—the most effective amulets for any important undertaking.

Thus, the propitiatory 'sacrifice of purity', during the foundation-laying, became an essential ritual during the implementation of major projects, such as the construction of forts, walls, bridges, and other strategic objects of the medieval city. In general, the tie between virginity or its loss on the one hand, and live burial or immurement on the other, is an ancient mythologem and practice. It suffices to recall the Ancient Greek myth about Danaë, whom her father shut up in a copper tower to protect her virginity, or about the Roman vestal virgins who were immured alive as punishment for breaking their oath of virginity.

If one takes a look at all the legends about immured virgins, old Europe begins to resemble a big cemetery: the walls, bridge piers, and foundations of many European buildings harbour human remains stemming from human sacrifices. The legend about the construction of the walls of medieval Copenhagen is a case in point. Pieces kept falling from the city walls until the builders turned to a radical measure: they constructed a niche in the walls and put a table with food and toys in it. They lured a hungry girl there and, while she ate and played, quickly walled up the niche and covered it with a vault. For several days, musicians played before the improvised burial chamber to drown out the moans of the innocent victim, after which the city walls ceased to crumble.

Many Czech castles are also built on sites of human sacrifices, mostly of women and children. Excavations at Troja Castle, Czech Sternberg, Konopiste Castle, and Karlstejn Castle have uncovered remains of women that were immured alive in walls and foundations. To strengthen a strategic bridge over the Morava, the beautiful wife of one of the builders was immured in its central pier in the sixteenth century. The technique proved effective: the bridge still stands today, although, according to local legend, it trembles from the wails and curses of the unfortunate victim at night.

In Scotland, in ancient times, there was a custom of sprinkling the walls and foundations of castles and towers with human blood. The legend of Vortigern, the king of England, tells that, hard pressed by his enemies, he fled westwards into Wales. He stopped at several places, looking for a secure fortress. The most famous of these castles is Dinas Emrys in the north of Wales. And that is where the most famous story connected with Vortigern starts: the king ordered his masons to build a fortress of Dinas Emrys, but the structure collapsed again and again overnight. To enable the building to stay upright, the druids or magicians advised Vortigern to sacrifice a 'fatherless' boy, whose blood had to be sprinkled over the walls. This boy, when found, proved to be the famous sorcerer Merlin, whose reputation may very well be the sole reason that we still remember Vortigern at all.[1]

When Liebenstein Castle was built in Thuringia, several adolescent girls were bought from among the local inhabitants and immured alive in the walls. A girl was buried alive during the construction of the Cathedral on Toomemägi, in the Estonian city of Tartu. Her spirit is said to roam about at night, looking for a living girl to replace her.

A poetic, though bloodthirsty, legend is connected to Marienburg (Alūksne) Castle in Latvia. 'Iron people' (German crusaders from the Livonian Order) attacked the castle from the west. Seeing that they could not resist the enemy, the city's dwellers set fire to the castle. They burned alive in it, and their souls turned into white birds. The conquerors tried to rebuild the castle on the same spot, yet whatever they constructed during the day was destroyed by the white birds at night. Then the 'iron people' hired a local girl called Maria as housekeeper. She was made drunk and was immured in the castle tower. The immured girl wailed terribly for nine days and nights, frightening the white birds away with her cries. During this time, the 'iron people' managed to finish the castle, which they called Marienburg—not in memory of their gullible victim, but in honour of the Holy Virgin.

The 'purely architectural murder' was often presented in a romantic light. For example, according to Finnish legend, a young maiden was wrongfully immured in the castle wall of Olavinlinna Castle as a punishment for treason. The subsequent growth of a rowan tree at the site of her execution, whose flowers were as white as her innocence and berries as red as her blood, inspired a folk ballad. A similar legend exists in the Irish county of Roscommon. The shadow of a young Catholic girl lives in the ruins of a local castle; the girl had fallen in love with a Protestant, for which she was immured alive in a wall by her own brother.

Legends about immured girls became the subject of historical ballads in many languages, especially in the poetry of the Balkan peoples. The folklore of many south-eastern European peoples refer to immurement as the method of death for victims sacrificed during the completion of a construction project, such as a bridge or fortress. Many Bulgarian and Romanian folk songs ('Three brothers were building a fortress', 'Immured Bride', et al.) describe a bride being offered for such purposes, and her subsequent pleas to the builders to leave her hands and breasts free so that she might still nurse her child. Later versions of the songs revise the bride's death; her fate to languish, entombed in the stones of the construction, is transmuted to her non-physical shadow—yet its loss leads to her pining away and eventually dying.

The ancient motif of stonemasons, making the foundation sacrifice of a woman, is often found in the literatures of Greek, Hungarian, Serbian, Romanian, and Albanian peoples. These folk ballads have expressive names that focus on the architectural structure, which had a primordial significance, rather than on the woman's fate, which was considered to be secondary: 'The bridge of Arta' (Greek), 'The Rozafat fortress' (Albanian), 'The building of Skadar' (Serbian), 'The Monastery of the Argeş River' (Romanian). The only exception is the name of the Bulgarian ballad, 'Immured Bride', which gave this chapter its title.

The Greek story, 'The Bridge of Arta', describes numerous failed attempts to build a bridge in the city of Arta. A vicious cycle, whereby a team of skilled builders toiled all day only to return the next morning to find their work demolished, was eventually ended when the master mason's wife was immured. According to the folk ballad, which stemmed from the acritic songs, 1300 builders, 60 apprentices, 45 craftsmen or masons, under the leadership of the Head Builder, tried to build a bridge every day, but its foundations would collapse each morning. Finally, a bird with a human voice informed the Head Builder that, for the bridge to remain standing, he must sacrifice his wife. As the wife was being killed and walled-up in the foundations of the construction, she uttered curses that concluded with blessings.[2]

The idea that a major edifice could not be built without a human sacrifice ('building in' of a person) was expressed in the Romanian legend of Meşterul Manole, the chief architect of the Curtea de Argeş Monastery in Wallachia. A master builder, being forced to sacrifice his wife in this way, is a common theme in folk songs.[3] A recurring plot element is the master builder's decision to sacrifice the first woman who comes to the building site bringing food. All but one break their promise and tell their wives to come late; it is the wife of the only honest one who is sacrificed. This is the plot of the popular Serbian ballad, 'The Building of Skadar'.[4]

Other variations include the Hungarian folk ballad, 'Kelemen the Stonemason'. This tale relates the story of 12 unfortunate stonemasons tasked with building the fort called Déva. To remedy its recurrent collapses, it is agreed that one of the builders must sacrifice his bride; the bride to be sacrificed should be the first one who comes to visit. Some versions of the ballad treat her relatively kindly, by burning her before building her ashes into the wall rather than walling her up alive.

As 'The fortress of Rozafat' tells, three brothers wanted to build a fortress to defend themselves from Turkish pirates. They worked in the daylight, building the walls. But, during the night, the wind destroyed everything. So, the brothers decided to sacrifice one of their wives to the fortress—the first one to bring them food the next morning. Only the younger brother respected the deal; it was his wife who arrived the next morning with food. The wife agreed to be buried in the foundations, but she asked that her single breast remain outside the walls so that she could continue to feed her baby. Even now, a milky liquid wets the stones of the fortress in Rozafat, at the location where the young woman was buried. And, it's at that site that childless women, for centuries, have brushed the stones with their fingers asking for the gift of motherhood.[5]

The close connection between a girl's death and a fort/tower/ castle is typical, not just in the legends of northern, central, and south-eastern Europe. A vivid example of this is the famous Maiden's Towers in Trans-Caucasia, Turkey, and the Crimea, with which the legends of the Turkic people are associated. The very name, 'Maiden's Tower' (Kiz Kulesi, Qiz Qalasi, and Kiz Kulle), refers to the tower's impregnability for invaders—a virtue that is common to both the tower and the maiden. Without a doubt, the legend of the Maiden's Tower is a version of the story of the immured virgin, for the tower is a synonym for the purity of the girl who was shut up within it. In these legends, the threat to the ideal of purity, and the violation of the taboo, lead to the heroine's death.

The legend of the Azerbaijani tower, Qiz Qalasi, fits in best with this interpretation. It recounts that a certain Shah fell in love with his own daughter and wanted to marry her. To delay the incestuous marriage, the girl asked her father to build a tower for her. The Shah did not change his mind, even after the tower was completed. So, the girl ascended the tower and jumped off the top, into the Caspian Sea. So, the tower protects her innocence from the threat of incest: the girl dies without her virginity being violated; she protects her chastity and leaves her *alter ego*—the Maiden's Tower—behind.

The famous Kiz Kulesi in Istanbul, which stands on an isle in the middle of the Bosporus, was built to protect a virgin from the threat of death. According to the most popular Turkish legend, a sultan had a much-beloved daughter. One day, an oracle prophesied that she would be killed by a venomous snake on her 18th birthday. The sultan, in an effort to thwart his daughter's early demise, had the tower built in the middle of the Bosphorus—so placing her away from land and so from any snakes—to protect her until her 18th birthday. The princess was placed in the tower, where she was frequently visited by only her father.

On the princess' 18th birthday, the sultan brought her a basket of exotic sumptuous fruits as a birthday gift, delighted that he had been able to prevent the prophecy. On reaching into the basket, however, an asp that had been hiding among the fruit bit the young princess and she died in her father's arms, just as the oracle had predicted. Nevertheless, it is clear that the tower acted as a guardian of innocence, here too.

The older name, Leander's Tower, comes from another story about a maiden: the ancient Greek myth of Hero and Leander. Hero was a priestess of Aphrodite who lived in a tower at the edge of the Hellespont (Dardanelles). Leander (Leandros), a young man who lived on the other side of the strait, fell in love with her and would swim across the Hellespont every night to be with her. Hero would light a lamp at the top of her tower, to guide his way. But, one stormy winter night, the waves tossed Leander about in the sea, the breezes blew out Hero's light, and Leander lost his way and was drowned. Hero threw herself from the tower in grief and died as well. The name, *Maiden's Tower*, might also have its origins in this ancient story. Despite the romanticism of the story of Hero and Leander, which was sung by generations of poets from Ovid to Schiller and Tennyson, it has no direct connection with the Maiden's Tower: Leander swam across the Dardanelles rather than the Bosporus, where the tower stands. Due to the vicinity and similarity of the Dardanelles and the Bosphorus, Leander's story was attributed to the tower by the ancient Greeks and later by the Byzantines.

The legend of the tower of Kiz Kulle, near the Crimean city of Sudak, also has Greek origins. The young daughter of the local ruler once waited for her beloved in the tower. The groom's arrival, from Miletus, was to be announced by a white sail on a ship's mast. However, the white sail was not hoisted in time, because of the father's machinations; the girl, believing that her beloved had betrayed her, jumped into the abyss from the tower. Here, the tower protected vows of love rather than the purity of the heroine herself, and it was the collapse of the amorous ideal that led to death.

The unassailable tower, as the abode of virginity, is not only a reflection of the aforementioned mytho-poetic notions of different peoples, but also of widespread historical practice. Although legends surrounding towers do not always contain sensational motifs (murder, suicide, immurement, etc.), they are almost always associated with women. An example is the famous Cypress Tomb (*Sarv-wala maqbara*) in Lahore, which got its name from the images of cypresses on its walls. Built in the eighteenth century, this tower belonged to Begum Sharafunnisa, the unmarried sister of Nawab Khan Bahadur Khan, the Mughal governor of Lahore. This pious girl prayed in the tower day and night, completely alone without any guards, protected solely by the Qu'ran and a sabre. It was Sharafunnisa's will to be buried in the Cypress Tower after her death; the Qu'ran, in a pure gold binding, and the gem-studded sabre that offered her spiritual and worldly protection during her lifetime came to adorn her sarcophagus. The Cypress Tower preserves the memory of her purity and piety.[6]

Another symbol of an unconquered woman is the Sumbeka (Söyembikä) Tower in Kazan. According to legend, Sumbeka, the last queen of Kazan (1520–1557), took charge of the defence of the city when Ivan the Terrible's troops approached its walls. Donning a helmet and armour, she went out to meet the enemy in person. The queen's courage roused the inhabitants of Kazan; Andrei Kurbsky, commander of the Russian army, was unable to take the city by storm for a long time, until he finally had a secret tunnel dug. When she learned that the defences had been breached and the enemy had entered the city, Sumbeka allegedly threw herself off the tower[7]— which served, here, as a substitute for the city's unassailability and the queen's honour.

The logic of the legend creates a stable correlation between the building, in which the woman died, and her name, historic or pseudo-historic image, or even the ghost that she became after her violent death or suicide. This leads to a 'cyclization' of legends around an architectural structure: the story of the 'victim of the building' is supplemented by independent tales of a phantom of a 'Woman in White', 'Black Lady', or 'Grey Nun' that perturb the inhabitants of old

European houses and castles and serve as an inexhaustible source of city folklore. In contrast to the well-known 'Phantom of the Opera', the 'phantom of the building' is almost always a woman. Most often, this is the phantom, not of an anonymous 'architectural victim', but of a concrete historical or pseudo-historical heroine who tragically died in the castle or tower. This phantom accompanies the building's cultural history for centuries, gradually shifting from the domain of legend to the subject matter of literature and art.

The subject transforms as it shifts into the domain of written literature: it is no longer merely a question of an innocent immured girl, but of the victim of unhappy love, domestic violence, parental despotism, or political intrigue. In this way, legendary motifs acquire social aspects, and gender issues become visible behind the stories' sinister and romantic images. However, the further evolution of the motif of the 'immured bride', that takes place in the domain of the mass media, is marked by aggressive commercialization rather than the deepening of these social motifs.

The more popular the legend about a female victim, the more culturally significant the building with which she is associated. And, vice-versa, buildings with the greatest cultural recognition have got the most popular female phantoms. In the twentieth century, the stable mutual connection between female victims and famous architectural structures has devolved from the empyrean of 'high' art to the shooting sets of movies, soap operas, and musicals. Today, this connection is supported by widely promoted tourist sites and commercial brands.

* * *

Like other old European and Asian cities, Lahore has its own legend about an 'immured bride'[8] which is dated back the reign of Akbar (1556–1605). Many Indians and Pakistanis still consider this legend to be a true story. There are several reasons for this: first of all, the legend's main characters—Emperor Akbar and his son Salim (the future emperor, Jahangir)—are undoubtedly historic figures; secondly, the tomb of the legend's heroine, Anarkali, is a Lahore landmark that was turned into the first Protestant parish church of St. James by the English; and, thirdly, 'Anarkali' also figures in the name of Anarkali Bazaar, a large and densely populated neighbourhood close to the Walled City.

Nevertheless, despite all this 'material' evidence, the story of Anarkali is purely apocryphal and is not substantiated by the chronicles and historical sources that were so abundant during the Great Mughal Empire. It is not mentioned in the memoirs of Emperor Jahangir, the lover hero of this legend. While Jahangir, like other medieval and especially royal authors, may not have wanted to write about his relations with women, he nevertheless did describe—in great detail—all the buildings that were constructed on his orders. Anarkali's Tomb is not in this list.

According to the legend, 'Anarkali'—which translates as 'Pomegranate Bud'—was the nickname of the court dancer, Nadira Begum or Sharafunnisa. Nadira was the daughter of an impoverished Persian merchant who came to India, in search of fortune, with his family. On the way, their caravan was attacked by brigands near Kabul; the merchant and other male members of the family were killed, and the women taken prisoners. Somehow, the incident came to the attention of the governor of Kabul at the time, the famous warrior Raja Man Singh. He punished the brigands, liberated the merchant's wife and daughter, and sent them to the emperor's harem in Lahore.[9] This prehistory suggests that Anarkali initially held the very modest position of a servitor or odalisque at the court.

However, her musical talent made her rise among the ranks: her gift as a singer and dancer was admired by the emperor himself, who gave her the nickname of 'Pomegranate Bud', apparently for her beauty and purity. Soon, the crown prince Salim fell in love with her, and she returned his feelings. Once, during a reception at the palace of Shish Mahal—where the ceiling and walls are covered with mirrors—Akbar saw the prince and dancing girl exchanging amorous looks. The emperor flew into a rage and threw Anarkali into jail. Salim rebelling against his father, intended to run away with his beloved and marry her. As such behaviour was tantamount to state treason, Akbar ordered that his son be arrested and that Anarkali, as the instigator of the rebellion, be immured alive in a wall.

The Anarkali legend clearly has a lot in common with the 'immured bride' motif that I have discussed in detail before. The heroine is sacrificed to the 'male' interests of power and succession to the throne; she dies at the same time as her hopes for love vanish; and her name is closely connected with famous architectural monuments—the Shish Mahal Palace, the architectural masterpiece of Lahore Fort[10] whose walls treacherously revealed the amorous secret, and the celebrated mausoleum that perpetuates her memory. Moreover, the Anarkali legend has a purely toponymic significance: the place where she was immured alive, and where her tomb was subsequently built, lies in the centre of the vast neighbourhood of Anarkali Bazaar. Finally, the Anarkali legend has a sensational aspect that is an indispensable part of such stories: rumours about famous historic figures, family scandal, adultery, and even a hint of incest.

Although Anarkali's execution entirely belongs to the domain of legend, the 'exact date' of this event is known: 1599. When Salim became emperor, after his father's death, he built a magnificent tomb on the site of the execution of his beloved in 1615 (although, by this time, he had already been happily married for five years to his favourite wife, Empress Nur Jahan). Anarkali's mausoleum is a typical example of Indian funerary architecture: an octagonal building whose dome rests on eight massive arches located inside. They are echoed on the outside by eight towers whose tops have the same form as the central cupola. The extraordinarily beautiful sarcophagus is carved out of monolithic marble, and covered with unique carving. Specialists consider this sarcophagus to be one of the best works of Mughal stone carving. The 99 names of Allah are inscribed on the sarcophagus; the following lines, below, were supposedly written by Jahangir himself:

> *tā qiyāmat shukr gūyam kardigār-i khīsh rā*
> *āh gar man bāz bīnam rū-yi yār-i khīsh rā*

> I would give thanks unto my God unto the Day of Resurrection
> Ah! could I behold the face of my beloved once more

One side of the sarcophagus bears the inscription *dar Lahur majnun Salim Akbar* ('In Lahore mad with love Salim, [son of] Akbar') and two dates written in Arabic letters and numbers: 1008 AH (AD 1599) and 1024 AH (AD 1615). The former date relates to Anarkali's execution, and the latter to the construction of her tomb.

Fiction and historical fact are closely intertwined in the Anarkali legend. The legend's heroine has a real tomb that bears a date, an epitaph, and the signature of a real historical figure. Such false tombs/cenotaphs were often built in the Indian Subcontinent, in honour of numerous Muslim saints, and became places of mass pilgrimage. The date of Anarkali's alleged execution is also known. Moreover, Prince Salim did foment a rebellion against his father in 1599; Akbar, who was in the Deccan at that time, had to return to the north with his army to bring the situation under control.

At the same time, later sources assert that when the English decided to turn Anarkali's mausoleum into a Christian church in the nineteenth century, they exhumed the mortal remains in the central hall and re-interred them under one of the corner towers.[11] Thus, there was a body in the tomb. In the light of such circumstances, the Anarkali legend may appear to be a deliberate hoax or mystification.

As with all apocrypha that purport to be true, the Anarkali legend evokes a lot of questions. Two questions, in particular, stand out. First of all, why was Anarkali so severely punished for her love affair with Salim? After all, women of her status—odalisques and courtesans/dancing girls—were obliged to simply gratify young dynasts. The earlier a young prince began his sexual life, the better one could judge his procreative potential, i.e., how many sons he could engender in the future so assuring the succession of the throne. In addition, liaison with a dancing girl, who had a special status in the traditional society of Muslim India, contributed to the social education of a young man. Relations with a courtesan (*tawaif*) could teach him etiquette and good manners, and make him appreciate music and poetry. Even if a prince, or the emperor himself, married an odalisque, there was nothing sacramental about it: she simply became a member of his large harem and did not disrupt the existing order. Sons from such marriages could vie for the throne on a par with the sons from the empresses. An example is the case of Prince Shahriar—a son from Jahangir's marriage to a concubine—who fought his stepbrother—the future emperor Shah Jahan, born out of 'lawful' wedlock with a Rajput princess—for power.

Everything historians know about Jalaluddin Muhammad Akbar also contradicts his role as a cruel tyrant and hardhearted father in the Anarkali legend. According to many chroniclers, the emperor was a magnanimous and lenient man who was not inclined to rash acts and sudden fits of anger. He forgave Salim his rebellion, pardoned his brother Hakim after the latter organized a conspiracy against him, tolerated the hostile intrigues of his wet nurse Maham Anga, and the outrageous behaviour of his foster brother Adham Khan for many years. Why then did Akbar, who became a model for clemency for subsequent Indian rulers, treat a helpless and powerless woman with such cruelty, rather than simply giving her to his son as a concubine in order to put an end to the conflict?

There was only one explanation: Anarkali would have deserved the death penalty if she had been a concubine or wife of Akbar, rather than a simple dancing girl. All women with whom the master of the harem had intimate liaisons were forbidden (*haram*) to other men, and so, Salim's love affair with his father's wife or concubine could have been viewed as state treason and incest—crimes that were punished very severely. In this case, the conflict between Akbar and Salim turns out to be more than a father's wrath against his disobedient son: it was also the result of the rivalry between two men over a woman.

This first disparity in the Anarkali story leads to the second question. If Salim was guilty of such serious crimes against his father and lord, why did he succeed to the throne? Akbar's male progeny were not numerous: two of his sons, Shah Murad and Danial, died young because of their addiction to alcohol; Akbar himself was also subject to this vice, while Salim (Jahangir) became a hopeless alcoholic in his old age despite his piety. At the same time, Salim was the firstborn and considered to be the heir apparent. Nevertheless, the strict rules of succession did not yet exist in Akbar's time, and the practice of power transfer was fairly flexible: if necessary, the throne could be inherited by a brother, son-in-law, nephew, or other male relative, who were always numerous in the Mughal dynasty.

Apparently, Salim's crimes against his father were not all that serious: his rebellion was pardoned, because rebellions and conspiracies by Mughal princes against their fathers were commonplace (one could say that Mughal dynasts passed the Oedipus complex down from generation to generation). For example, Jahangir himself was confronted with the rebellions of two of his sons during his reign

(1605–1627): Khosrow (who was blinded as punishment) and Khurram (the future emperor, Shah Jahan). In turn, Shah Jahan became hostage to the struggle for power between his sons Dara Shikoh, Sultan Shuja, Murad Bakhsh, and Aurangzeb.

At the same time, Jahangir's memoirs show that, by the end of Akbar's reign, relations between father and son had become quite close. 'At this crisis my father desiring me to draw near, threw his arms about my neck, and addressed me in the following terms', wrote Jahangir: 'My dear boy (baba), take this my last farewell, for here we never meet again. Beware that thou dost not withdraw thy protecting regard from those that are secluded in my harem; that thou continue the same allowance for subsistence as was allotted by myself. Although my departure must cast a heavy burden upon thy mind, let not the words that are past be at once forgotten. There are many a vow between us; break not the pledge which thou hast given me, forget it not. Beware; many are the claims which I have upon thy soul. Be they great or be they small, do not thou forget them. Call to the remembrance my deeds of martial glory. Forget not the exertions of that bounty which distributed so many a jewel. My servants and dependants, when I am gone, do not thou forget, nor the afflicted in the hour of need. Ponder word for word on all that I have said, do thou bear all in mind; and again, forget me not.'[12]

No matter what Akbar's words 'many are the claims which I have upon thy soul' mean, it is clear that he truly loved Salim and was ready to bequeath his military glory and harem, along with his throne, to him. The Anarkali legend, which is based on jealousy and hidden rivalry between father and son over a woman, fits in poorly with such patriarchal relations consecrated by blood ties.

From the start, the Anarkali legend has had such a strong melodramatic appeal augmented by the participation of famous historical figures that people wanted to believe in it unconditionally. This was the case of European visitors to Lahore who, in their travel notes, described Anarkali (sometimes without mentioning her name) as a real woman who had been executed.

The first to leave behind such a description was the abovementioned William Finch, who travelled in the Punjab in 1611–1616, i.e., during the construction of Anarkali's tomb. He wrote,

'Passing the Sugar Gonge in a faire miskite built by Sheeke
Fereed beyond it […] is a faire monument for Don Sha
his mother, one of Akbar's wives, with whom it is said
Sha Selim had to do (her name was Immacque Kelle, or
Pomegranate Kernell); upon notice of which the King
(Akbar) caused her to be inclosed quicke within a wall
in his moholl, where she died, and the King (Jahangir),
in token of his love, commands a sumptuous tomb to be
built of stone in the midst of a foure square garden richly
walled, with a gate and divers rooms over it. The convexity
of the tomb he hath willed to be wrought in works of
gold, with a large faire Jounter with rooms overhead.'[13]

The heroine of the story that Finch heard from Anarkali's
contemporaries, in the early seventeenth century, was one of Akbar's
wives. Finch's memoirs are extremely valuable as he visited Lahore
during Jahangir's reign, and heard Anarkali's story relatively soon
after the alleged events took place. His account has several unclear
moments. Firstly, one can only guess at who Don Sha(h), described
by Finch as Anarkali's son, was. Abraham Eraly, a specialist on Mughal
India, has conjectured that Finch was referring to Prince Danial,
Akbar's son who died at a young age. In this case, Salim truly had an
incestuous relationship with one of the wives of his father.

Abraham Eraly supported his hypothesis by quoting an incident
recorded by Abul Fazl. According to the court historian, Salim was
beaten up, one evening, by guards from the royal harem of Akbar. The
story is that a mad man had wandered into Akbar's harem, because of
the carelessness of the guards. Salim caught the man, but was himself
mistaken for the intruder. The emperor arrived upon the scene and
was about to strike, with his sword, when he recognized Salim. Most
probably, the intruder was no other than Prince Salim, and the story
of the mad man was concocted to put a veil on the Prince's indecency.
Eraly concluded that there was an 'Oedipal conflict' between Akbar
and the crown prince.[14]

A few years after Finch's stay in Lahore, the Englishman Edward
Terry visited the city. Terry wrote that Akbar had threatened to
deprive Salim of the right of succession, for his liaison with Akbar's
wife (whose name is not cited), before pardoning Salim on his death

bed.[15] In 1842, two centuries after Finch and Terry, the Russian artist and traveller Prince Alexy Soltykoff came to Lahore. He mentioned Anarkali as an undoubtedly historical figure: 'I haven't yet written to you about a miserable woman who was walled-up alive for adultery. Her tomb is not far from our camp. Later it turned out that she was innocent, and a beautiful mausoleum was erected over her grave.'[16] As Soltykoff spent only a few days in Lahore, at the court of the Sikh ruler Sher Singh, he clearly heard Anarkali's story in a very general form.

The historian of Lahore, Muhammad Baqir, believes that 'Anarkali' was originally the name of the garden in which the tomb of one of Jahangir's wives was built. She bore the title 'Mistress of Beauty' (*Sahib-i Jamal*) and was the mother of Prince Parvez. Over time, the name of the garden came to be applied to the person buried in the tomb. This conjecture is fairly plausible, all the more as a garden called 'Anarkali' is mentioned in Prince Dara Shikoh's hagiographic work, *Sakinat al-awliya*, as the place where Mian Mir, the patron saint of Lahore, meditated.[17]

In his chronicle, *Akbar-namah*, Abul Fazl wrote that Salim married *Sahib-i Jamal* in June 1596, and that she was the daughter of the Mughal nobleman, Zain Khan Koka. Abul Fazl noted that Akbar initially objected to this marriage; Muhammad Baqir explains this by the fact that the crown prince had previously married Zain Khan Koka's niece, and marriages with second-degree relatives were looked down upon. However, when Akbar saw that his son's heart was smitten with love for the girl, he reluctantly agreed.[18] It should be said that Baqir's argumentation is not entirely convincing as Salim's first wife, whom he married in 1585, was the Rajput princess Man Bai, his cousin on his mother's side.

Jahangir had twenty wives, not counting concubines, in his harem. If we are to assume that one of them was buried in the tomb, the emperor's verses engraved on the sarcophagus would turn out to be totally inappropriate: no Mughal emperor would have ever said that he was 'madly in love' with his lawful wife, and that he dreamt of meeting her in the afterlife. In seventeenth-century Muslim India, such romantic and poetic license would have been impossible in the relations between husband and wife, especially of such high standing.

The Sikhs, who ruled the Punjab from the late eighteenth to the mid-nineteenth centuries, preserved most of the Mughal buildings, even if they stripped their marble facings and architectural ornamentation and changed their functions. Anarkali's Tomb was subject to the same fate. It became the residence of Kharak Singh, Ranjit Singh's eldest son and successor, and then of the Italian mercenary general, Ventura, who served in the Sikh army. The same fate was in store for the tomb of Anarkali's beloved: Jahangir's famous mausoleum in Shahdara became the villa of another Sikh mercenary, the French general Emis.[19] Both Sikhs and Christians were clearly not disturbed by the fact that some Muslims were buried inside their homes. These 'transformed' buildings subsequently led the English to coin a strange term for a certain type of Muslim mausoleum in the Indian Subcontinent—the 'residential tomb'.

In 1846, after the end of the First Anglo-Sikh war and the conclusion of the Treaty of Lahore, the British army consolidated its presence in Lahore, which was still under the formal power of the Sikhs. Barracks and bungalows were erected for soldiers and officers of the garrison in the city quarter around Anarkali's Tomb. The Residency (now the Punjab Secretariat) was built here for the British Resident, Henry Lawrence (1806–1857).[20] This led to the establishment of the Cantonment—the first military station that marked the beginning of English military settlement in Lahore. In 1849, the Punjab was annexed by the English; the ceremony of the transfer of power took place in the same eventful palace, Shish Mahal. Upon gaining power over Lahore, the English immediately found an application for Anarkali's Tomb, which they transformed into the first parish church in 1850. Ever since, the whole neighbourhood and adjoining streets came to be known as 'Anarkali', out of which the new colonial Lahore has grown.

This time around, the tomb was subject to significant changes: the large organ, suspended wooden ceiling, and benches for worshippers totally changed the interior of the central hall; the openings in the upper gallery were walled up; high windows were cut in the walls. The mausoleum was plastered over, and painted with whitewash, leaving no traces of the gilded dome and glazed tiles that decorated the façade.

At the same time, the sarcophagus was removed from the central hall and the mortal remains beneath it were re-interred.

In 1880, the British oriental scholar E.B. Eastwick found the marble sarcophagus, black with dirt, in the basement of the parish church while gathering materials for his guidebook to north-western India. Realizing the artistic and historical value of his discovery, Eastwick gave a detailed and sentimental account of the legend of the 'immured bride' of the Mughals in his guidebook.[21] From that time on, Anarkali's Tomb figured on the list of Lahore's historical sights and became a favourite subject for European artists visiting the city.[22] After the construction of the new Protestant church, Anarkali's Tomb was handed over, in 1891, to the Punjab government to house the records of the Punjab Civil Secretariat. It still serves this function today.

In 1960, the Pakistani government attempted to restore the historic monument and open it to the public. Little came of this endeavour as the Museum of the Punjab Civil Secretariat was set up in the mausoleum's central hall, and its valuable collection of documents made it necessary to limit visiting hours to several hours a week for the public-at-large. The marble sarcophagus, which was cleaned up a bit, has not been returned to its original place and gathers dust in one of the aisles.

As other variations on the motif of the 'immured bride', the Anarkali legend has been widely portrayed in literature and art. The professional artists of the Indian Subcontinent have paid their honours to the heroine of the Lahore legend: in the early twentieth century, the doyen of Indian miniaturists Hajji Muhammad Sharif, the former court painter of the Maharaja of Patiala, created the famous miniature *Salim and Anarkali on the Balcony*.

The image of Anarkali, by the classic Pakistani painter 'Abdur Rahman Chughtai (1894–1975), is a lot more expressive. In his usual style, combining the traditionalism of the Bengali Renaissance with the refinement of European Art Nouveau, Chughtai depicted Anarkali not as a romantic heroine but as an experienced courtesan with a deceitful smile and an enticing and crafty gaze. Anarkali's tresses writhe ominously and she holds a broken flower in her hand—details that refer to her fatal role in the Lahore legend.

The romantic tragedy '*Anarkali*' by the Urdu playwright Imtiaz 'Ali Taj (1900–1970) holds a prominent place among the works of fiction inspired by the Lahore legend. It was Taj who asked his friend 'Abdur Rahman Chughtai to paint the aforementioned portrait of the Lahore beauty as an illustration for his play. The play was published in 1931, almost a decade after it was written. The reason for this delay was described, by the author, in the preface: 'I wrote *Anarkali* in 1922, yet the theatres of the day did not accept it. The changes that they asked to make in the play did not suit me. I also hesitated to publish it at that time. Only now, after seeing how the situation in theatre has changed, I have no reserves about my play being published.'[23] There is no doubt that Imtiaz 'Ali Taj's play was greatly ahead of its time in its poetics and dramatic conflict.

Although Taj's play has been widely imitated, and gave rise to the genre of 'Mughal melodrama', it was a typical *Lesedrama* (play for reading only) and was staged in an abridged form (it takes over five hours to perform fully). At the same time, Taj's play became a major source of quotes for the creators of the numerous screen versions of the Anarkali legend. Indeed, the legend's subject seems custom-made for cinema. It has all the conceivable elements of a costume drama: fateful passions, harem secrets, palace receptions, luxurious costumes, large-scale battle scenes, and musical acts with singing and dancing.

Of special significance was the fact that Taj's play created a definite version of the well-known legend and reproduced the 'Mughal' atmosphere—a set of stage devices, requisites, and musical means that are still used in historic films by Indian and Pakistani filmmakers. Taj supplemented the story with fictitious main and secondary characters, new episodes, and plot twists. The following characters, introduced by Taj, became part of all subsequent film versions of the Anarkali legend: Salim's loving mother, Rani Jodha Bai (or Jodhi Bibi);[24]Anarkali's faithful sister (or mother), Soraya; the upright military commander, Raja Man Singh; the treacherous antagonist, Dilaram; and Salim's true friend, Bakhtiar.[25]

The inception of Indian cinema is traditionally dated to 1913, when the Indian first film director, Dadasaheb Phalke, shot *Raja Harishchandra*. Films about the Anarkali legend began to appear in the 1920s; the first was *Loves of a Mughal Prince*, produced by

Prafulla Roy at the Great Eastern Film Company. Subsequently, films based on the subject began to appear regularly on the screen—about twice a decade—bringing great fame to their actors. The best-known Anarkali, in Indian cinema in the 1920s and 1930s, was Sulochana (1910–1983), a stunningly beautiful Christian of mixed descent (her real name was Ruby Myers). She was the only actress to have starred in three films about Anarkali: twice as the main heroine (in the silent movie *Loves of a Mughal Prince* in 1928, and in R.S. Chaudhri's talkies in 1935) and, at an advanced age, as Salim's mother in Nandalal Jaswantlal's film (1953).

Pradeep Kumar (1924–2001) gained celebrity as Salim—a role he played twice in the 1940s and 1950s: the first time, in Nandalal Jaswantlal's film, with Bina Roy as Anarkali; the second time, with Anjali Devi. Pradeep Kumar's exquisite appearance and irreproachable manners made him perfectly suited for roles of royalty: after gaining success as Salim, he played princes and emperors in historical melodramas for many years. Pradeep Kumar's constant partner was the popular film star Meena Kumari, who also starred as Empress Nur Jahan in Indian cinema. Thanks to the large number of screen versions, the role of Anarkali has been performed by famous film stars as well as by professional dancers and singers. An example is the outstanding vocalist and 'queen of melody', Nur Jahan (1926–2000), who played the main role in Anwar Kamal Pasha's *Anarkali* (1958).

Nevertheless, the popularity of these films and actors cannot match the thundering success of the cult film *The Great Mughal* (*Mughal-e Azam*), directed and produced by Karim Asif (1960). *The Great Mughal* is a national cinematographic myth on which generations of Indian and Pakistani viewers grew up, amid the collective image of 'love in the Indian style' set in the backdrop of the country's history. Its place, in the popular culture of the Indian Subcontinent, is comparable to the role of David Selznick's *Gone with the Wind* in American culture, and Marcel Carné's *Children of Paradise* in French culture. Numerous polls have shown that *The Great Mughal* is considered to be the best Indian film of all time.

The Great Mughal was Bollywood's most ambitious project, and was meant to be a challenge to its elder brother, Hollywood. It cost three million dollars to make the film, while the production cost of an average Indian movie, in the 1950s, did not surpass two hundred thousand. Work on the film began in colonial India in 1944, and continued for over fifteen years. After the Partition in 1947, project financing stopped; shooting did not resume until 1951, with the new and definite cast of Prithviraj Kapoor (Akbar), Dilip Kumar (Salim), and Madhubala (Anarkali).

The shooting, however, proceeded extremely slowly, whether on account of the difficulties of the first years of independence or due to the director's personal style of work. When shooting was finally complete, in 1957, Asif was struck by the idea of re-shooting the film in colour. He managed to re-shoot about fifteen percent of the film before the producers finally lost patience and refused to continue financing such a drawn-out enterprise. The premiere of *The Great Mughal* finally took place in 1960. It appeared on screen in black and white, with three episodes in colour. Apparently, in an effort to appeal to viewers, Asif, who was also one of the film's screenwriters, changed the legend's end: at the last moment, Akbar pardoned Anarkali and banished her from his empire—her life was saved at the price of exile as, for Salim, she was lost forever.

The first thing that struck the audience of the film was its unprecedented grandeur, its sumptuous decorations, and its meticulous re-creation of a historic period—in other words, the same attributes that marked Hollywood blockbusters. To make the picture as authentic as possible, Asif brought the best craftsmen from across the country to the Bombay film studio. Tailors from Delhi stitched the costumes, with the exception of Anarkali's and Rani Jodha Bai's clothes which were loaned from the Salar Jung Museum in Hyderabad. Embroiderers from Surat decorated the costumes with gold and silver thread, Hyderabadi goldsmiths made the jewellery, Rajasthani ironsmiths crafted the weapons, and cobblers from Agra sewed the footwear. The statue of Lord Krishna, in the Maharani's chamber, was made of pure gold. Finally, with the permission of the Ministry of Defence, 8000 soldiers from the regular army, 4000 horses, and 2000 camels were used for the battle scenes.

Such grandeur and expensive opulence are quite characteristic for the cinematographic development of the 'immured bride' plot: in mass culture, the death of the female victim serves as a pretence for demonstrating luxury and exoticism.

Another of the film's great merits was its music, written by the prominent Indian composer 'Ali Naushad (1919–2006). The songs, composed to the lyrics of Shakeel Badayuni, continue to be popular with several generations of South Asians. Naushad called on the services of the best classical singers of the day: Ustad Bade Ghulam 'Ali Khan, Mohammed Rafi, Lata Mangeshkar, and Shamshad Begum. The sound recording technology of the time did not allow for reverberation; to create the effect of echoing in the Shish Mahal in the *mahfil* (musical gathering) scene, Naushad had Lata Mangeshkar sing the famous hit *Pyar Kiya to Darna Kya* ('Having Loved, So What Is There To be Afraid of?') from the studio's bathroom. The soloist, Mohammed Rafi, sang the hit *Ay Mohabbat Zindabad* ('Long Live Love!') with a chorus of 120 singers. All this created an enormous impression on the audience.

Naturally, the cinematographic language of *The Great Mughal* is quite simple and traditional, in keeping with the general development of Indian cinema at that time. The three-hour-long film consists of a simple succession of close-ups and long shots that are 'livened up' by their content (dances, palace receptions, battle scenes, etc.) rather than by montage as was used in European cinema. Nevertheless, some of the film's episodes would have done honour to many of the Western directors of the 1950s. Among them is the scene when the two protagonists meet for the first time in a dark chamber; as they pass each other, a candle lights up their faces from unusual angles, creating an atmosphere of reticence and mystery. Another wonderful scene was shot by gradually zooming in on Anarkali, as she was reading a letter from the prince, while backing the camera and facing a white wall.

Despite the omnipresence of love scenes, Indian cinema was quite puritan at the time. Hence, the tryst scene—in which the hero caresses the heroine, as she lies in his arms, by slowly drawing a white ostrich feather across her face—shocked many viewers as it was an eloquent metaphor for intimacy and restrained passion. Finally, the famous episode of the last *mahfil* shows Anarkali's dance reflected in the rotating mirror kaleidoscope of the Shish Mahal.

Nevertheless, the main reason for the film's resounding success was the actors who starred in the lead roles. Prithviraj Kapoor (1904–1972), the founder of the famous Kapoor dynasty of actors, made his debut in the first Indian talkie, *Alam Ara*, in 1931. Prithviraj's wonderful acting ability, imposing figure, and deep and resounding voice made him wonderfully suited to the roles of mythological heroes and emperors. At the same time, he was a serious theatre actor and director who founded his own 'Theatre of the Earth' (Prithvi Theatre) in which he staged topical political plays about the Partition.

In *The Great Mughal*, Prithviraj depicted the tragedy of power: his Akbar is torn between his pride as the ruler of an enormous empire, and his inborn magnanimity and natural fatherly feelings. The vividness and noble grandeur of his screen personality, the characteristic modulations of his unforgettable voice, and his somewhat affected and expansive manner of acting were often copied to the point of becoming a cliché. Subsequently, acting in the 'Prithviraj style' meant roaring, brandishing one's fists, and assuming a fighting posture.

Salim was played by Dilip Kumar (born 1922), a living legend of Indian cinema, who appeared in films over many decades and ended his screen career at the age of 77. Dilip Kumar set a record for the number of Filmfare Best Actor Awards (given to the best actor of the year) that he received throughout his career. He also received the Dadasaheb Phalke Award, the country's highest cinematographic prize. In addition, he was a member of the Indian parliament and the head of a number of charitable associations. In his time, Dilip Kumar rejected an invitation to go to Hollywood: he had been invited to star in David Lean's production of *Lawrence of Arabia*—the role that was subsequently played by Omar Sharif. Dilip Kumar's appeal and charm (which may appear somewhat syrupy to the European viewer) have long become a truism: the Bombay idiom 'You're my Dilip Kumar' simply means 'You're my hero'.

As with many film stars of the older generation, Dilip Kumar came from a Muslim family—his real name is Muhammad Yusuf Khan—yet he adopted a Hindu name on moving to Bombay from his native Peshawar, so adapting to the realities of independent India and the tastes of the mass audience. Already successful in his earlier roles, he became nationally known after the release of Bimal Roy's film, *Devdas* (1951). Dilip Kumar often incarnated the image of the tragic rebel fighting against the vicissitudes of fortune and the tyranny of the powers that be—a role that was in keeping with the social attitudes of the time and appealed to millions of viewers.

This may explain why Prince Salim, in Dilip Kumar's interpretation, is more a fearless fighter against tyranny, embodied by Akbar, than a romantic lover. Dilip Kumar is more impressive and convincing in episodes of struggle and opposition than in love scenes. Although the prince's rebellion against his father's power and the dictatorship of the state is doomed to fail, he wins the moral victory in the pathetic finale that is brilliantly performed by the actor.

But, the excellent leading male stars in the film notwithstanding, the soul of the production was Madhubala (1933–1969), who has become identified with the role of Anarkali in the minds of both Indians and Pakistanis. Madhubala died very young, from a grave heart disease that she had concealed for a long time from those around her. This disease may explain why she differed so greatly from contemporary Bombay film stars—in her fragile vulnerability, her mat pallor that is so rare for Indian women, and her fathomless eyes with their expression of doom. Madhubala was wonderful in the roles of suffering heroines who were surrounded by a halo of mystery and were too precious for this cruel world. Her acting was marked by a nervous impetuousness, rapid changes of tone, and a magical energy.

The role of Anarkali made considerable physical and nervous demands on the actress. Bent on authenticity, Asif spent a lot of time shooting Madhubala in real iron chains and shackles in the scenes of her imprisonment. After one such scene, she was taken to the hospital directly from the film set.

As with Dilip Kumar, Madhubala was a Muslim by birth—her real name was Mumtaz Jahan—and she came from a poor family with many children. When Madhubala was born, a certain holy man (*pir*) told her father that the girl would become rich and famous, yet would be unhappy and die young. From this prophecy, her father retained only the word 'rich', and soon brought his daughter to Bombay, from Delhi, for her to be closer to the Indian film industry. Madhubala began to appear in films from the age of one. By the time she was twelve, as Baby Mumtaz, she had become widely known as a performer of children's roles. The pretty girl came to the attention of the film star Devika Rani, who recommended that she change her name to Madhubala to appeal better to Indian viewers.

In 1951, the young beauty got acquainted with Dilip Kumar during the filming of *Tarana*. In keeping with the heroines of Indian romance, she sent him a red rose with a note asking him to accept the flower only if he was willing to accept her love too. Several scenes in *The Great Mughal* play on the symbolism of the rose. Following the performance of the song *Teri Mahfil Mein Qismat Azma Kar Hum Bhi Dekhen Ge*, in the scene of the musical contest between Anarkali and her conniving antagonist Bahar, the prince gives Bahar a rose flower, and Anarkali a rose stem with thorns so predicting her future suffering. During the protagonists' last meeting, Anarkali, on Akbar's order, gives Salim a rose—sprinkled with sleeping powder—to smell; and so, the prince faints.

Yet, everything was simpler in real life: the intrigued and flattered Dilip Kumar accepted Madhubala's rose and a tumultuous love affair began between them, lasting for seven years. It ended in a scandalous separation and legal case.[26] By the end of the shooting of *The Great Mughal*, relations between the former lovers were irrevocably spoiled.

In 1960, when *The Great Mughal* was released, Madhubala married the singer/actor Kishore Kumar. This marriage was unhappy, for religious reasons among others: Madhubala was rejected by her husband's Hindu family, while her husband was boycotted by her Muslim relatives. In the meanwhile, the actress's health deteriorated rapidly; she had several heart attacks and died while waiting for heart surgery. Without a doubt, the complicated relations between Madhubala and Dilip Kumar influenced their performance, giving their characters' emotions the depth and tension of a real-life drama. On top of everything, *The Great Mughal* is a monument to Madhubala. Anyone who has seen the film will long remember her beautiful and tender face, reflected in the mirrors of the Shish Mahal, while she sings *Chup Na Sakega 'Ishq Hamara* ('My Love Cannot be Concealed').

Although it is no secret that films become outdated, at least technically, *The Great Mughal* was given the rare chance to live a second life in our century. In 2002, the Indian Academy of Arts and Animation decided to restore and colourize the film using digital technology. Sound engineers re-recorded the soundtrack in Dolby Digital. Given the great length of the film (three hours), this was a unique experiment in international cinematography which was made possible because of the rapid development of technology in India. Thus, Asif's dream of making a colour version of the film was realized fifty years later. In 2005, the world premiere of *The Great Mughal* took place in India, Great Britain, and the USA, and then came to Pakistan. This was the first distribution of an Indian film, since 1981, in this country. And thus, the Anarkali legend came back to where it arose—to Lahore.

Thanks to *The Great Mughal*, the Anarkali story quickly turned into a commercial brand—as befits legends about 'immured brides'. There are countless restaurants, beauty parlours, and women's clothing stores called 'Anarkali' in Pakistan, India, and even New York and Birmingham. The story is actively used by television and show business. A few years ago, the Pakistani Ministry of Culture and Tourism commissioned the director Shoaib Mansoor to make a short music video, with the strange Anglo-Persian title *Supreme 'ishq* ('Supreme Love'), in the setting of the actual Shish Mahal and against the backdrop of Anarkali's Tomb, as it has looked through the ages. (The video is available on the Internet on the popular site YouTube.)

Another glamour production, called *Anarkali through the Eyes of Noor Jahan*, was recently staged on Broadway by the Pakistani designer and couturier Rizwan Baig, to raise funds for the UN Human Development Fund. The extravagant production was an example of the aforementioned trend of relating the traditional story of the death of the female victim with fashion shows on the red carpet and catwalk. This version of the Lahore legend also shows that present-day viewers prefer happy ends: it claims that Anarkali did not die but married the prince and became world-famous as Empress Nur Jahan.

However, the biggest TV project so far, intended for a new generation of Subcontinental viewers, was conceived by the London-based media magnate Akbar Asif, son of the director of *The Great Mughal*. In 2006, he launched the reality show 'In Search of Anarkali' (*Anarkali ki talash*) in the popular TV format of a beauty and talent contest. For an entire year, young Indian beauties competed in singing, dancing, and the ability to seduce modern princes. The winner got a prize of eleven million rupees (about $250,000) and a contract for the main role in the remake of *The Great Mughal*. Akbar Asif's show was broadcast in India, Pakistan, and Great Britain, and the proceeds given to charity: Asif evidently inherited his father's extravagance and ambition.

The destiny of the legend of the 'immured bride' is similar everywhere. In Lahore, too, it is undergoing the same historical evolution, from a romantic legend and an artistic image that people know and love from childhood, to yet another 'star factory' in which anyone can become the one and only Anarkali.

* * *

I have taken the reader far from my original theme, of the city legend, in an attempt to describe the evolution of the motif of the 'immured bride'. This evolution leads to a functional and role-based relationship between legendary images, historical figures, and classical heroines of different periods. This relation is based on the Jungian 'collective unconscious' of the patriarchal society, where women are assigned the role of victims: propitiatory victims if they are sacrificed in the interests, and for the good of, 'male society', or expiatory victims if they are sacrificed for the sins of this society, which are usually ascribed to the women themselves.

The heroines of legends and ballads have died as foundation sacrifices, because their lives and innocence were necessary for constructive male activity, such as the building of towers, castles, and cities, and also because they become obstacles in male political and power-related games. The murder or suicide of the female characters, in the literary and cinematographic versions of such legends, is furthermore based on the laws of the psychology of art: no one has invented a more heartrending theme, so far, than the sacrificial death of a loving woman. This explains why stories of this sort are so easily commercialized and adapted by mass culture.

The 'woman-victim' seems to be the secret desire of every man, and an ancient practice of a society dominated by men. Such a society has always tolerated the murder of brides, wives, mistresses, and even daughters, as a repressive measure in retribution for betrayal, disobedience, imprudence, or other offences, no matter how much this contradicts the doctrines of all world religions. Although such a society might legally condemn the men for murdering women 'out of passion', it empathizes with the former, believing that the moral torments of executioners are more important than the very lives of their victims. The readers of the famous *The Ballad of Reading Gaol* are interested only in the fate of the hero, who was sentenced to death for the murder of his beloved one, and care little about the slain woman–all the more as crimes against women are a law of society, as the epigraph to this chapter shows.

Street vendor in Lahore.

CHAPTER SIX

'Bread and Games!'

Before the partition of India, Lahore was often called the 'The Paris of the East'. In their authoritative guidebook to nineteenth-century Lahore, John Lockwood Kipling and Thomas Thornton often compared the city to the French capital.[1] The similarity lay not in the city's outward appearance or its historic role but in the joyous and carefree atmosphere that marked Lahore's cultural life, with its numerous cafés and restaurants, noisy receptions and festivals, and elegantly dressed crowds strolling on the Mall. This corresponded to the image, in the Indian mind, of a merry and carefree Paris before the First World War. In the 1920s and 1930s, Lahore continued to set the fashion for a certain type of lifestyle: 'Lahore by now had acquired the reputation of being the Paris of India. Fashion ruled the life of its people whose lifestyles, habits and customs were considered to be most admirable', recalls Pran Nevile, a contemporary chronicler of Lahore.[2]

Another interesting account belongs to the outstanding Urdu writer Ismat Chughtai (1915–1991), who was summoned to appear before the Supreme Court in Lahore in 1944 on charges of indecency for her short story *Quilt* (*Lihaf*).[3] Despite such difficult circumstances necessitating her visit to Lahore, Ismat Chughtai wrote,

'How beautiful Lahore was! Still invigorating, full of laughter, its arms spread out in welcome, embracing all those who arrive here, the city of cheerful people who

135

love unconditionally, without reserve, the "heart of the Punjab". [...] This was the time when words of praise issued forth spontaneously from my heart for the King of Britain, because he had brought a case against us and thus afforded us the golden opportunity of having a festive time in Lahore. We began to wait impatiently for our second appearance in court. We no longer cared if we were to be hanged. If we were hanged in Lahore we would attain the status of martyrs and the Lahore-wallahs would take out our funeral processions with great pomp and show. [...] Lahore. What a savoury word it is. Lahori salt! Like gems. White and pink. I feel like stringing the tiny chunks into a glimmering necklace and draping it around the slender white neck of a Punjabi belle. [...] There is a glow in the atmosphere of Lahore, silent bells tinkle, and the orange blossoms [...] fill the air with fragrance.'[4]

Quite a few periods in Lahore's history were not carefree for its inhabitants: invasions, plundering, and destruction during the medieval period; the troubled reign of the harsh and bellicose Sikhs; and, finally, the tragedy of the 1947 Partition that sapped the Punjab, including Lahore. Nevertheless, 'a glow', 'silent bells tinkle', and 'the orange blossoms' mentioned by Ismat Chughtai were constantly felt in the city, as a constitutive part of its *topophilia*.

As with many other cities of the Indian Subcontinent, street life in Lahore resembles a 'human broth' of sorts, in which the daily life, work, and amusements of the vast majority of its urban dwellers take place outside the home and before the eyes of other people. While women spend their time in seclusion, behind high walls and closed shutters, men—no matter whether rich or poor, young or old— 'simmer' in this broth and live, seen by all, in the bazaars, street cafés, parks, courtyards of the mosques, or simply at the busy crossroads. Every day, long noisy processions (whether religious, funerary, or celebratory) pass through the city, attracting thousands of voluntary participants or simply onlookers. Many celebrations, whether private or public, are marked by entire neighbourhoods. On hot days, people take a nap on the ground in central public places such as Hazuri Bagh, Data Darbar, and the Kashmiri and Delhi Gates. When the heat subsides in the evening, people fill the restaurants, surround the food stands and open-air grills, and crowd under the awnings of snack bars. Generally speaking, Lahoris react to any important news, whether good or bad, by going out into the streets—an innate electoral instinct of which Pakistani politicians have often taken advantage. Western visitors frequently get the impression that most Lahoris feel more at ease in the street than at home.

Quite a few of the people walking down the streets of Lahore are strolling aimlessly, simply whiling away their time. This sets Lahoris apart from the inhabitants of other big South Asian cities, where only tourists stroll for pleasure. The presence of a large number of *flâneurs* in the city crowd brings us back to *psychogeography*, which we discussed in Chapter 1. The *flâneur* plays a primordial role in the sensation, experience, and description of the city's atmosphere. Saadat Hasan Manto, Intizar Hussain, Bapsi Sidhwa, and other writers were *flâneurs* in the modern sense of the term and left behind vivid descriptions of Lahore in their works.

The very term *flânerie* (strolling aimlessly about a city in order to discover and experience it) was invented by Charles Baudelaire to describe the pastimes of Parisians. The comparisons between Lahore and Paris are most likely based on the predilection of their inhabitants to stroll aimlessly. In the West, the idea of *flânerie* is closely connected to the modern urban environment, with its diverse arcades, plazas, malls, and other vast and complex spaces of commercial architecture that offer unexpected discoveries and new impressions to *flâneurs*. In the East, the centuries-old tradition of the bazaar—a multifunctional complex with open spaces, crossroads (*chowks*), arcades, narrow passageways, side streets, and covered galleries—laid the foundation for *flânerie* long ago.

The *flâneur* is a participant in events, a 'man in the crowd', and an onlooker who aesthetically experiences city life and records all that is unusual about it. According to many scholars, this trait is purely French:

> 'There is no English equivalent for the term, just as there is no Anglo-Saxon counterpart of that essentially Gallic individual, the deliberately aimless pedestrian,

unencumbered by any obligation or sense of urgency, who, being French and therefore frugal, wastes nothing, including his time which he spends with the leisurely discrimination of a gourmet, savoring the multiple flavors of his city.'[5]

Nevertheless, the ability to savour 'multiple flavors of the city' is not restricted to the French. The contemporary Pakistani writer Samina Quraishi writes about the hero of her story,

> 'Aziz Ahmed knows the Old City well. He is so familiar with the sounds and smells of each lane that he once bet his cousin that if he were to be placed anywhere within the city walls blindfolded, he would still be able to tell the spot. He knows where the best place is to view a wedding procession. He knows where to buy the finest sweetmeats, the tangiest pickles and the tastiest *seekh kababs*. He can get from the Lohari Gate to the Delhi Gate in less than 10 minutes, a journey which is normally traversed in no less than twenty minutes. Yet he prefers to stroll slowly through the various *muhallahs*, surveying each widely divergent market area and marvelling at how the merchants have stayed together in their traditional locations over the centuries, despite rivalries and disputes. [...] He knows everything that his grandfather taught him of the city history; stories about the *muhallahs*, their vendors, their resident heroes or saints; about the city's legendary rulers, past glories, and semi-mythical wealth and power; all the folk tales, myths, songs, traditions, and stories about Lahore. They mix in his head as he walks, swirling and blending with what surrounds him, with all that he perceives, with all his senses.'[6]

The hero's lifestyle, as described in the story, is true *flânerie* or *dérive*, in spite of the fact that the Urdu and Punjabi languages, as is the case with English too, do not have a precise equivalent of this notion.

Lahore's 'Parisian spirit' is also embodied in its inhabitants' habit of spending time in the literary and artistic cafés, where artists and writers used to gather. The best-known among them is the Pak Tea

House, located in the very centre of the city, on the Mall, near Anarkali Bazaar. This gathering place, for several generations of Urdu writers, has been the equivalent of the celebrated Café de Flore and Café 'Les Deux Magots' in Paris, and the Caffè Greco in Rome, which attracted the creme de la creme of European literature and art. Although the Pak Tea House had become popular among writers during the colonial era—it was called The India Coffee House back then—it acquired its real fame after Partition. At different times, famous Urdu writers such as Miraji, Faiz Ahmed Faiz, Saadat Hasan Manto, Munir Niyazi, Ahmad Faraz, Intizar Hussain, and Qayum Nazar, have spent hours arguing about literature and politics over a cup of tea. According to Intizar Hussain, a frequenter since 1949, 'no literary institute in the country, including the Literary Academy, has such authority as the Pak Tea House'.[7]

The well-known scholar Muhammad Umar Memon, publisher of the prestigious American journal *The Annual of Urdu Studies*, wrote,

> The Pak Tea House was not merely a place where writers hung out and passionately discussed literature, the arts, and politics, or where they held their literary meetings and dreamed their brave, fragile dreams, or where they stopped on their way to and from work every day for a brief chat, it was unique as a gathering place which never denied its hospitality to anyone, even those who could not afford to pay for a cup of tea. It chose to operate at a loss rather than submit to the indignity of closing its doors to the nation's destitute and chronically disenfranchised intellectuals. It was everything the society at large was not—and above all it was a place where dreams could be dreamed, where time and history could be held at bay.[8]

Unfortunately, the Pak Tea House found itself on the verge of bankruptcy in 2000. The writers' community made an appeal, to the Punjab government, to save this historical centre of Lahore's culture. The government, in response, proposed financial assistance to the café's owner to compensate him for his losses. However, it was too late to save the café. After having survived the difficult times of the dictatorships of Ayub Khan and Zia-ul-Haq, the Pak Tea House is nothing but a dilapidated lifeless building today.

In Chapter 4, I mentioned that Lahori aristocrats in the past led a predominantly 'garden' lifestyle. The modern Lahori is literally a 'man on the street'.[9] In the gardens and on the streets, he primarily looks for sights, amusements, celebrations, and games. For this reason, the Lahore inhabitant can also be called *homo ludens* ('playing man'). Lahore's main celebration (which also contains elements of gambling) is the annual 'spring festival' (*jashn-e baharan*), better known as *basant*. *Basant* (literally 'spring') is celebrated from late January to the first half of February—its date is fixed each year by the Lahore municipality. *Basant* marks the change of seasons: as the Punjabi saying goes, '*basant* has come, and winter has gone' (*aya basant pala udant*). Lahore celebrates *basant* largely as a kite-flying festival rather than a seasonal or religious holiday, as is the case in India.

Basant has pre-Islamic roots, tracing its history to a Hindu religious festival in honour of the goddess Sarasvati—*Vasant Panchami*. In India, it is celebrated on the fifth day (*Panchami*) of the Hindu month, Magh—corresponds to January–February—and is considered the first day of spring. As Sarasvati is the goddess of wisdom and learning, *basant* in India is mostly organized, and celebrated, by school and university students and their parents and teachers. Before Partition, Punjabi Hindus celebrated *basant* in the same way as their other co-religionists. A particularity of the *basant* celebrations in Lahore was the kite-flying competitions—a sight that was so colourful, captivating, and exciting that *basant* continued to be the favourite celebration of Lahoris, even after the creation of Pakistan and the exodus of the Hindus.

It should be mentioned that Indian Muslims got acquainted with *basant* as far back as the Middle Ages, thanks to the cultural tolerance and syncretism of the Sufis. During the Delhi Sultanate, *basant* was celebrated in the major Sufi *dargahs* of Nizamuddin Auliya and Qutub-ud-Din Bahtiyar Kaki in Delhi. Dara Shikoh mentioned the '*Basant* of Amir Khosrow', which was celebrated at the great poet's tomb, and cited his poems dedicated to the *basant*:

āj basant manā le suhāgan āj basant manā le
anjān manjan kar piyā morī lambe kes lagā le
tū kyā sove nīnd kī māsī so jāge tere bhāg
āj basant manā le suhāgan āj basant manā le [10]

Celebrate *basant* today, o beautiful wife, celebrate *basant* today!
Darken your eyelids with collyrium; rub yourself with incense,
my beloved,
Arrange your long tresses.
Why are you sleeping, sleepyhead? Your fate does not slumber
Celebrate *basant* today, o beautiful wife, celebrate *basant* today!

During the Mughal era, *basant* celebrations with kite-flying also took place in the abodes of the great Punjabi saints: Mian Mir and Shah Hussain in Lahore, Bulleh Shah in Kasur, and Sultan Bahu in Sargodha. During the *basant*, pilgrims wore yellow clothing and offered garlands of yellow flowers, including mustard flowers (*basant phulna*), to the saints. In the poetry of the Punjabi mystics (in particular, in Shah Hussain's *kafis*), *basant* customs are often given a Sufi semantic:

sājan de hāth dor asadī main sājan dī guddī

The Beloved holds the string in his hand, and I am his kite. [11]

The quasi-historical legend of how *basant* came to be celebrated in Lahore reflects the dissatisfaction some Muslim circles viewed this Hindu (i.e., pagan) festival with. Legend has it that when Zakariya Khan (1707–1759) was governor of the Punjab, a Hindu youth called Haqiqat Rai Puri, who was constantly mocked by his Muslim peers, publicly offended the Prophet and his daughter Fatimah. For this, he was summoned before the Lahore court which sentenced him to death for blasphemy. Although the Hindu inhabitants of the city appealed to the governor for mercy, the sentence was upheld. Lahori Hindus declared a period of mourning, in memory of the executed youth, and a rich merchant named Kalu Ram established an annual spring fair (*basant mela*) in his honour. This legend leads some conservative Muslims to claim that, during the *basant*, people fly 'banners of blasphemy and paganism' rather than innocuous kites. [12]

Initially, the kite festival—*basant-bash*—was only celebrated in the Walled City, whose very architecture was suited for this activity: closely spaced buildings with flat 'living' roofs on which people slept during the hot nights. From these 'launching pads', children and young people launched homemade kites (*patang* or *guddi*), easily moving from rooftop to rooftop, joyously shouting '*Bo kata!*' ('I cut you off!'). Today, *basant* is celebrated on a national scale and has become an industry that gets the support of city's authorities and major companies.

This applies, above all, to the production of kites, in which a large number of the city's craftsmen are engaged. Although one can buy a *guddi* at the last moment from any bazaar, the affluent have them made-to-order ahead of time. To see the *basant*, lovers of spectacles and gawkers come from all over Pakistan, India, and even from Europe and America where the Pakistani diaspora exists. The income of hotel and restaurant owners are greatly augmented; the roofs of tall office buildings and hotels, with good views, are reserved long before the start of festivities; tens of thousands of festively dressed people gather in the brightly lit Shahi Qila at night, men wear a special yellow scarf called a *basanti chunni* while women wear yellow flower bracelets (*gajra*) on their wrists. Lifting their heads, they watch myriads of bright squares, triangles, dragons, fantastic birds, and other flying objects of the most extraordinary shapes dart here and there in the moving beams of light shone into the sky for hours on end. Thundering music resounds everywhere: drumbeats and trumpet fanfares celebrate the victories of participants who succeed in cutting off the others' kites. Firecrackers and fireworks (*patake*) fly into the sky with a bang. City restaurants sell snacks and drinks on the street. Excited competitors and spectators drink gallons of *lassi* (cold milk drink) and eat tons of *kheer* (rice dessert), covering the streets with a carpet of paper cups by dawn.

In the affluent suburbs of Lahore, such as Gulberg, Defence, and Model Town, *basant* is celebrated at garden parties, which are much loved in Pakistan. These parties differ from the street celebrations, with an abundance of various kinds of food and performances by professional female singers and dancers (*mujra*). Even film stars from the local 'dream factory', Lollywood, perform in the luxurious *hawelis* of the major politicians and businessmen. Members of the upper social strata can visit up to a dozen such parties during a single night, as being invited to *basant* is an indication of status; the number of invitations is directly proportional to the guest's social standing.

In Pakistan, a country constantly shaken by political crises and ruled by the military for long periods of time, the position of the conservative Muslim parties is extremely strong, and private and public behaviour is regulated by fairly strict restrictions. In such a context, *basant* resembles a medieval carnival in Mikhail Bakhtin's interpretation. It is simultaneously a social protest against ideological pressure as well as a diversion that simply allows people to 'let off steam'. Naturally, Pakistan is not Brazil and the celebration of *basant* never turns into a mass orgy. Nevertheless, the festival is a time when certain taboos are lifted and people savour the feeling of temporary freedom from centuries-old conventions, making *basant* a unique phenomenon for a Muslim state. It is no coincidence that in other provinces, such as Balochistan or the Sarhad, where the level of secularism is a lot lower than in the Punjab, *basant* is not celebrated at all.

I have already written about kite-flying in my book about old Lucknow, where it was also a favourite activity of both the rich and poor. Before the competition (*patang-bazi*), the kite line (*manjha*) is smeared with glue on one side and then covered with crushed glass. A well-manoeuvred *guddi* is brought, at considerable speed, to the clean side of the competitor's kite line. The kite operator pulls on his kite sharply, and the crushed glass cuts his opponent's line. The downed kite is considered to be a trophy that can be sold, reused, or returned to its owner for a reward. During kite fights, people place bets so making the competition particularly exciting. The champion of a street or neighbourhood is the person who cuts off most kites. In addition to the amateur enthusiasts, professionals—who engage in the game all their lives and earn quite a lot of money each year—also participate in the competitions.

Today, covering kite lines with crushed glass is strictly prohibited; kites are sold with a reel of simple fishing line. However, ardent kite fighters ignore this ban and sometimes go so far as using wire. Every year, after *basant* ends, city newspapers publish reports that resemble news coverage from a battlefield: accounts about children falling to their death from roofs while chasing kites; reports about cuts, bruises, cut-off fingers and even heads (!) of unfortunate victims who got in the way of the sharp wires. Also, some district or the other of Lahore is invariably plunged into sudden darkness during the *basant* because wires, dragged at high speed by thousands of kites, cut a power transmission line. So, opponents of the *basant* have more than enough arguments in favour of banning the celebration.

In 2005, when the number of *basant* victims exceeded a hundred, the Lahore Supreme Court promulgated a total ban on kite-flying in the city. In its verdict, it specified that, first of all, *basant* is a Hindu religious ritual that was never part of the Muslim cultural heritage. Secondly, the festival causes too much damage—from the cost to human lives to the expenditure incurred in restoring damaged power lines. Thirdly, in a country with such a low per capita income and such a poor standard of public health and education, the state and private corporations should spend their millions of rupees on raising the standard of living of the population rather than on public amusements.

The verdict of the Supreme Court evoked the wrath of the very population it was meant to protect. The latter went out onto the streets, blocking all access to the court building. Looking for a compromise, Punjab's chief minister declared a 'temporary moratorium' on the Supreme Court's decision. Although *basant* is still officially banned today, anyone who has visited Lahore has seen multi-coloured kites flying on the horizon, even on ordinary days of the year.

While *basant* lasts for only one week a year, the favourite daily pastime of Lahoris is to eat copiously at any time of the day—except during the month of Ramadan. In essence, life in Lahore is an endless dinner party with an unpredictable number of participants. For Lahoris, eating means more than simply satisfying the bodily need for nourishment: it is the centre of social life, allowing people to spend time with their friends or strike up new business and personal ties. Food is not only an object of gourmandise but also a favourite subject of conversation, somewhat like the weather in England: people speak about what they ate, when and where they ate, and how the food was made. The upper-middle-class city dweller spends his evenings hosting dinner parties at his home or attending dinner parties at the homes of family or friends or, if worst comes to worst, going to a restaurant.

Lahoris' daily eating habits, and the quantities consumed by them, shock Europeans and Americans who are used to low-calorie diets and healthy food habits. Vegetarians have a difficult time in Lahore, for the main food here is fried or stewed meat (except pork, of course) which is cooked for a long time, until it releases an extract or thick sauce to which lots of drawn butter (*ghee*) is added. The average Lahori starts his day with spicy roast beef or lamb (*nihari* from *nahar* 'morning') and finishes it late at night with an assortment of meat dishes that tend to include *kebabs*, *murgi tikka* (marinated boneless pieces of chicken baked in *tandoor*), *halim* (meat with lentils stewed to a paste-like consistency), and meat *pulao/biriyani*. Such a 'diet' makes one conclude that Lahoris are either immune to atherosclerosis or universally suffer from cardiovascular disease. Of course, this observation is a kind of exaggeration which reflects the opinion or prejudice of many Westerners about Pakistani food in general and Lahori cuisine, in particular.

Punjabi cuisine is a mixture of North Indian food ('Mughlai cuisine') and purely local dishes, such as *roh-di-kheer* (rice cooked in sugarcane syrup), *karahi-gosht* (thick casserole of goat meat prepared in a wok-like utensil), and the dubious delicacy *kapura* (fried goat's testicles). Common flavourings in Punjabi cuisine are a rich yogurt sauce with onion, garlic, or ginger, and *tangi masala* (a mixture of dry tomatoes with mango powder and pomegranate seeds). Generally speaking, many Anglo-Indian dishes (such as *tandoori*, *nan*, *pakora*, and *panir*) have become popular in the West thanks to the Punjabis.

In Lahore, there are many traditional places that specialize in a certain type of dish and where gourmands come at any time of the day or night. The ragout *gurda-kapura* is prepared on huge flat frying pans on Abbot Road; the best *nihari* in town is cooked next to Bhati Gate; the Hira Mandi quarter is famous for its *payas*; and people visit the Old Anarkali Bazaar to buy a special type of marinated fish (*machli-ka-achar*) and Mozang for the frozen *kulfi*. Finally, the confectioners of *Halwai* caste have many shops in the city, where traditional Punjabi sweets, such as *balu-shahi*, *patisa*, and *mungi-de-laddu*, are made and sold. While they are not as popular in the West as Bengali sweets, nevertheless there is a great demand for them.

This culinary map of the city is a vestige of the Middle Ages and corresponds to the traditional distribution of the groups of artisans. Naturally, there are many modern restaurants in Lahore where one can taste different Punjabi dishes without having to travel all over the city. Yet. the Lahori *flâneur* is a man on the street who prefers to buy his food from its immediate producer and is wary of restaurants, which he suspects of simplifying traditional recipes.

Food Street, near the Walled City in the Gawalmandi neighbourhood—an area of well-preserved old architecture—provided a comfortable eating experience for the city's gourmands and a tourist attraction for its foreign visitors. Here, a vast panorama of Punjabi cuisine unfurled every evening, under awnings and on stands and tables. As the historical name of the neighbourhood suggests (*gawal* is a caste that milks cows and produces milk; *mandi* means a 'bazaar' and forms a part of many Lahori toponyms), Gawalmandi used to be a milk market and was considered to be an 'environmentally clean' place for producing and selling food products. Food Street resembled any other busy Lahore street during the day; yet, it was closed off, with boom gates, to all vehicles from eight o'clock in the evening.

Apart from Shahi Qila, the Mall, and the government buildings, Food Street was the only street in Lahore where the buildings' façades were lit up at night. It was lined, on both sides, with narrow and closely spaced three-and four-storey buildings decorated with numerous carved balconies, gables and columns in relief, *jharoka* windows with fancy frames, and massive encrusted doors. This entire architectural decoration was lit up, level by level, creating the illusion of elongated buildings that grew upwards. Most of the windows had closed shutters, which made the houses seem deserted despite the bright lighting, and augmented the theatrical effect.

At the beginning and end of Food Street stood the *panwala* shops that sold *pan*—a chewing mixture of betel leaf, slaked lime, and spices. *Pan* is traditionally chewed at the end of dinner: it freshens up the breath and gives the tongue and teeth a dark red colour, which was considered beautiful in South Asia. Simple plastic tables and chairs lined both sides of the street, creating a homely atmosphere. The crowd, while moving down the centre of the street, got thicker with each passing hour. Whereas men usually predominate in public places of Lahore, entire families came to Food Street: parents with smartly dressed children in front, followed by the older generation—bearded old men leaning on sticks and old women wrapped in shawls from head to foot. From time to time, they stopped at a stand, piled heaps of food on plastic trays, and sat down at the nearest table.

The mixture of different sexes, ages, social groups, and nationalities in the crowd moving down Food Street was a unique phenomenon for Pakistan. This place was marked by the spirit of friendly cheer and spontaneous casualness, which is not found in any other public setting.

Another gastronomic or, more precisely, cultural sight of Lahore is Cuckoo's Den restaurant, next to Roshnai Gate near the Badshahi Masjid. In the evenings, a wonderful view of the lit-up Shahi Qila and old city is visible from the open veranda on the restaurant's roof. Both the restaurant, and the building in which it is located (a narrow three-storey house, typical for the Walled City, with balconies overhanging the street), belong to the well-known artist, Iqbal Hussain, the 'Pakistani Toulouse-Lautrec'. Born to a *kanjari* caste mother in the red-light area of Hira Mandi, Iqbal Hussain, thanks to his talent, avoided the typical fate of men of his caste—becoming a procurer or guardian of a lady of pleasure. Iqbal Hussain received an arts education and became a professor at the National College of Arts. He became famous, far beyond Pakistan, for his paintings which depict the characters, life, and mores of Lahore's brothels. Iqbal Hussain's personality and artistic career are so uncommon for a person of his origins that he became a prototype of the artist, and the hero of the modern French novel *Hira Mandi*.[13]

Iqbal Hussain turned the house that he inherited (located between the fort and the Hira Mandi) into a studio, with an art gallery and a fashionable restaurant that is a gathering place for Lahore's bohemia and a must-see for foreign visitors to the city. Iqbal Hussain's own works are exhibited on the first floor; they mostly portray tired and morose women with lifeless faces, covered by numerous layers of make-up, and gloomy eyes that evoke the viewer's compassion. As Toulouse-Lautrec did before him, Hussain portrays everyday life in the brothel: women comb each other's hair, mend clothing, look in the mirror, and gossip. Only the profusion of make-up on their faces, their revealing dresses, and the dim gloominess suffusing the room suggest, to the viewer, that something is not right about these women and that they are not the usual respectable middle-class ladies.

Next to the studio is a gallery of artefacts, collected by Hussain in both Pakistan and India. A steep spiral staircase, leading from the gallery, circles the inner rooms of the house and takes guests to the roof where 'Cuckoo's Den' is situated. Just as on Food Street, it is furnished with long plastic tables and highly uncomfortable chairs with hard seats and prickly metal backs. Yet, the restaurant's 'specialty' is not its interior but its breathtaking panorama of the Walled City, which seems a hand's length away. There is no kitchen in the restaurant building, as the heat and cooking fumes could damage the artworks in the house. The food is cooked on the street and lifted, with copper chains, to the roof where it is placed into huge trays (*thaals*).

Cuckoo's Den lures its patrons not only because of its traditional food, elite clientele, and splendid panorama, but because it lies in immediate proximity to the prostitutes' quarter (Hira Mandi) which, its ill-fame notwithstanding, is on the list of Lahore's attractions. Hira Mandi is located in the very heart of the Walled City, between the Roshnai Gate to the north and the Bhati Gate to the south, although the road leading to the neighbourhood passes through the Taxali Gate. According to popular etymology, the neighbourhood's name means 'diamond bazaar' (from *hira* 'diamond' and *mandi* 'bazaar'), where 'diamonds' are a euphemism for 'living goods' (in the poetic style, the quarter is sometimes called 'beauty bazaar' *bazaar-e husn*).

At the same time, the toponym has much more mundane origins: it was named after a certain Hira Singh who was the neighbourhood's overseer (*nazim*) during Ranjit Singh's reign, in the eighteenth century, and introduced certain restrictions on the activities of its inhabitants, including a ban on singing and playing musical instruments at night.[14] The neighbourhood is also known by the medieval name, Shahi Mohalla ('Imperial Quarter'), indicating that the court courtesans and dancers (*tawaif*)—who performed at the nearby palace of the Mughal emperors and enjoyed their support—lived there long ago.

The term 'red-light area' arose in the 1890s in America and has purely Western origins. According to cultural anthropologists, the term stems from the Biblical story of the pious harlot, Rahab, who helped Joshua conquer the city of Jericho by hiding his spies in her house and giving them a signal by hanging a red cord out of her window (Joshua 2:6–16). According to a more banal historical account, American trackwalkers left their red lights at brothel entrances to make it easier to find them if there was an accident on the railway.[15] There is an equivalent term in the Urdu and Punjabi languages, *chakla*, which originally simply meant 'district' or 'city quarter' and eventually only came to be applied to the districts where prostitutes lived.

Chakla, or 'red-light districts', appeared in all major South Asian cities. Some of these districts were very large and had lots of 'personnel': Sonagachi in Calcutta, Kamathipura in Bombay, and G.B. Road in Delhi. They developed in different ways from the Shahi Mohalla. In most South Asian cities, 'red-light districts' appeared during the colonial era, at the initiative and under the patronage of the colonial governments, to cater to the sepoys—the soldiers of the colonial army—and the lower level of the administrative apparatus that was recruited from among the local inhabitants (such as the Bengali *babus*).[16] In contrast, the Shahi Mohalla quarter, just as with the Chowk in Lucknow, Rangila Maidan in Faizabad, and Sanchi Mandir in Dacca, emerged during the Mughal era, under imperial patronage, as a place where numerous female singers and dancers as well as musicians (all of whom were greatly in demand at the court and, more generally, part of the traditional culture of the time) lived and were trained.

As a rule, salaried female singers and dancers, generally called *tawaif*, were maintained by patrons. Thus, professional music, singing, and dancing on the one hand, and venal love on the other, became very closely connected in South Asian culture, beginning with the Hindu temple dancers—the *devadasi*. The *tawaif* got an excellent education—one that was beyond comparison with the rudimentary knowledge that girls from respectable families received. They were guardians, of sorts, of the traditional genres of art, including the *ghazal* and other classical and semi-classical vocal forms as well as of dance, *kathak*. Consorting with a *tawaif* (not necessarily in an intimate way)—somewhat like conversing with an Athenian hetaera—

was one of the stages of education for a young man from a noble family, and an important part of the social life of an adult man.

In traditional Indian society, quarters settled by dancers were considered worthy of admiration. 'The lavishness of a district where dancers live is a source of wealth for everyone who comes here. Spending time with beauties with refined manners and exquisite habits changes the behaviour of the guest and enriches his heart with invaluable treasures', wrote the nineteenth-century Urdu writer Rajab Ali Beg Suroor about the Chowk in Lucknow.[17] An anonymous Lahori poet sang similar praises of Tibbi, an area of Shahi Mohalla:

> *Tibbī men chal ke jalwa-e parwardigār dekh*
> *are yeh dekhne kī chīz hai ise bār bār dekh*[18]

Come to the Tibbi to see the magnificence of the Almighty.
Yes, it is worth seeing; go there again and again.

Such prostitution had ancient historical roots and was socially condoned because of its patrons' royal status and the courtesan dancers' artistic mastery—leading to comparisons between a *tawaif* and Lahore itself. Bapsi Sidhwa, in her novel *The Pakistani Bride* wrote, 'Lahore—the ancient whore, the handmaiden of dimly remembered Hindu kings, the courtesan of Mughal emperors—bedecked and bejewelled, savaged by marauding hordes—healed by the caressing hands of successive lovers. A little shoddy, as Qasim[19] saw her; like an attractive but aging concubine, ready to bestow surprising delights on those who cared to court her—proudly displaying Royal gifts.'[20] In contrast to Christian invectives comparing Rome and Babylon to whores, the contemporary comparison between Lahore and a *tawaif* is, on the whole, complementary in nature.

In different regions, the term *tawaif* referred to women from different castes/vocational groups: *domni, kanchani, chunapazni, mirasan, paturi,* etc. The men in these castes were artisans, whose skills ranged from weaving baskets (*doms*) to firing bricks (*chunapazes*), while the women were hereditary singers and dancers who also offered intimate services. In the Punjab as a whole, and in the Shahi Mohalla in particular, singers-dancers-courtesans mostly belonged to the caste of the *kanjars*. As weavers and sellers of ropes, the *kanjars* were considered to be a very low caste: legend had it that they ate snakes and corpses. Over time, male *kanjars* abandoned their hereditary profession and began to work as procurers for their women, while the word *kanjari* (feminine form of *kanjar*) has become a synonym for 'prostitute'. At the same time, the *kanjari* are a structured sub-caste who describe themselves as a *baradari* ('brotherhood', although it is more of a 'sisterhood') that functions according to its own centuries-old laws.

After the annexation of the Punjab by the British crown, the golden age of the Shahi Mohalla came to an end. Still, the English turned a blind eye to the red-light area, although they considered prostitution to be a social vice. Sometimes, during military operations, dancers were listed in army registers as 'camp followers', yet the English were totally indifferent to the art of the *tawaif*, calling them 'nautch girls' (a garbled derivative of the verb *nachna* 'to dance'). Nevertheless, the new local elite—civil servants recruited from among the Indian population, and members of the national bourgeoisie that were loyal to the English—could not imagine celebrating important events in their public and private lives, such as weddings, the birth of sons, the opening of new businesses, job promotions, and awards, without a *mujra*—a traditional performance by dancers, accompanied by musicians. As the state, naturally, was not about to support the world's oldest profession, the *kanjari* communities (*baradari*) began to organize their business themselves, on the basis of the laws of preservation, reproduction, and development that exist in each caste.

After Partition in 1947, and the formation of Pakistan, the affairs of the Shahi Mohalla temporarily improved. Muslim migrants came to Lahore from cultural centres, such as Delhi, Lucknow, Hyderabad (Deccan), and Allahabad, where the traditions of *kathak, ghazal, thumri*, as well as of other vocal and dance genres performed by the *tawaif*, had existed for centuries and were considered to be true art. In the 1950s, a galaxy of outstanding musicians came to Pakistan from India: the singer and film star, Nur Jahan (1926–2000), called the 'Queen of Melodies'; the singers Malika Pukhraj (1912–2004) and Iqbal Bano (born in 1935); the composer Ghulam Ahmed Chishti (or Babaji, died in 1984); and the legendary singer and classical music performer, Ustad Bade Ghulam Ali Khan (1902–1968), who subsequently returned to India. At a certain stage in their careers, all of them worked in Lahore and had rehearsal studios (*baithak*) in the Shahi Mohalla.

Mujra, during which *ghazal*, *thumri*, and other traditional vocal-poetic forms are performed, is not a classical vocal recital where a performer is accompanied by musicians sitting on the floor in a static pose. During a *mujra*, the singer makes use of coded facial expressions, eye movements, and gestures, dances in the *kathak* style, and accompanies the rhythmic figures of the dance with the ringing of foot bells (*ghungru*). *Mujra* is an entertaining show that can be refined or quite vulgar, depending on the repertoire and the singer's professional training.

Today, *mujras* are mostly travelling shows: through agents (*dalals*), dancers are invited to private homes, leased auditoriums, or hotels, where they perform for an agreed fee. Nevertheless, the traditional and 'correct' place for *mujra* performances is the *kotha*—a performance room is situated in the building where the dancers live. Indeed, by the rules of their 'brotherhood', they must perform and receive clients without leaving their houses—an echo of seclusion or staying 'behind the *parda*' that is the mark of respectable women.

Over the past three decades, the state has become intolerant towards traditional prostitution. After the introduction of laws defining 'the limits of permitted behaviour' (the so-called Hudood Ordinance of 1979) by President Zia-ul-Haq (1978–1988), that brought the civil and criminal codes into line with the Shari'a,[21] many dancers left the Hira Mandi and moved to respectable suburbs. From the standpoint of the *kanjari* community, they violated the laws of the 'brotherhood' in doing so and will have to pay the price sooner or later.

The dictionary meaning of *kotha* is a room on the upper floor of a house or on a flat roof. In Shahi Mohalla, the *kothas* are located on the ground floor, and clients enter them directly from the street. If you drive along the streets of Hira Mandi in the evening (walking here is risky for women in general, and European women in particular), and look in through the brightly lit windows, you will see floors with white coverlets, long cushions on which one leans while sitting, musical instruments—harmonium, *tabla*, and *dholak* drums—lying in the corner, scattered foot bells, trays laid with tea ware, and sagging sofas on which the *kanjari* sit or recline with a bored air while waiting for their clients. The direct entrance from the street, and the high brightly lit windows, are a showcase that demonstrate that, in the *kotha*, one engages in artistic pleasures only. Clients coming for intimate services enter from the courtyard, as rooms for intimate meetings are located at the back of the building.

Previously, *mujra* was a show reserved for male viewers only. This gave rise to the euphemistic term 'viewer' (*tamashbin*) for a prostitute's client. Today, in liberal circles in Lahore, women attend public *mujras* (for example, during wedding receptions). It is commonly held that the artistic level of the *mujra* declines with each passing year: the singers' repertoire increasingly consists of popular songs from Punjabi films (often sung with a recorded accompaniment) rather than classical *ghazals*, and group dances that have little to do with the *kathak*, as they are performed in the 'Indian disco' style, with a fair bit of eroticism thrown in—which viewers are familiar with from watching the movies.[22]

An ancient ritual that has come down to our time is the showering of the dancers with money (*vail*). Viewers pour a shower of banknotes (from small denominations of a hundred rupees to large denominations of a thousand rupees) on the dancer, or put a large banknote on the head of one of the guests who the dancer approaches and takes the money from at close range. *Vail* is a bonus that the dancer receives, in addition to the agreed on sum, and depends entirely on the success of the performance and the generosity of the audience. *Vail* is a custom that is derived from Mughal musical gatherings (*mahfil*) during which the emperor showered the singer or dancer that pleased him with gold and jewellery.[23]

In the relatively liberal 1950s, all the female inhabitants of Hira Mandi were given the status of 'artistes and musicians' by a ruling of the Supreme Court, allowing them to perform legally, and to semi-legally engage in the world's oldest profession. Subsequently, Zia-ul-Haq's draconian laws had a devastating effect on all aspects of life in the area: *kotha* dancing and singing could only be performed during three hours of the day (from eight to eleven o'clock in the evening); police posts were set up in all the Hira Mandi bazaars, with the right to register night-time visitors. All this drove away the clientele, who came to the neighbourhood to see the art of the *mujra*, in large numbers.

An integral part of the Hudood Ordinance, the Law on Adultery (Zina Ordinance) declared that all extramarital relations are criminal acts, and forced prostitutes to conceal themselves and hide their activities from the outer world. While public politicians may refer to them as 'dirty whores' (*gandi gashti*), the inhabitants of the Hira Mandi describe themselves only as 'dancers' (*nachnewali*); they refer to their profession as 'business' (instead of the previously used Indian equivalent *dhandha*), to the *kotha* as 'office', and to their clients as 'admirers' ('*ashiq*) and spouses (*shohar*). The transition from one 'spouse' to another is called a new 'marriage' (*shadi*).[24] At the same time, most inhabitants of the Shahi Mohalla are Shias and often enter into temporary marriages (*mut'a*), which are permitted by Shias yet prohibited by the Qu'ran and the Sunnah.

Quite a few *kanjari* are well-to-do house owners and observe many of the rules of behaviour of respectable women: they do not go out of the house unaccompanied, do not walk bareheaded in the streets, regularly visit *Data Darbar* (the main Sufi shrine of Lahore),[25] and zealously observe the days of mourning for the Shia martyrs during the month of *Muharram*. Yet, the police continue to harass them, fining, beating, and arresting them on the slightest pretext.

The paintings of Iqbal Hussain, the aforementioned portraitist of the life of Hira Mandi, reflect the highly vulnerable and stigmatized position of the prostitutes. One of his paintings, *Hudood Ordinance*, depicts a policeman pulling a woman, who is lying on the ground, roughly by her hair—while none of the people, on the lively street, pay any attention to the cruel and lawless action taking place before their eyes. Another painting, *Thana* ('Police Station'), shows the incorporeal semi-clothed figures of women, who were apparently tortured at the station, rising up like phantoms behind the backs of the policemen who are armed with helmets and shields.

It is difficult to say how the Hira Mandi would have survived the crisis of the past decades, had it not been for the unexpected financial support from the United Arab Emirates. While the highest strata of *kanjari* (the most beautiful and talented women) have long found work in Lahore's Lollywood and on television, girls with more modest merits and incomes dream of travelling to Dubai or Abu-Dhabi. There, they find numerous grateful viewers among the Pakistani blue and white-collar workers who are homesick and dream of hearing *mujra* in their native language and of having a good time with an affordable fellow countrywoman. Sometimes, Arab sheikhs set their eyes on newly-arrived Lahori women; especially girls aged thirteen or fourteen, and pay large amounts of money (by Pakistani standards) for the 'right of the first night'.

Many stars of the Pakistani (and Indian) cinema have come from communities of professional prostitutes; it is their origins that have been romanticized, in the image of the *tawaif*, in film. An example is the numerous screen versions of the classical novel by Mirza Muhammad Hadi Ruswa, titled *Umrao Jan Ada*, which recounts the life of a Lucknow *tawaif* who became a talented poetess. In the Pakistani version, as compared to the original novel, the heroine falls in love with her first client and eventually marries him after various tribulations. Films about *tawaif* show scenes of musical gatherings and *mujra* that greatly appeal to the viewers. From the moral standpoint, these films tend to be quite chaste and moralistic: the heroines defend their innocence to the end and do not want to become courtesans, resisting the pressure of their avaricious female relatives (stepmother, aunt, or stepsister) who are attempting to lead them down the path of vice.

A classic example of a film about the life of a *tawaif* is Kamal Amrohi's *Pakeezah* (lit. *Pure*, or *Pure of Heart* 1972) starring famous Indian movie stars—Meena Kumari, Ashok Kumar, and Raj Kumar— in the title roles. The film owed its spectacular success to Naushad's music, Lata Mangeshkar's singing, and verses by the famous poets Majrooh Sultanpuri and Kaifi Azmi. *Pakeezah* is a heart-rending melodrama about the lives of two generations of *tawaif* (the roles of both the mother and daughter were performed by Meena Kumari). In the film, the courtesan Nargis falls in love with Shahabuddin (Ashok Kumar) who belongs to a *nawabi* family. She runs away from the *kotha* with him. Shahabuddin's family does not accept the 'fallen woman'; dejected and disheartened Nargis leaves Shahabuddin and dies from grief. Before dying she writes a letter to Shahabuddin asking him to take care of their newborn daughter Sahibjan. Nargis's sister

Nawabjan (played by Veena), the owner of a *kotha*, finds Sahibjan and trains her to become a *tawaif*. When Shahabuddin comes in search of his daughter, Nawabjan decides to move to another city. While they are travelling by a train, Sahibjan meets a forest officer called Salim (Raj Kumar) and her life changes from that day onwards. While trying to escape from being raped Sahibjan again meets Salim; this time he proposes to her. She tells him that she is a *tawaif* but he still loves her and wants to marry her. He brings Sahibjan to his house but Salim's grandfather refuses to accept Sahibjan in his family. She returns to Nawabjan and resumes the life of a *tawaif*. Salim then invites her to perform at his wedding, which she accepts. Salim turns out to be the nephew of Shahabuddin. Seeing Shahabuddin at the wedding, Nawabjan reveals to him that the *tawaif* performing at his nephew's wedding is his own daughter. In a furious rage Shahabuddin's father tries to kill Sahibjan but Shahabuddin shields her and takes the bullet on his body. As a dying wish Shahabuddin asks Salim to marry Sahibjan which he agrees to.

To this day, *Pakeezah* is the favourite film of all *kanjaris*, and still makes them cry. However, the film has little to do with reality. Girls become prostitutes, in real life, thanks not to a scheming procuress or a drug-addicted panderer (although this happens, too) but to a loving mother or grandmother, for it is the female side of the family that assures the continuity of the profession and the very existence of the community of 'hereditary (*khandani*) *kanjari*'.

In a country as rigidly patriarchal as Pakistan is, where women's sexuality is strictly controlled by society, the *kanjari* is the only group that lives according to matriarchal dictates. Only the birth of a girl is greeted with joy in the family; it is the girls who perpetuate the family's line and profession (*dhandha*), and who get all the hereditary rights to the real estate and other family property. The more girls that are born in a family, the more thriving the family and community as a whole eventually becomes.

Sons, so coveted in all other castes and traditional groups of Indian and Pakistani society, are dead-weights and extra mouths to feed for the *kanjari*. In their childhood, male *kanjars* run petty errands (particularly, bringing food from the nearby market; while the *kanjari* 'does business' she does not attend to household matters); in their youth, they loaf about, doing odd jobs; and, when they grow up, they help their female relatives as drivers, guards, and intermediaries. Society has good reason to call *kanjars* pimps, and they are the butt of many derisive jokes and satirical songs, such as:

> *jāt ke the nīm julāe*
> *us pe bangaye darzī*
> *lote pote ke bangaye kanjar*
> *zi khudā kī marzī*

> From his birth, he was a bad weaver
> And then became a tailor.
> When he saw life, he became a pimp
> By God's will.[26]

Kanjari rarely want to enter into lawful marriage (as defined by the Shari'a), as it is not condoned by the community's laws. Returning once again to the film *Pakeezah*, it is hard to say which side would have opposed the protagonists' marriage more: the groom's respectable family or the bride's dubious relatives. Naturally, there are always exceptions to the rule: Ranjit Singh himself married, at an advanced age, the professional *tawaif* Gul Begum, who ran a *kotha* near Mochi Gate. She died in 1865, until which the English paid her a regular pension, as they did to the other wives of the Sikh rulers.

Generally speaking, one of the key myths surrounding the world's oldest profession is the myth of a prostitute being saved by a client who falls in love with her and takes the poor wretch out of the meshes of vice and makes her a 'respectable' woman. This is a beloved theme of cinema, from *Blue Angel* with Marlene Dietrich to *Pretty Woman* with Julia Roberts. The *kanjari* is a caste group that considers, as its goal, not lawful wedlock but the best possible performance of its caste's duties for its clients, family, and community.

Moreover, far from being jealous of married women, most *kanjari* consider that the former (not without reason) have less freedom, being the lifelong slaves of their husbands and their husbands' relatives. Indeed, the fate of some married women in Pakistan is unenviable: until recently, courts in the rural regions of Sindh, the Sarhad, and Balochistan exonerated husbands who killed their wives in 'honour killings' (*Karo Kari, Siyah Kari*, or *Tor Tora*)—killings that are often uncorroborated and simply based on a suspicion or rumour. *Kanjari* are theoretically exempt from this. While they are young and attractive, they must work: their mothers or grandmothers find them 'spouses', who succeed each other and support the entire families for a certain period of time. However, by the time a *kanjari* is thirty years old, her chances of earning her livelihood are virtually nil, unless she has made an independent career as a singer and dancer. Thus, she, in turn, begins to live off the growing younger generation—daughters, granddaughters, and nieces.

Male *kanjars* can marry whenever and whoever they wish; their wives are usually village girls whose parents do not understand what awaits their daughters in this milieu. The new bride lives in strict seclusion and takes over all the household duties. Daughters born out of such a marriage—called 'daughters of the daughter-in-law'—are taken away from their mother and brought up by the mother-in-law, aunt, and other relatives, according to the laws of the *baradari*. The 'daughters of the daughter-in-law' always have a smaller share in the inheritance, than the direct descendants of a *kanjari* along the female line.

All important decisions concerning the family are taken by the *kotha*'s owner, known as the *nayika*. Curiously, the owner or 'madam' of a Muslim brothel is called by a lofty Sanskrit term that refers to the main heroine in classical poetry and drama, who usually has a high social status—a woman of royal descent or a celestial maiden. The word *nayika*—literally 'main female character', 'heroine', or 'wife of the hero *nayaka*'—was most likely borrowed by the *kanjari* from the terminology of Indian dance, where the role of the *nayika* was played by a solo dancer.

All the inhabitants of the *kotha*—men, women, and children—obey the *nayika* unquestioningly. She organizes *mujras*, agrees on travelling performances, bargains over fees, deals with musicians, finds the best clients, gives bribes to policemen and, most importantly, decides who, when, and on what conditions they should engage in 'business'. In the *kanjari* profession, the most expensive, and short-lived, good is virginity; all the profits from its 'sale', which is marked by the ceremony of the *nath utarwai*—literally, 'removing the nose ring'—belong entirely to the *nayika*.

Also in Hira Mandi, there lives another caste group without whom the *kanjari* cannot perform their work: the *mirasi* or hereditary musicians. The initial (dictionary) meaning of the word *mirasi* is 'hereditary' or 'handed down from generation to generation'. In contrast to the *kanjari*, the *mirasi* caste is organized in the 'correct' or patriarchal way: men play the lead roles, and the profession of instrumental musician or vocalist is handed down from father to son. In other parts of the Subcontinent, the women of this caste (*mirasan*) are also singers who perform before female audiences. But, in the Punjab as a whole, and in Hira Mandi in particular, the *mirasan* are simply spouses and housewives. Both the *kanjari* and the *mirasi* are endogamous caste groups: their close professional contacts notwithstanding, marriages between them are forbidden; an affair between a *kanjari* dancer and a *mirasi* musician evokes the strong disapproval of both communities.

The *kanjari* get to know the *mirasi* from childhood on: from this caste group, they choose an *ustad*, or mentor, who teaches them music and singing for many years. With the exception of the *nayika*, the *ustad* is the most authoritative figure in a dancer's life. Today, most dancers confine themselves to a basic musical education, which they receive at the *baithak* (rehearsal room that is located, like the *kotha*, in the building where the musicians live) several times a week. However, if a girl has talent and determination, the *ustad* recommends her to his colleagues in radio, television, or the cinema, and organizes an audition or casting. If she is successful, her career can take a different path from the traditional 'business'.

Although most *mirasi* prefer to live and work in the Shahi Mohalla, they are a lot freer in their social contacts, less stigmatized, and more in demand than the *kanjari*. Today, their primary source of income is no longer the *mujra*, as it was in the past. Many musicians work in the cinema where they record film soundtracks, or participate in large variety shows where they accompany singers and perform melodies of popular Punjabi songs from Pakistani films.

Every *mirasi* dreams of having an independent solo career. This is a lot more attractive than participating in *mujra*, spending hours in the *kotha* waiting for *tamashbins* to come, and wringing their pay from the *nayika*. The role-model and ideal for all *mirasi* is Ustad

Bade Ghulam 'Ali Khan, who began as a *sapardai*, or accompanier, for a dancer-courtesan in the provincial town of Kasur; eventually, he became a living legend, the founder of his own school (*gharana*), and the recipient of the highest awards of India and Pakistan as well as international prizes.

Pakistani society has an ambivalent attitude towards the Hira Mandi. Intellectuals and artists have appealed to the state, to 'save' the area by turning it into a reserve of national music and traditional arts that would be without parallel in South Asia. In a nutshell, they propose applying Iqbal Hussain's experiment to the entire neighbourhood.

Conservative circles and state law-enforcement bodies take a radical stance: they say that it is time to put an end to the Shahi Mohalla, raze all the *kothas*, and replace them with office buildings. This would deprive the *kanjaris* of a place to do their work, sap the foundations of centralized prostitution, and prevent the inflow of new recruits into the 'business'. However, as one has seen in the Lahori suburbs, such measures encourage prostitution to spread all over the city and take on the Western form of 'call girls'.

Finally, human rights activists, social workers, and feminist organizations advocate protecting the neighbourhood's female inhabitants, from the police's arbitrary rule and brutality, in conformity with international law; prohibiting the participation of minors in prostitution; and conducting a broad health awareness campaign—most *kanjari* believe that they can save themselves from AIDS simply through prayers and ablutions.[27] Indeed, the neighbourhood has streets with extremely squalid establishments and terrible slums where one can 'buy' a woman for fifty rupees (less than a dollar); the notorious Tibbi Gali lane, whose merits were once sung by an anonymous poet, and where the police does not dare to enter, is an example.

No matter what future is in store for the Shahi Mohalla, it remains an accentuated place for Lahoris. For the religious-minded, especially the women, the place is stigmatized and taboo. However, for most middle-aged and older men, it is coloured by nostalgic memories of the forbidden desires and risky adventures of their youth. The Shahi Mohalla is an ambivalent cultural and spatial image, where lofty feelings inspired by music and poetry are combined with the most basic instincts. Nevertheless, in this tangled bundle of emotions, admiration tends to prevail over censure. In other words, the sublimatory aspect of art is highly pronounced here: art as a means of pacifying the 'seething cauldron of excitations' of the unconscious. For the sake of aesthetic pleasure, and in memory of the glorious past, Lahoris are willing to pardon all sins, as a Punjabi saying goes:

naīn rīsān shehr lahūr diyān
īthe vigaṛiyān galān sonwar diyān

There is no city like Lahore:
Everything that is wrong is set right here.

Kim's Gun, Lahore.

CHAPTER SEVEN

The City of Dreadful Night

As is the case with the other ancient cities of the world, the historical and geographic images of Lahore have been adopted by literature and the fine arts, which have turned it into an artistic image. The artistic image of a city greatly augments the general capacity of the *topophilia* to reveal the emotional connection between man and his environment, and effaces the phenomenological barriers between the subject and the object. The reflection and dream, allusions and associations, imagination and invention that are employed by creative thought considerably transform and expand the chorological notions of a city.

I have already mentioned that Lahore made its way into Western literature, in John Milton's work, as far back as the seventeenth century. In the national literary tradition—first in Urdu and then in Punjabi—the artistic image of Lahore took shape only in the late nineteenth century. Naturally, these 'inner' and 'outer' images of the city differ greatly. The latter are marked by exoticism, pronounced idealization, or, in contrast, demonization, while reflection and associative imagery predominate in the former.

The first 'outer' artistic image of Lahore appears in the poem *Lalla Rookh* (1817) by Thomas Moore, who paints an exotic oriental picture in the spirit of European romanticism. The main plot line of Moore's poem has a pseudo-historic 'Mughal colour': the poem's heroine is said to be Emperor Aurangzeb's daughter,[1] who makes a long voyage from Delhi to Kashmir to marry the son of the ruler of Bukhara. It is known that the historical Aurangzeb-'Alamgir had five daughters from three official wives[2] and that none of them was called Lalla Rookh or was the daughter-in-law of the Khan of Bukhara. On its way to Kashmir, the luxurious imperial procession makes a stop in Lahore, in keeping with traditional Mughal practice. Moore gives a brief description of the city, excerpt from which I have already cited in Chapter 4 in connection with Shalimar Gardens.

This description greatly resembles the images of ceremonial processions that were *loci communes* in Persian and Urdu tales:

> 'The arrival of the young Bride at Lahore was celebrated in the most enthusiastic manner. The Rajas and Omras in her train, who had kept at a certain distance during the journey and never encamped nearer to the Princess than was strictly necessary for her safeguard here rode in splendid cavalcade through the city and distributed the most costly presents to the crowd. Engines were erected in all the squares which cast forth showers of confectionery among the people, while the artisans in chariots adorned with tinsel and flying streamers exhibited the badges of their respective trades through the streets. Such brilliant displays of life and pageantry among the palaces and domes and gilded minarets of Lahore made the city altogether like a place of enchantment; particularly on the day when Lalla Rookh set out again upon her journey, when she was accompanied to the gate by all the fairest and richest of the nobility and rode along between ranks of beautiful boys and girls who kept waving over their heads plates of gold and silver flowers, and then threw them around to be gathered by the populace.'[3]

In this excerpt, the city is depicted as a procession. No specific or characteristic features of Lahore are given because palaces, domes, and gilded minarets were part of the standard image of every Muslim city, for the Europeans, in the nineteenth century and later. Nevertheless, as he says in his notes to the poem, Moore made use of available historical and literary sources, even if they did not have a direct bearing on Lahore. For example, he learnt about the custom of scattering gold and silver flowers, as alms, from the English translation of Firishta's chronicle, published by Jonathan Scott in 1794.[4]

In the corresponding note, Moore wrote, upon the passage of Firishta from which this is taken, 'small coins, stamped with the figure of a flower. They are still used in India to distribute in charity and on occasion thrown by the purse-bearers of the great among the populace.'[5] Speaking about 'chariots adorned with tinsel and flying streamers', Moore referred to John Hoppner's popular book *Oriental Tales* (1805), which was a digest of tales from the Persian storybook *Parrot's Tales* (*Tuti-namah*) and the Sanskrit *Hitopadesha*.[6]

Thomas Moore also mentioned certain details about the geographic location of Lahore, in particular, the surroundings of the Grand Trunk Road. Further, he wrote, 'Fadladeen felt the loss of the good road they had hitherto travelled and was very near cursing Jehan-Guire (of blessed memory!) for not having continued his delectable alley of trees a least as far as the mountains of Cashmere.'[7] Moore got his information, about the Imperial Highway, from Bernier's book,[8] which he cited in his notes: 'The fine road made by the Emperor Jehan-Guire from Agra to Lahore, planted with trees on each side. This road is 250 leagues in length. It has "little pyramids or turrets", says Bernier, "erected every half league, to mark the ways, and frequent wells to afford drink to passengers, and to water the young trees".'[9] Here, Bernier made a mistake that Moore unwittingly made his hero—the courtier Fadladeen—repeat: the 'little pyramids or turrets' (*kos-minars*) that were located approximately three kilometres apart on the Grand Trunk Road appeared during the reign of Akbar rather than of Jahangir. One of these *kos-minars*, still preserved near the tomb of 'Ali Mardan Khan, is a tourist attraction of Lahore.

Curiously, Moore's description of Lahore, as a procession, coincides with the image of Lahore in the drawings of Moore's younger contemporary, the Russian traveller and artist, A. Soltykoff (1806–1859). Soltykoff visited Lahore in 1842 and made several sketches, of which *Lahore Street*, housed in the British Library, is of particular interest. A cavalcade of horsemen and mounted elephants, quickly moving down a narrow street to a gate arch, takes up the greater part of the sheet. A young person of noble descent, leaning on a bow, sits on the biggest elephant; he is apparently on his way to a hunt. His mounted companions are armed to the teeth, with bows, sabres, and spears. In the background, one sees a long building, supposedly in the Lahore-style with scalloped balconies and wide windows (which never actually existed in Lahore), in which viewers stand, including barefaced female dancers in whom Soltykoff took a particular interest. Local colour is also provided by a group in the foreground, on the left, consisting of two bare-chested dervishes and a bearded *akali* with a lance in his hand.

The following letter, by Soltykoff, can be considered a commentary of sorts for his drawing:

> 'You mount an elephant and make your way with difficulty through the narrow streets, constantly waiting for one of the rickety five-storey buildings to fall on you together with dwellers and balconies. On both sides [...] loiter creatures without clothing or in rags and with long beards: loathsome eunuchs and fakirs covered with ashes [...] Everywhere you hear the sound of knocking, roaring, and weapons clanking [...] Yet, if you look up, you see in the windows and on the balconies the impudent gazes of venal beauties and dancers covered with gems and gold.'[10]

Without a doubt, the framework narrative of *Lalla Rookh*, which repeatedly mentions Lahore and other Indian toponyms, was neither central to Thomas Moore's conception nor the main merit of his work. The tale of a 'Mughal' princess who falls in love with the poet, Feramors, on the way to her wedding and learns, upon her arrival, that he is in fact her groom, the Bukhara prince Aliris, is nothing but a setting, in prose, for four famous interpolated poems: *The Veiled Prophet of Khorassan, Paradise and the Peri, The Fire-Worshipers*, and *The Light of the Harem*. These poems made Moore famous and were often imitated and paraphrased.

Translations of Thomas Moore's poems, by Russian writers, stimulated the development of Orientalism in Russia, and increased the interest in Eastern literature among readers. Moore's work had a marked influence on Russian poetry in the 1820s and 1830s. Russian poets often borrowed from the *Irish Melodies* and *Lalla Rookh*. Thomas Moore's works penetrated into the consciousness of Russian readers, where they occupied a special niche thanks to the rise of the Romantic Movement, the strengthening of Oriental trends in literature, and the reception of Moore's writings in a more general context, together with the work of his friend and great contemporary, George Gordon Byron.

Orientalism marked the development of not only literature, but also of music, leading to the appearance in the mid-nineteenth century of operas on Eastern and, in particular, Indian themes. The forerunner of this trend in European opera was Mozart's Singspiel, *The Abduction from the Seraglio* (1782), which is set in Ottoman Turkey. Oriental exoticism readily penetrated into opera on account of this genre's predilection for exotic scenery, vivid costumes, and pompous spectacle. Model Italian 'exotic' operas were Domenico Cimarosa's *Cleopatra* and *The Sun Virgin* (1789) and Gaspare Spontini's *Nurmahal or the Rose Festival in Kashmir* (1829) based on the poem *Lalla Rookh*.

However, the real founder of Orientalism in opera was the Frenchman Félicien David, with his operas *The Pearl of Brazil* (1851) and *Lalla Rookh* (1862). They were followed by such classic works as Charles Gounod's *The Queen of Sheba* (1862), Georges Bizet's *The Pearl Fishers* (1863), Giacomo Meyerbeer's *The African Woman* (1865), Giuseppe Verdi's *Aida* (1871), and Léo Delibes' *Lakmé* (1883). This list also includes Jules Massenet's *The King of Lahore* (*Le Roi de Lahore*), which offers a fantastic and exotic image of Lahore.

The premiere of this opera took place in April 1877 at the Opéra Garnier (Grand Opéra); it was immediately acclaimed by not only the public at large, but also by Massenet's most exacting musical colleagues. Shortly after the premiere, Massenet was appointed as professor at the Paris Conservatory and elected to the Institut Français. 'The King of Lahore' made Massenet world famous as an operatic composer. After Bizet's early death in 1875, Massenet became the doyen of French composers.

In *The King of Lahore*, Massenet made use of the music of his earlier unfinished or unperformed works, especially his opera *The Cup of the King of Thule* which had never been staged. *The King of Lahore* was performed at opera theatres in many European and American cities, including St. Petersburg in 1882. Pyotr Tchaikovsky was very impressed by Massenet's music and wrote to his brother Modest, 'I play excerpts from *The King of Lahore* with immense pleasure. How much taste and chic these Frenchmen have! I recommend that you get yourself a copy.'[11] Nevertheless, *The King of Lahore* still bears the mark of the style of the 'grand opera'—a traditional genre of French musical theatre that had largely worn itself out by that time. This explains why music lovers today mostly know of Massenet for his *Manon* and *Werther*, in which he shows himself as a lyric composer giving an intimate and chamber interpretation of the subject matter as well as a development of romantic female images.[12]

The plot of *The King of Lahore* (libretto by Louis Gallet) is set in the eleventh century during the conquest of Mahmud Ghaznavi. At the same time, the plot makes use of many stereotyped and banal turns and anachronisms.

The first act of *The King of Lahore* opens with a scene before the Temple of the god Indra, in Lahore. People gather next to the temple to beseech Indra to save the city from the Muslim invasion led by Mahmud. Then Indra's head priest, with the non-Hindu name of Timur, and the head minister, Scindia, enter the stage. Scindia (also transcribed as Sindhia or Shinde) was the historical name of the Marathi dynasty that ruled the Gwalior Principality in the eighteenth and nineteenth centuries, and had nothing to do with Lahore. This Scindia, who somehow appears in eleventh-century Lahore, is the opera's chief villain. He is in love with his niece, Sita (the only character in the opera with a 'correct' Hindu name), a priestess of Indra who has taken the vows of chastity—this motif, most likely, appeared under the influence of Spontini's opera *The Vestal Virgin* (1807), which was fashionable at the time. Scindia wants to marry Sita; yet, her vow could be annulled by only the king of Lahore, who bears, for some reason, the Arabic name Alim ('knowing, educated'). However, Sita rejects Scindia's proposal as she and Alim love each other and meet secretly.

The second act opens with a scene in the Thol (Thal) Desert, where the royal camp has been pitched. Sita is anxiously waiting for Alim to return from the battlefield. She is consoled by the young servant of the king, called Kaled (more likely, 'Khalid'—yet another Arabic name), whose role is sung by a mezzo-soprano. Alim, covered with blood, appears: he has been treacherously wounded by Scindia. Alim curses the traitor and dies. Scindia declares himself king and, taking the lamenting Sita prisoner, leaves for Lahore.

The opera's third act brings the viewer to Indra's paradise, where the celestial maidens (*apsaras*) sing and dance. According to Hindu belief, the heavens—or Indra's paradise (*Svarga*)—are located on Mount Meru. Brave warriors, who die a glorious death in honest combat, go to *Svarga* where they take pleasure in the singing of the celestial beauties and savour the heavenly food. Alim appears and begs Indra to let him return to earth to reunite with Sita. Indra is touched by his love and allows him to go on two conditions: Alim will return to earth as a beggar instead of as a king; his life will depend on Sita's life—if she dies, so will he.

The fourth act opens with a scene in the royal palace, where Sita is languishing in captivity. She is ready to commit suicide, to escape Scindia's advances. Dressed in rags, Alim is sleeping in the square before the palace. A crowd has gathered to greet Scindia, the new king of Lahore. It turns out that the threat of invasion has subsided: the Muslim army has decided not to storm the city and has disappeared into the desert. The crowd joyously celebrate their victory and greet the new king. Alim awakes and sees Scindia, whom he loudly denounces as a traitor and usurper. The crowd is stunned by the remarkable similarity between the beggar and the late king. Scindia orders that Alim be arrested, yet the head priest Timur receives a revelation from Indra and intercedes on Alim's behalf, sheltering him in the temple.

The fifth act is set, once again, in the Temple of Indra where Sita is hiding having run away from the palace. She is listening to a hymn that the priestesses are singing, and recalls the days when the king came to see her in the temple. Alim appears, and the lovers embrace each other. They decide to flee from the city through a secret passage, yet Scindia appears and bars their way. Seeing that their path to freedom has been blocked, Sita stabs herself with a dagger; Alim dies too, as Indra has predicted. The walls of the palace disappear, and one sees Indra's paradise. Extolled by the singing *apsaras*, Sita and Alim are resurrected next to the god's altar. In despair, Scindia confesses to his wrongdoings.

As we see, the image of Lahore in the opera is highly conditional and lacks all local colour. The librettist may have chosen Lahore as the opera's setting to relate the plot to early Muslim conquests; otherwise, the opera could have just as easily been called 'The King of Delhi' or 'The King of Kashmir'. The pseudo-Hindu colour of the action— temples, the god Indra, *apsaras*, and priests—is violated in the most absurd way by the Arabic-Muslim names of the characters (it suffices to recall the head priest, Timur). Naturally, the 'Indian' subject matter did not influence Massenet's music, which lacks Oriental melodies— in contrast to the opera by Mikhail Glinka *Ruslan and Ludmila* (1842) with its stylized Eastern 'Persian Chorus' and 'Chernomor's March'.

The King of Lahore is a typical 'grand opera' with a quasi-historic plot, a bloody and tragic ending, pompous crowd scenes, depictions of processions and temple rituals, visions of paradise, choruses of priests, city dwellers, soldiers, and *apsaras*, ensemble singing, and a traditional five-act structure. As with other examples of this genre, the cast was determined by the necessity to include all the traditional vocal roles: the noble hero Alim (tenor), the true and tender heroine Sita (soprano),[13] the villain Scindia (baritone), the raisonneur Timur (bass), and the travesti Kaled (mezzo-soprano).

One can apply, to *The King of Lahore*, the stern words that Leo Tolstoy wrote with regard to another opera along an 'Indian' plot. On 19 April 1897, Tolstoy attended a dress rehearsal of Anton Rubinstein's opera *Feramors*, based on the same *Lalla Rookh*. After the rehearsal, Tolstoy wrote a brief description of the opera, and then incorporated its expanded version into the first chapter of his famous treatise, *What is Art?* (1897–1898).

The printed version of Tolstoy's treatise does not mention the work on which the opera's libretto is based or the Russian composer who set it to music. Nevertheless, there is no doubt that Tolstoy was referring to Moore's *Lalla Rookh*, and to Rubinstein's opera *Feramors* which was based on this poem. Tolstoy wrote,

> 'I remember being once at the rehearsal of one of the most ordinary of the new operas which are produced at all the opera houses of Europe and America […] The performance had already commenced, and on the stage

a procession of Indians who had brought home a bride was being represented [...] The opera he was rehearsing was one of the most ordinary of operas for people who are accustomed to them, but also one of the most gigantic absurdities that could possibly be devised. An Indian king wants to marry; they bring him a bride; he disguises himself as a minstrel; the bride falls in love with the minstrel and is in despair, but afterwards discovers that the minstrel is the king, and everyone is highly delighted.'[14]

Tolstoy then proceeded to say something that was aimed at Rubinstein's opera yet could be read as a denouncement of opera in general:

'That there never were, or could be, such Indians, and that they were not only unlike Indians, but that what they were doing was unlike anything on earth except other operas, was beyond all manner of doubt; that people do not converse in such a way as recitative, and do not place themselves at fixed distances, in a quartet, waving their arms to express their emotions; that nowhere, except in theatres, do people walk about in such a manner, in pairs, with tinfoil halberds and in slippers; that no one ever gets angry in such a way, or is affected in such a way, or laughs in such a way, or cries in such a way; and that no one on earth can be moved by such performances; all this is beyond the possibility of doubt. Instinctively the question presents itself: For whom is this being done? Whom can it please? If there are, occasionally, good melodies in the opera, to which it is pleasant to listen, they could have been sung simply, without these stupid costumes and all the processions and recitatives and hand-wavings.'[15]

Tolstoy's invective did not attack Thomas Moore or his poem specifically but the art of opera in general, no matter what plot it was based on. Still, it clearly shows Tolstoy's indifference to the 'Oriental' material that he used as the grounds for his polemic. An abyss opened between the Russian romantic poets, who were charmed by the themes of *Lalla Rookh* and took pleasure in the music of Spontini's opera *Nurmahal or the Rose Festival in Kashmir*, and Tolstoy who rejected the genre of the opera, the 'Indian' atmosphere and, more generally, all conventionalism on stage.

Paraphrasing Tolstoy, 'there never was, or could be' such a Lahore as was portrayed in *The King of Lahore* for it is a compendium of 'the most gigantic absurdities'. Nevertheless, Tolstoy was essentially outraged by the magic of opera—an art form that transforms life and enchants the viewer with its synthesis of music, singing, drama, and scenography, in which the plot plays an important, though not the main, role. In the final analysis, the 'phoney' Lahore of Massenet's opera differs little in its conventionalism from the Egypt of *Aida*, the Ceylon of *The Pearl Fishers*, and the Japan of *Madam Butterfly*, because the Oriental exoticism of classical opera only serves as a pretext for creating a colourful spectacle and a costume drama that has as little to do with reality as possible.

It is no coincidence that the image of Lahore—with its architecture and natural surroundings, and the customs and costumes of its inhabitants—made nineteenth-century Europeans think of opera. The founder of theosophy, Helena Blavatsky, wrote about the *darbar* of the viceroy of India in Lahore, which she attended in 1880: 'Before us, almost at our feet, and seemingly at one and the same time, scenes from the greatest European theatres seemed to unfold, with their "Africans", "Aidas", "Kings of Lahore" and the tutti quanti of various operas and ballets portraying Oriental life. The most gorgeous decorations under the sun ever seen by Europeans were displayed before us.'[16] On another occasion, Blavatsky compared Shia religious hymns to opera: 'As we passed under the windows of the house where they had retired to complete their mysterious ceremonies, we heard their singing again, this time loud and sharp, resounding through the deep silence of the nocturnal air, like some invisible threat. For some unknown reason I was reminded of the scene and chorus from *The Huguenots*: "La bénédiction des poignards".'[17]

With respect to Lahore, one can say that European nineteenth-century fiction was based on pre-existing documentary literature—travelogues, memoirs, diaries, and letters by colonial officials that I have often cited in this book. Among the numerous English authors who wrote about India, the women of the Victorian period play a special role. They astonish modern scholars with their tenacity in ordeal, benevolent curiosity, and unprejudiced attitude towards the culturally 'other' inhabitants of India, and their mores and customs. Whereas male English memoirists never forgot about their mission to criticize and improve 'barbarian' colonial society, women wrote their letters and diaries for their kinfolk back home and treated everything they saw with spontaneity, compassion, and even admiration. Some of these books—such as those written by Mrs Mir Hasan Ali (an Englishwoman who married an Indian Muslim), Emily Eden (sister of Governor-General Lord Auckland), Fanny Parks (who lived in India for twenty-five years and, in contrast to most of her countrywomen, was fluent in Urdu), and Mrs Harris (witness to the dramatic siege of the Residency at Lucknow)—are rightly considered to be classics in their genre.

The influence of this collective experience of English travellers and memoirists is apparent in the work of the main portrayer of colonial India, and the creator of a vivid and authentic image of Lahore, Rudyard Kipling (1865–1936).

Kipling was born in Bombay, where his father taught at the J.J. School of Arts—one of the first arts schools in the Subcontinent. As a child, Kipling grew up surrounded by native servants, and spoke Urdu before he had learnt English. One can say that India was in his blood. In 1871, Kipling and his younger sister were sent to England for their education, and his happy Indian childhood came to an end. It was customary among the English families working in India—who called themselves 'Anglo-Indians'—to send their children to their home country for their schooling: in India, children were brought up by local nannies and male servants, who spoilt, and never punished, them. This was contrary to Victorian notions about the correct (i.e., strict) upbringing of young ladies and gentlemen. Furthermore, children from colonial families spoke English badly, and with a marked accent.

Kipling himself recalled, at an advanced age, in 1935: 'In the afternoon heats before we took our sleep, she [their Portuguese Roman Catholic nanny] or Meeta [their Hindu bearer] would tell us stories and Indian nursery songs all unforgotten, and we were sent into the dining-room after we had been dressed, with the caution "Speak English now to Papa and Mamma." So one spoke "English", haltingly translated out of the vernacular idiom that one thought and dreamed in.'[18]

In 1875, while Kipling was in England, his parents moved from Bombay to Lahore, where John Lockwood Kipling was appointed curator of the Museum of Indian Art and became the director of the Mayo School of Art (today, the National College of Arts). After leaving school, Rudyard did not enrol in the civil service, or join the army, because of his poor eyesight. His parents lacked the means to send him to college. Thus, at the age of sixteen, he returned to Lahore where he found work as an assistant to the editor of an evening newspaper, *The Civil and Military Gazette*. The long title of the newspaper stemmed from the fact that the European part of Lahore consisted of the Civil Lanes (where the personnel of the Indian civil service lived) and the Cantonment (which was inhabited by the military)—as was the case in the other cities of British India as well. Each part of this vast British community had its own news and readers. Kipling wrote a fiction column in the newspaper. He quickly integrated into the Anglo-Indian society of Lahore, spending all his free time at the Punjab Club on the Mall where he learnt all the details about the lives of the colonial civil servants, officers, doctors, and engineers—characters in his early short stories.

Kipling was a born *flâneur* and strolled all over Lahore. While wandering about the city and talking to its inhabitants, he learnt many things that most English people in India were unaware of. Some traits of Kipling's personality, and his in-depth knowledge of the psychology and customs of the different groups of Indian society, were reflected in his favourite character—the policeman Strickland, a talented scholar of India, an actor who could assume any guise, and a clever detective.

In all, Kipling lived in Lahore for five years: in 1887, he was transferred to Allahabad to the editorial office of the larger newspaper *The Pioneer*. In Lahore, Kipling was happy in his family circle, although he preferred his native Bombay to all other Indian cities.[19] It was in Lahore that Kipling became a writer and where the short stories that made up his first prose collection, *Plain Tales from the Hills* (1888), were written and published in the newspaper.

As a well-defined literary and spatial image, Lahore appears in the very first short story in the collection. The story is entitled 'The Gate of A Hundred Sorrows' and takes the form of the confession of an opium-smoker, who spends his life in a Chinese opium den called The Gate of a Hundred Sorrows. The choice of subject matter and style reflect the influence of the autobiographical tale by Thomas de Quincey (1785–1859), *Confessions of an English Opium-Eater* (1822), which was popular at the time. The opium den, where the story's hero lives out his days, is situated deep in the labyrinth of streets of the Walled City, behind Delhi Gate:

> 'It lies between the Copper-smith's Gully and the pipe-stem sellers' quarter, within a hundred yards, too, as the crow flies, of the Mosque of Wazir Khan. I don't mind telling any one this much, but I defy him to find the Gate, however well he may think he knows the City. You might even go through the very gully it stands in a hundred times, and be none the wiser. We used to call the gully, "the Gully of the Black Smoke", but its native name is altogether different of course. A loaded donkey couldn't pass between the walls; and, at one point, just before you reach the Gate, a bulged house-front makes people go along all sideways.'[20]

This excerpt is marked by a descriptive style that is typical of the early Kipling, stemming from his experiences as a journalist and the documentalism that is often found in his early prose and, more generally, in the English short story of the day. After becoming popular in the US and Europe, this genre lingered on in England. Kipling's early short stories greatly resemble 'physiological sketches'—Dickens' *Sketches by Boz* was the model—of Indian life, abounding in details and Urdu words that were understandable to the Anglo-Indians only; the vividly drawn characters seemed to be taken from everyday life.

Even more importantly, beginning with 'The Gate of a Hundred Sorrows', Kipling systematically drew an infernal and demonized image of Lahore, as a city of vice and death. This trend also marked his other stories set in Lahore: 'Without Benefit of Clergy', 'On the City Wall', 'The City of Dreadful Night', 'In the House of Suddhoo', etc.

Whereas 'The Gate of a Hundred Sorrows' depicted Lahore as a city of vice, full of 'stifling, sweltering chandoo-khanas' (i.e., Indian hemp dens), the short story 'Without Benefit of Clergy' painted a portrait of a city of terrible diseases and epidemics which destroys the happiness of the Englishman, Holden, and his Indian beloved, Ameera. They settle in a secluded house on the outskirts of Lahore, in an attempt to hide their love from the eyes of the people and gods, yet the lethal air of the city reaches them and kills first their child and then Ameera herself.

In Kipling's stories, Lahore appears as a mortal foe of man, evoking dread through its frightening sounds and foul smells. In words, from the standpoint of *topophobia*, it is presented as:

> 'They sat together and laughed, calling each other openly by every pet name that could move the wrath of the gods. The city below them was locked up in its own torments. Sulphur fires blazed in the streets; the conches in the Hindu temples screamed and bellowed, for the gods were inattentive in those days. There was a service in the great Mahomedan shrine, and the call to prayer from the minarets was almost unceasing. They heard the wailing in the houses of the dead, and once the shriek of a mother who had lost a child and was calling for its return. In the grey dawn they saw the dead borne out through the city gates, each litter with its own little knot of mourners. Wherefore they kissed each other and shivered.'[21]

The story 'On the City Wall' depicts Lahore as a city of violence and religious conflict, which foretells the future partition of the Subcontinent. In Lahore, and in particular in the Shahi Mohalla, one still sees tall and narrow old houses that adjoin the remains of the city walls. The upper floors of these houses formerly opened directly onto the walls, projecting somewhat like birdhouses over the lower floors, and constituting a scenic feature of the city landscape. Such a house, in which the courtesan Lalun lives, is the setting of the short story:

> If you fell from the broad window-seat you dropped thirty feet sheer into the City Ditch. But if you stayed where

you should and looked forth, you saw all the cattle of
the City being driven down to water, the students of the
Government College playing cricket, the high grass and
trees that fringed the river-bank, the great sand bars that
ribbed the river, the red tombs of dead Emperors beyond
the river, and very far away through the blue heat-haze, a
glint of the snows of the Himalayas.[22]

This short description of the view from the window allows us to
identify the narrator's location: to the south, he sees the Shahalami
(or Bherwala) Gate, behind which the pastures lay; to the west, the
campus of Government College on the Mall;[23] to the north-west, the
Shahdara funerary complex on the other side of the Ravi; and, to the
north, the glimmer of Himalayan snows. This vast panorama can only
be seen from the eastern wall of the city, between the Delhi and the
old Akbari Darwaza.

In contrast to the journalistic precision of his earlier prose, Kipling
tried to 'encrypt' city toponyms in 'On the City Wall'. He called Shahi
Qila, the Fort Amara; Akbari Darwaza, Padshahi Gate; Sheranwala
Darwaza, Kumharsen Gate; and Shahalami Darwaza, the Gate of
Butchers (after the meat bazaar located next to it). However, this
did not fool anyone who knew Lahore. After Lahore became British,
the Fort was used to house the garrison artillery, and served as an
arsenal and prison for state prisoners. The story's main character,
Khem Singh, an old fighter against the colonial regime, is detained
in the prison. The story's narrator, an Englishman, unwittingly helps
him to run away, deceived by Lalun's feigned affection.

In the narrator's description, the fort is a gloomy place that
preserves the memory of its rulers' numerous crimes: 'No man knows
the precise extent of Fort Amara. Three kings built it hundreds of
years ago, and they say that there are miles of underground rooms
beneath its walls. It is peopled with many ghosts, a detachment of
Garrison Artillery and a Company of Infantry. In its prime it held
ten thousand men and filled its ditches with corpses.'[24] The toponym
'Kumharsen Gate' (i.e., Potters' Gate) is just as transparent. Khem
Singh, who has not seen the city for a long time, passes by it and says,
'The Kumharsen Gate is new. Who pulled down the stone lions?'

As the reader will recall, stone lions were placed at the Lion Gate (Sheranwala Darwaza) during Ranjit Singh's rule.

The story is set during *Muharram*, the time when Shias organize mourning processions in the streets, in memory of their martyrs, and carry huge replicas of Imam Hussain's tomb in Karbala (*taziya*). As it is often the case today too, a religious conflict flares up between the Shias and Hindus. Although the English, and the colonial troops loyal to them, try to quash it, the conflict escalates into a massacre, the city is overcome with panic, and the people are wounded and dying. As with Kipling's other stories, Lahore once again appears as a city of violence and death.

> 'The six or eight Policemen with each tazia drew their batons, and struck as long as they could in the hope of forcing the mob forward, but they were overpowered, and as contingents of Hindus poured into the streets, the fight became general. [...] The priests at the corners of the streets knocked the legs from the bedsteads that supported their pulpits and smote for the Faith, while stones fell from the silent houses upon friend and foe [...] Tazia after tazia, some burning, others torn to pieces, hurried past us and the mob with them, howling, shrieking, and striking at the house doors in their flight. [...] The clamor in the City redoubled. The Hindus had descended into the streets in real earnest and ere long the mob returned. [...] Everywhere men struck aimlessly with sticks, grasping each other by the throat, howling and foaming with rage, or beat with their bare hands on the doors of the houses.'[25]

Still, the most expressive, memorable, as well as terrifying, literary image of Lahore is found in Kipling's short story, 'The City of Dreadful Night.' Kipling borrowed the story's title from the poem of the same name, written by the Scotsman James Thomson (1834–1882) in 1870–73, and read by Kipling during his school vacations. Although a second-rate Victorian author, Thomson managed to convey, in his poem devoted to London, an atmosphere of deep melancholy and black despair—a fashionable and 'purely English' mood at the time. The poem's title apparently appealed to Kipling a great deal, for he used it twice—as the title of his short story about Lahore and for a series of sketches about life in Calcutta. It should be mentioned that O. Henry also used this title for one of his short stories about New York.

Kipling's short story also contains an unacknowledged quote from Thomson's poem. The story ends with the sentence: 'So the city was of Death as well as Night after all.' This is a paraphrase of Thomson's lines:

> The City is of Night; perchance of Death,
> But certainly of Night.[26]

'The City of Dreadful Night' is a story without a plot—a sketch that arose from the nightly wanderings of the author while suffering from the torrid summer heat. He describes Lahore as a city of the dead where sleeping people lie in the street like corpses, yellow stray dogs roam, rats swarm in dark holes in courtyards, and vultures slumber on minarets waiting for prey—in other words, a real hell, and a space that is inimical to man and frightening in its *topophobia*.

'Straight as a bar of polished steel', the road brings the narrator through Delhi Gate to the Wazir Khan Mosque:

> 'The open square in front of the Mosque is crowded
> with corpses; and a man must pick his way carefully
> for fear of treading on them. The moonlight stripes the
> Mosque's high front of coloured enamel work in broad
> diagonal bands; and each separate dreaming pigeon in
> the niches and corners of the masonry throws a squab
> little shadow.'[27]

Kipling wrote that Gustav Doré, in his engravings, could have depicted Lahore at night; he was apparently referring to Doré's illustrations for Dante's *Inferno* (1885). Kipling himself saw Lahore in the changing contrasts of black and white, pallid moonlight and dark shadows:

> 'The pitiless Moon shows it all. Shows, too, the plains
> outside the city, and here and there a hand's-breadth of

the Ravee without the walls. Shows lastly, a splash of
glittering silver on a house-top almost directly below the
mosque Minar. [...] A small cloud passes over the face of
the Moon, and the city and its inhabitants—clear drawn
in black and white before—fade into masses of black and
deeper black.'[28]

Truth be told, Kipling's descriptions recall not Doré's neoclassical
engravings but the expressive dynamic etchings drawn by, for
example, Kipling's contemporary, the famous Welsh artist Frank
Brangwyn, who depicted the gloomy districts of London and other
industrial cities.

The climax of the dreadful night in Lahore becomes the narrator's
encounter with a funeral procession: a woman who died from the heat
at midnight is being carried to the burning *ghat* to be cremated. The
City of Night turned out, indeed, to be the City of Death—death
that, up to then, only appeared to the narrator in the immobile bodies
sleeping in the streets.

Nevertheless, there were places on Kipling's 'mental map' of Lahore
that were flooded with *topophilia*—places connected to his beloved
parents and his happy years of working at the newspaper. He recalled
these places in his *magnum opus*—the novel *Kim* (1900). The image
of Lahore transforms, with the change of genre from short story to
novel. Employing the traditions of the European 'grand road novel',
with its Quixotic pair—the noble idealist Lama and the cunning
trickster Kim—Kipling unfurled, before the reader's eyes, a panoramic
picture of the cultural pluralism of Indian life and the sensitivity and
openness of the people of the country to all that surrounds them. In
his novel, Kipling presented an image of India that was in keeping
with the conception of 'Unity in Diversity'—something that was
subsequently worked out by the country's national leaders with respect
to its cultural heritage. Naturally, in conformity with these new goals,
Kipling could not permit himself to demonize Indian cultural and
geographic images as he did in his 'physiological sketches' of Lahore
and Calcutta.

The novel begins on the Mall, Lahore's main street, next to the Museum across from which the old cannon Zamzama still stands today:

> 'He [Kim] sat, in defiance of municipal orders, astride the gun Zam-Zammah on her brick platform opposite the old Ajaib-Gher—the Wonder House, as the natives call the Lahore Museum. Who hold Zam-Zammah, that "fire-breathing dragon",[29] hold the Punjab, for the great green-bronze piece is always first of the conqueror's loot.'[30]

The cannon Zamzama ('Lion's Roar') was placed in its current position in 1870, on the occasion of the Duke of Edinburgh's visit to Lahore. Often called the symbol of British rule (*Raj*) in India, the cannon was actually cast in 1757 by Indian gun makers on the orders of Ahmad Shah Durrani and under the supervision of his vizier Shah Wali Khan. Zamzama is made of an alloy of copper and brass: a metal vessel was taken as Jazia—a capitation tax for infidels—from every Hindu house in the city, to manufacture the cannon.[31] Ahmad Shah Durrani first used Zamzama in the famous battle at Panipat in 1761. When he returned to Kabul, he left the cannon, as it was too heavy to be transported, with his governor, Khwaja Ubaid.

A year later, the Sikh military commander Hari Singh Bhangi launched a campaign against the Afghan governor and plundered the Lahore arsenal, taking the cannon as a military trophy. From that time on, Zamzama became known by the Punjabi name *Bhangiyan di top* ('Cannon of the Bhangi Clan'), although it is more commonly referred to as 'Kim's Gun' today. The cannon had been kept in Shah Burj in Lahore Fort until the 'Sikh Triumvirate' of *sardars*, of the Bhangi clan, seized power. Zamzama became the subject of discord between the different Sikh clans who moved it from one military command post to another: from Gujranwala to Gujrat, and from Rasul Nagar to Amritsar. Rulers began to treat Zamzama as a symbol of power and a talisman that brought military success; moreover, the Hindus considered the cannon to be an incarnation of Mahadeva, the god Shiva. Ranjit Singh repeatedly used the cannon in his military campaigns. The cannon was greatly damaged, and became unfit for military use, during the storming of Multan Fort. In 1848, the English returned Zamzama to Lahore; initially, it was placed next to the Delhi Gate, and later brought to its current location. A Persian inscription is engraved around the cannon's muzzle:

> *ba amr-i durr-i daurān shāh walī khān vazīr*
> *sākht tūp-i zamzama-nām-i qal'a-gīr*
>
> At the order of the Pearl of Time (i.e., Durrani), the
> vizier Shah Wali Khan
> Made the cannon by the name of Zamzama, the
> capture of strongholds.[32]

Next to Zamzama, fate brings Kim together with Lama, who comes to Lahore from Tibet. Kim accompanies Lama to *Ajaib-Ghar*, the Museum, where they meet a grey-bearded Englishman—the wise and kind 'Keeper of the Images'—in whom Kipling portrays his father. Lama is thrilled by the Museum's Buddhist collection:

> 'In the entrance-hall stood the larger figures of the Greco-
> Buddhist sculptures done, savants know how long since,
> by forgotten workmen whose hands were feeling, and
> not unskillfully, for the mysteriously transmitted Grecian
> touch. There were hundreds of pieces, friezes of figures
> in relief, fragments of statues and slabs crowded with
> figures that had encrusted the brick walls of the Buddhist
> stupas and viharas of the North Country and now, dug
> up and labeled, made the pride of the Museum. In open-
> mouthed wonder the lama turned to this and that, and
> finally checked in rapt attention before a large alto-relief
> representing a coronation or apotheosis of the Lord
> Buddha.'[33]

Kipling's father, who amassed a collection of Gandharan art, wrote about it in 1860:

> 'Entering the arts and manufacture division, the
> visitor will find in the aisle to the left the sculptured
> remains from Yusafzai which are the chief and most

valuable possessions of the Museum. [...] The Buddhist paintings and sculptures belong to the flourishing period of the Indo-Scythian rule. [...] The human form is delineated with truth, and occasionally with spirit and freedom of action; some of the heads are so vigorously and expressively carved that there can be no doubt of their being contemporary portraits; the details of costume are accurately rendered, and scenes of actual life are represented with considerable dramatic power. The vitality of style, the more remarkable from its contrast with the inane vagueness and monstrosity of ordinary Hindu sculpture, may be partly explained by the greater purity and simplicity of the early forms of Buddhist creed, but the influence of the Greek is still more plainly visible.'[34]

The museum that Kim and Lama visited was located in an old building known as Tollinton Market. This was a temporary exhibition pavilion that had been built for the First Industrial Exhibition in Lahore in 1864. The exhibition was part of a vast program aimed at demonstrating the technical and technological achievements of England and its colonies; it was held in all the large cities of the British Empire, after the 1851 World Exhibition had been held in London. When the exhibition ended in Lahore, some of the exhibits were taken to Tollinton Market, where they were kept until 1890. Meanwhile, the collection grew: it came to incorporate archaeological finds, inscriptions, weapons, cloth, decorative and applied art, and miniature painting. So, it became necessary to find new exhibition premises.

The Museum's current red-brick building, with its white marble portico over the main entrance, was built in the so-called 'Anglo-Indian style' in 1887, on the occasion of the fiftieth anniversary of Queen Victoria's coronation. The Queen's grandson Albert Victor, Duke of Clarence (who according to rumours and gossip was suspected of being Jack the Ripper), came from England for the foundation stone-laying ceremony. The building was designed by John Lockwood Kipling and the architect and designer Bhai Ram Singh, one of the first graduates of the National College of Arts and creator of the architectural style of colonial Lahore.

Standing next to Zamzama, Kim saw another building with which he (as well as the author himself) felt a certain affinity: 'over yonder behind the Museum, in the big blue-and-white Jadoo-Gher—the Magic House, as we name the Masonic Lodge', where people engage in 'great magic'.[35] He was speaking about Freemasonry and the Grand Lodge of the Punjab Province, which was also located on the Mall. The Kiplings, both father and son, were members of the Lodge. In the late nineteenth century, there were seventeen Masonic lodges from Delhi to Peshawar:

> 'There is a Masonic educational institution maintained by the masons of the Punjab. [...] It educates, clothes, and maintains eight children [...] Such boys in its care as display special talent are sent to the Roorkee Engineering College with a view of passing out as civil engineers. In Lahore there are two lodges, "Hope and Perseverance" and "Ravi," both thriving and popular bodies. There is also a lodge, "Industry" at Naulakha, and "St. John the Evangelist" at Meean Meer.'[36]

The Masonic code of behaviour, with its strict secrecy, struggle for covert influence over political events, codes and passwords, solidarity and mutual assistance is reflected in many places in the novel. The actions of its English characters—Colonel Creighton and Lurgan—and their influence on Kim, whom they try to turn into a 'Sahib' or participant in the 'Great Game', were not only motivated by the interests of the secret service but also by the traditions of the Freemasons.

Kipling's description of Lahore, in the novel, is not limited to the official colonial Mall and its elegant buildings: Kim takes his Lama to the very heart of the Walled City—Kashmiri Gate—where they find an abode in a caravanserai, which I have already mentioned in Chapter 2. Like his hero, Kipling was attracted to the 'hot and crowded bazaars' blazing with light and the crowds with 'all manner of Northern folk'; far from frightening the writer, they gave him new material for his descriptions of Indian mores, customs, and characters.

Kim and Lama set off on their long trip, across the country, from Lahore Railway Station:

'They entered the fort-like railway station, black in the end of night; the electrics sizzling over the goods-yard where they handle the heavy Northern grain-traffic. "This is the work of devils!" said the lama, recoiling from the hollow echoing darkness, the glimmer of rails between the masonry platforms, and the maze of girders above. He stood in a gigantic stone hall paved, it seemed, with the sheeted dead third-class passengers who had taken their tickets overnight and were sleeping in the waiting-rooms. [...] The lama, not so well used to trains as he had pretended, started as the 3.25 a.m. south-bound roared in. The sleepers sprang to life, and the station filled with clamour and shoutings, cries of water and sweetmeat vendors, shouts of native policemen, and shrill yells of women gathering up their baskets, their families, and their husbands.'[37]

Lahore Railway Station was designed by the British architect William Brunton, on the commission of the British government. The station was meant to be a fort, with a walled courtyard and bastions with towers from whose loopholes one could fire at the enemy. In a state of emergency, the railway station could easily be transformed into a fort. Government officials did not like the building's façade; so, Muhammad Sultan Chaghatai—a direct descendant of the Great Mughals and the owner of the majority of caravanserais along the Grand Trunk Road—rebuilt the façade at his own expense. The railway station stands near Delhi Gate, and is always packed today as the overwhelming majority of Pakistanis cannot afford to travel by air. It is interesting to note that, after Partition, only one train travelled between Pakistan and India—the *Samjhota Express* (Express of Agreement); it always departed from, and arrived at, the first of the station's eleven platforms. This train appears in many works by Indian and Pakistani writers, as a symbol of the fragile ties between relatives and friends living on either side of the border.[38]

Kipling's image of Lahore is without parallel in European literature. Precise down to the smallest detail, yet vividly exotic, this image is made up of direct impressions (in the short stories) and recollections (in the novel *Kim*) that stemmed from the writer's youth and passed through the idealizing prism of memory. Kipling did not create his novelistic image of Lahore immediately after his stay in India; he postponed it, and let it ripen, before returning to it during the most productive (American) period of his work. For decades, Kipling kept the image of Lahore as alive and vivid, as if he were still living there. This, in fact, was the case to a certain extent—Kipling called his house in Vermont 'Naulakha', after the famous palace-pavilion in Lahore Fort.

Lahore is rarely mentioned in subsequent twentieth-century European literature, in which it figures, at best, simply as an exotic toponym. In the works of Jorge Luis Borges (1899–1986), who often set his short stories in Indian towns that are little known to the general reader (such as Jaisalmer or Bikaner),[39] Lahore appears in the short story *Blue Tigers* (1977), a philosophical parable about the choice between the 'abnormality' of the miracle and the norm of common sense. Before speaking about Lahore,[40] Borges justly recalls Kipling:

> 'When the Jungle Books were revealed to me I was upset that the tiger, Shere Khan, was the hero's enemy. As the years passed, this strange fascination never left me; it survived my paradoxical desire to become a hunter as it did all common human vicissitudes. Until not long ago (the date feels distant but it really is not), it co-existed peacefully with my day-to-day labours at the University of Lahore. I am a professor of Eastern and Western logic, and I consecrate my Sundays to a seminar on the philosophy of Spinoza. I should add that I am a Scotsman; it may have been my love of tigers that brought me from Aberdeen to Punjab.'[41]

Obsessed by his search for the legendary blue tiger, the story's hero comes to a remote Punjab village where the tiger lives (or so rumour has it) and finds strange blue stones that have the miraculous property of reproducing themselves. As he marks, and counts, the new stones appearing in his pocket, the narrator becomes convinced that he is going insane because he is incapable of understanding what is taking place. Salvation comes to him at the Wazir Khan Mosque:

'I did not sleep the night of 10 February. After a walk that led me far into the dawn, I passed through the gates of the mosque of Wazir Khan. It was the hour at which light has not yet revealed the colours of things. There was not a soul in the courtyard. Not knowing why, I plunged my hands into the water of the fountain of ablutions. Inside the mosque, it occurred to me that God and Allah are two names for a single, inconceivable Being, and I prayed aloud that I be freed from my burden.'[42]

The narrator's prayer was heard: a blind beggar in the mosque takes the stones as alms. Yet, what the narrator considers liberation from his nightmare and trouble is, according to the beggar, a return to the indigence of the everyday and a rejection of the miracle granted from above. 'I do not yet know what your gift to me is,' says the beggar, 'but mine to you is an awesome one. You may keep your days and nights, and keep wisdom, habits, the world.'[43]

Borges' choice of Lahore, and the Wazir Khan Mosque, is not accidental. His parable echoes Sufi notions of the advantages of insanity, which liberate the mystic from the hardships of the physical world and over the banal common sense of spiritually unenlightened people.

Lahore, a beggar, and the Wazir Khan Mosque appear once again in one of Borges' last short stories, entitled *Shakespeare's Memory*:

'In Punjab,' said the major in the course of our conversation, 'a fellow once pointed out a beggar to me. Islamic legend apparently has it, you know, that King Solomon owned a ring that allowed him to understand the language of the birds. And this beggar, so everyone believed, had somehow come into possession of that ring. The value of the thing was so beyond all reckoning that the poor bugger could never sell it, and he died in one of the courtyards of the mosque of Wazil Khan, in Lahore.'[44]

The story's hero is a modest man of letters who devotes his life to reading and solitude. With the help of a simple ruse—a technique that Borges often uses to make the action seem more fantastic—he gets hold of Shakespeare's memoirs, which turn out to be similar to 'Solomon's ring', i.e., a priceless yet useless and cumbersome gift. Shakespeare's recollections gradually replace his own memory, and he loses his personality, sensing himself to be on the verge of insanity. Many of Borges' stories treat this theme of the unreliability of recollections, the inventiveness of life, and the fabrication of experience. The key to Borges' universe is not amnesia and forgetfulness but manipulation of memory and personality.

Yet, what do Lahore and the Wazir Khan Mosque have to do with it? Possibly, before Borges' hero took on 'Shakespeare's memory', he used the 'memory' of Kipling. Borges wrote about him, in the *Blue Tigers*: 'Surely one of the pages of Kipling contains that village of my adventure, since all of India, all the world somehow, can be found there.'[45] The spiritual shock that the narrator experiences in the Wazir Khan Mosque in Lahore is a hidden yet recognizable reference to 'The City of Dreadful Night'; the fact that Borges, who often created his works out of others' books, twice places his characters in the same setting cannot be a simple coincidence—all the more as the image of Lahore in the *Blue Tigers* coincides with Kipling's view of Lahore as a city of paranoid and insane night.

There is nothing extraordinary about Lahore's evolution, in European literature and art, in the nineteenth and twentieth centuries: every age and generation of writers—from Thomas Moore to Borges— had its own Lahore that corresponded both to changing cultural and geographic notions of the world and to new types of artistic thinking. From the decorative city of festive processions (*Lalla Rookh*) to the phantom city of paranormal events (*Blue Tigers*) lay a very long road that stretched from Early Romanticism to Postmodernism.

* * *

In conclusion, I would like to say a few words about the literary image of Lahore, created by Urdu writers and poets, i.e., Lahore as seen from within the tradition. This theme could be the subject of a separate research, which would go beyond the framework of my book. One of the first Urdu prose writers to re-create the image of Mughal Lahore is the classic author and enlightener Muhammad Husain Azad

(1830–1910), who wrote the book *Akbar's Court* (*Darbar-e akbari*, 1898) which combines fiction and historical prose.[46] In the twentieth century, many outstanding Urdu authors wrote about Lahore: most of Saadat Hasan Manto's short stories, including his famous *Toba Tek Singh*, are set in Lahore. Nevertheless, Urdu literature mostly consists of poetic works, and poetry is more authoritative than any other literary genre in this language. For this reason, it may be best to compare the images of Lahore created by the Europeans, with the images of the city found in the work of twentieth century Urdu classic poets—Muhammad Iqbal (1877–1938) and Faiz Ahmed Faiz (1911–1984). Such a comparison also fits into the temporal framework: Iqbal was a younger contemporary of Kipling, and Faiz a younger contemporary of Borges.

In the poem 'On the Bank of the Ravi' (*Kinar-e Ravi*)[47] from the collection *The Sound of Caravan Bell* (*Bang-e dara*, 1924), the poet-philosopher Iqbal employed the image of Lahore as a starting point for profound meditations about the world, time, and human life:

> In the evening's serenity the Ravi melodious is
> Do not ask me what the condition of my heart is
> This became message of prostration's rise and fall to me
> The whole world became precincts of the *haram* to me
> I am standing at the bank of the running water
> However, I do not know where I am standing
> The red wine has coloured the skirt of the evening
> The aged sky is holding wine cup in its trembling hand
> The day's fast moving caravan is advancing to its end
> The evening's twilight is the sun's flower so to say
> In the distance those solitary structures are standing
> They are the minarets of the Mughal emperors' tombs
> This place is the tale of revolution's tyranny
> This place is some book of the bygone age
> This place is a silent orchestra so to say
> Not trees! But it is a serene assembly so to say
> A fast moving boat is sailing on its surface
> Whose sailor is fighting fiercely with the waves
> This boat is in fast speed like the sight
> Getting out of sight, it has gone far away
> The ship of Man's life is sailing in the same way

It is present as well as hidden in eternity's sea
It never gets acquainted with defeat
It is concealed from sight but is not effaced![48]

Iqbal's lyrical hero, standing on the bank of the Ravi, sees the same landscape as the narrator in Kipling's short story 'On the City Wall'— the Shahdara memorial ensemble on the other side of the river. Yet, what were simply 'the red tombs of dead Emperors beyond the river' for Kipling were, for Iqbal, the remains of the former glory of his motherland—the Great Mughal Empire—with which he felt a genetic tie. Shahdara is described as 'the minarets of the tomb of the magnificent horseman [from the kin] of the Chaghtai', i.e., of the Great Mughal Jahangir (*minār-e khwābgah-e shahsawār-e chaghtā'ī*). The 'solitary structures' of the minarets remind the poet of the frailty of worldly glory, the inexorable progression of history, and the vicissitudes of human fate:

> *fasāna-e sitam-e inqilāb hai yeh mahal*
> *ko'ī zamān-e salaf kī kitāb hai yeh mahal*

> This place is the tale of revolution's tyranny
> This place is some book of the bygone age

Although *nazm*—the genre in which Iqbal's poem is written—is certainly not descriptive, the image of Lahore found here is extremely precise emotionally: relicts of the Mughal capital have always led viewers to reflect on the past greatness of its rulers and the faded splendour of its glory. This is particularly true of Shahdara, with its abandoned architectural monuments that were barbarically stripped of their marble decoration—this had already happened in Iqbal's time—and the gardens that stand desolate for most of the year.

Faiz' poem 'City of Lights' (*Ai roshniyon ke shahr*)[49] from the collection *Book of Jail* (*Zindan-namah*, 1956) was written in 1952 in dramatic circumstances: in 1951, Faiz was arrested and sentenced to prison for participating in the so-called Rawalpindi Conspiracy Case. He served time in Sargodha, Karachi, and Montgomery (today Sahiwal) jails, as well as in Lahore Jail which was located in the Fort.

From his prison window, the poet looked out at the evening lights of Lahore, of which he had so many happy recollections:

> On each patch of green, from one shade to the next,
> the noon is erasing itself by wiping out all colour,
> becoming pale, desolation everywhere,
> the poison of exile painted on the walls.
> In the distance,
> there are terrible sorrows, like tides:
> they draw back, swell, become full, subside.
> They've turned the horizon to mist.
> And behind that mist is the city of lights,
> my city of many lights.
>
> How will I return to you, my city,
> where is the road to your lights? My hopes
> are in retreat, exhausted by these unlit, broken walls,
> and my heart, their leader, is in terrible doubt.
> But let all be well, my city, if under
> cover of darkness, in a final attack,
> my heart leads its reserves of longings
> and storms you tonight. Just tell all your lovers
> to turn the wicks of their lamps high
> so that I may find you, Oh, city,
> my city of many lights.[50]

In the Urdu original, Faiz compared the state of depression in prison with 'a dull wave of cheerless pain that looks like mist' (*kuhar kī sūrat be-raunaq dardon kī gadlī lahr*) and the 'poison of solitude that is licking the prison walls' (*dīvāron ko chāt rahā hai tanhā'ī kā zahr*). His inner despair was echoed by the bleak view from the window: 'Flaccid withered plants. Dull yellow noon' (*sabza sabza sūkh rahī hai phīkī zard dopahar*). The prisoner is lured by the 'City of Lights' (*roshnīyon kā shahr*) in the distance—a term that recurs in the poem like a refrain or spell. Even if one did not know where, and in what circumstances, the poem was written, the 'City of Lights' is a generally accepted name for Lahore, derived from the annual religious festival of *Mela-yi chiraghan* (Festival of Lights) which is celebrated here every year in honour of the Punjabi saints Shah Hussain and Madho Lal.

In the 'City of Lights', live beautiful women who wait for their lovers with burning lamps—including, most probably, the poet's beloved. However, he is unable to enter this city of love because of 'guards of passion' and 'gloomy walls of separation' (lit. *shahr-panāh* 'city wall')—euphemisms for real guards and fortress walls. As the lyric hero is unable to go to the City of Lights himself, the stream of his longings may well manage to enter it if the longings are sufficiently strong and unafraid to take the city by storm at night (*shabkhūn se munh pher na jāye irmānon kī rau*).

As we can note, Faiz gave no description of Lahore as such, not even in a laconic way—as Iqbal did in a few lines. However, the poetic image of a city that is illuminated by lights and populated by beautiful beloved women, and to which the poet's 'longings' go, was so precise and universal, from the emotional point of view, that it expressed the feelings of many despite its subjectivity. Later Urdu poets who wrote about Lahore after Faiz, such as Munir Niyazi and Kishwar Naheed. spoke, whether consciously or not, as Faiz did, about the city of love or beloved city that was the object of their desires.

Clearly, the images of Lahore, in the Urdu poems cited above, accent its *topophilia*, i.e., the profound emotional tie between the city and the poet's inner world. Poetic Lahore is a chorological concept that is not just an object of the poet's consciousness and imagination (like Indian toponyms in Kipling's poetry) but also acts as a subject that sets down certain parameters of the artistic image in the widest sense of the term. In Iqbal's poem, it is a leitmotif of co-belonging and cultural/historic memory that brings together time, society, and individual; for Faiz, it is an omnipresent theme of the City as a symbol of liberation and the abode of light, i.e., the city of one's dreams.

Courtyard, National College of Arts, Lahore.

CHAPTER **EIGHT**

Down the Cool Street

It would not be an overstatement to say that a single street has been the centre of cultural life in Lahore from the mid-nineteenth century on: the Mall Road,[1] which is made up of the Upper Mall and the Lower Mall. The name 'Mall Road' clearly refers to the city's colonial past, which is why the street has been re-named in honour of Pakistan's founder Muhammad 'Ali Jinnah—*Shahrah-e Quaid-i A'zam* (Avenue of Great Leader). However, in the vernacular, and especially among the lower classes, the avenue is still called Cool Street (*Thandi Sarak*). The Mall represents the triumph of the imperial style of architecture—a grand ensemble, the likes of which are only found in Calcutta and New Delhi, of buildings in the Neogothic, Neoclassical, Anglo-Indian, and 'Moorish' (Saracenic) styles.

The construction of the Mall began in 1851 when, following the annexation of the Punjab, the province was ruled by the British administrative council consisting of the brothers Henry and John Lawrence[2] and Charles Mansel.[3] At that time, General Charles Napier, Commander-in-Chief of the British Army in India,[4] visited Lahore. He ordered that the Cantonment be transferred from the Anarkali station, which was believed to be 'insalubrious', to the Mian-Mir area.[5]

Bosworth Smith, John Lawrence's biographer, wrote:

'One day, towards the end of his stay in Lahore, the three members of the Board and Montgomery,[6] who was the

Commissioner of the Lahore Division, happened to be taking their early morning ride together, when in the distance they saw the Commander-in-Chief [Sir Charles Napier] and his Staff similarly employed. "Let us go straight up to him," said Henry to John Lawrence, "and see if we cannot manage to get an answer out of him at last about the cantonments for Lahore." They did so. "You want to know where the cantonments are to be, do you?" said Sir Charles; "follow me then;" and, as he spoke, he dug his spurs into his horse and rode as hard as he could go, neck or nothing, across country some three or four miles. At last the old General reined in his horse in the middle of the plain, to all appearance at simple haphazard, and the last of the long pursuit came up, he cried out from the midst of the smoking steeds and breathless riders, "You asked me where the cantonments are to be; they are to be here." As ill luck would have it, he had pitched on a bit of ground which was particularly marshy and pestilential. But the word was spoken, and it was only by a stretch of authority that the Engineers employed to construct the cantonments managed to draw them back a little from a rather more to a rather less unhealthy spot. Such was the origin of the famous cantonments of Mean Meer!'[7]

The road leading from west to east, and connecting the old Cantonment in Anarkali with the new one in Mian-Mir, became the main street of the new Lahore. The Anarkali area, which begins right outside the Walled City, beyond Bhati Gate, was called the Lower Mall. The Lower Mall includes, among others, the Punjab Secretariat, the tomb of Jahangir's legendary beloved (described in Chapter 5), Government College, and the Chauburji Gate.

The future Mall was lined with waste grounds, dumps, and large plots of abandoned 'no man's land'—such was the general state of Lahore during the period of Sikh strife. In 1876, Thornton wrote:

'To the south of the city extends in a vast semicircle with a radius of some three or four miles, as uneven expanse interspersed with the crumbling remains of mosques,

tombs and gateways, and huge shapeless mounds of
rubbish from old brick kilns. Within the last few years
an immense change has taken place in this region, which
was utterly waste and desolate for a long time after the
annexation in 1849. Immense quantities of old bricks
have been removed and used in road making and as
ballast for the railways [...] while the European houses
and gardens in Donald Town,[8] the metalled roads
overshadowed by trees, and the vegetation consequent
on the introduction of irrigation, have transformed a part
of the artificial desert on this side of the city into a suburb
which reminded a recent French traveller of Enghien or
Passy, near Paris.'[9]

In the early nineteenth century, the building practices and techniques
of the Great Mughals were apparently irrevocably lost. The new
architecture of colonial cities seemed eclectic and bland—a second-
rate imitation of British metropolitan architecture. 'If the mercantile
classes of native society are distinguished by their conservative
adherence to ancestral usage, the landed gentry, who are on visiting
terms with European officials, cherish equally strong aspirations in
the opposite direction. To relieve the monotony of their eventless
life, many of them spend large sums of money every year in building,
and keep a native architect as a regular member of their domestic
establishment. But he is warned that nothing in the Indian style
can be tolerated; and some government office in the civil station, or
the latest new barracks in the nearest military cantonments, are the
palatial edifices which he is expected to emulate.'[10]

The architecture of the Mall provides vivid evidence of the priorities
of the English while building the new colonial Lahore: they built
public edifices that served the needs of education, public health, and
justice. This street had four educational institutions (three colleges
and one university), a hospital, two courts, two libraries, a museum,
an exhibition hall, and, of course, a church. Such public buildings
had no architectural precedents in the Indian tradition of urban
planning and design. For this reason, British architects constructed
them in the Neogothic, Neoclassical, and Baroque styles and then,
with the assistance of native architects (*mistri*), gave the buildings a

'Mughal' or 'Hindu' appearance by adding overhanging balconies, arched balustrades, openwork screens, and domed pavilions. Thus, the buildings of the Lahore Museum, High Court, and General Post Office were as 'Mughal' in style as the British Parliament in Westminster, which was built in the mid-nineteenth century, was 'Gothic'.

The official architecture of colonial India was a stage in the development of English, rather than Indian, architecture. Despite their magnificence and external similarity to native architecture, the pseudo-Mughal palaces on the Mall derived from the same trend of European Orientalism as the 'Chinese pagodas' in Kew Gardens and the 'Indian' Royal Pavilion in Brighton.

Nevertheless, just as during the Mughal period, colonial mainstream architecture did not do away with regional, provincial, and local architectural traditions (the so-called *desi*), whose patrons were 'the mercantile classes of native society'. The style in which the houses of rich Lahori tradesmen and businessmen were built, and decorated, came to be known as the 'Imperial vernacular', and differed greatly from the 'Anglo-Indian' style of public buildings.

These private houses, built in the late nineteenth and early twentieth centuries, were meant to demonstrate the financial standing and aesthetic 'self-awareness' of the native commercial and financial elite. They were simultaneously similar and dissimilar to colonial architecture. The 'similarity' lay in their monumentality and Western building techniques; the 'dissimilarity' in their traditional approach to architectural ornamentation and to the decoration of the tall and long façades—with numerous overhanging balconies, *jharoka* windows, openwork shutters, reliefs, pilasters, and balustrades—giving the façades a dynamic, curved, and 'sculptural' appearance. William Finch, who I have cited on numerous occasions in this book, wrote, as far back as the seventeenth century, about the high quality of stonework and woodwork on the famous Punjabi windows and doors: 'The buildings [in Lahore] are fair and high of brick, with much curious carvings about the doors and windows.'[11]

The old *hawelis* of Dhoni Chand, Jan Muhammad, Sir Ganga Ram,[12] Dayal Singh,[13] and Ghulam Rasul on the Upper Mall—which, today, are home to stores, offices, and restaurants—strike visitors with their Punjabi 'mannerisms'. The vivid imagination of the stonecutters turned cornices into twisting garlands of leaves and flowers, wall vases into gigantic lotus bulbs, and balustrades into interlaced writhing stalks. The naturalistic depiction of the traditional decorative elements of flowers and plants overshadow their architectural functionality, turning the buildings into enormous artefacts that showcase the virtuoso art of the craftsmen.

Still, the overall decline of national architecture, and of decorative and applied arts, led to the establishment of four schools of 'industrial arts'; their mission was to train Indian specialists in architectural design. The first school opened in 1850 in Madras, initially as a private educational establishment directed by Alexander Hunter. In 1854, a school of 'industrial arts' was founded in Calcutta. It adopted a broader approach by offering not only 'industrial' disciplines but also easel painting, lithography, and sculpture. In 1857, the J.J. School of Art opened in Bombay. Its alumni include several generations of outstanding artists of the Subcontinent. The school's name was an abbreviation of the name of its founder—the rich Parsee philanthropist and arts patron Jamshetji Jeejebhoy. It also offered classes in decorative art and architectural drawing. Before his transfer to Lahore, John Lockwood Kipling taught a class on architectural sculpture at the J.J. School of Art.

Finally, the Mayo School of Industrial Arts opened in Lahore in 1874. It was named after the Viceroy of India, Richard Bourke, the 6th Earl of Mayo (1822–1872). The Earl of Mayo was assassinated by a Pathan life-prisoner during a visit to the Andaman Islands, where convicts were imprisoned; in memory of the tragically killed viceroy, a large hospital, a park, and an arts school in Lahore bear his name. As has already been mentioned, John Lockwood Kipling was the school's first director.

In fact, the very term 'art', as it was applied in the Indian context by the British, seldom meant the higher or fine arts, but rather artifice, craftsmanship, manufacture, and industry. The latter's national traditions were greatly affected by the long-term competition with English goods and were in need of revival.

The main 'academic' disciplines that were taught at the Mayo School of Industrial Arts were architectural drawing and drafting; students who majored in drafting found jobs more easily than other graduates of the school. In spite of specialized classes in architecture, the school trained assistants rather than 'professional' architects:

> 'The students were drawn from the artisan classes, and the intention remained "the development and improvement of the indigenous arts of the Punjab, and the training of skilled assistants to meet the requirements of the Raj". Thus, the Architectural Classes proudly announced by the School in 1919 were in fact "founded to give students a thorough training in architectural draughtsmanship in order to qualify them to become Architectural Assistants".'[14]

The school's first alumni were the sons of caste artisans—stonecutters, blacksmiths, weavers, carpenters, and potters.

One of those hereditary craftsmen was the aforementioned Bhai Ram Singh,[15] a carpenter's son who rose to the position of the leading architect of Lahore and the director of the Mayo School of Industrial Arts. In the 1880s, John Lockwood Kipling and Bhai Ram Singh designed a new building for the school, next to the Museum. Both these edifices constitute a single ensemble in a pseudo-Mughal style; they are among the finest pieces of architecture on the Mall. The project engineers were Indians: Sir Ganga Ram and Rai Bahadur Kanhaya Lal.

Initially, the school had only six rooms, and housed the departments of drawing, design, woodcarving, and plaster modelling. The school subsequently expanded, acquiring modern equipment and building new workshops for printing, binding, pottery-making, woodworking, metalworking, weaving, carpet-making, etc. In 1958, the school was upgraded into the National College of Arts (NCA). The craft and industry oriented structure of the school, which had provided much-needed early nurturance to individuals pursuing diverse occupations, as carpenters, lacquer-workers, blacksmiths, goldsmiths, potters, architectural draftsmen, civil engineers and commercial artists, was updated and confined to three departments—Fine Arts, Design, and Architecture. In the late twentieth century, the college's programme incorporated new disciplines and areas of study, such as multimedia art, communications and cultural studies, theatre art, and advertising.

According to the NCA website,

> 'Lockwood Kipling's preoccupation with indigenous art and his effort to save its tradition from becoming polluted with a cheap imitation of British Victorian fashions set the tone of the Mayo School and later, of the college itself. Two great Pakistani painters, Abdur Rahman Chughtai and Shakir Ali, both associated with the College, were a kind of culmination of this inspiration. Chughtai represented the revival and development of the Mughal tradition while Shakir Ali constituted a link between the Pakistani sensibility and the world of international art.'[16]

Haji Muhammad Sharif, once the miniature painter at the court of the Maharaja of Patiala, gave a firm foundation to the teaching of the dying art of miniature. After him, Sheikh Shujaullah carried on the tradition of miniature painting, leaving behind, on his death, pupils like Bashir Ahmad who, today, is the prized representative of the art.

The entrance to the college's campus resembles a traditional high portal with a deep, arched passageway. The oldest building of the college is located immediately behind the entrance arch—the Kipling Block, which houses the administration. It is surrounded by a large inner courtyard, planted with old trees and a green lawn, with an elegant fountain designed by Bhai Ram Singh in the centre. A covered gallery—an architectural allusion to the traditional *riwaq*—runs along the inner façade of the Kipling Block, opening out into the courtyard. The college's workshops, lecture halls, studios, and auxiliary rooms are connected in the traditional style, by arched passageways and inner courtyards. The administrative building houses the famous Principal's Office, which has changed little since Kipling's day. It is a large spacious room with openwork shutters, and old portraits and artefacts on the walls; among these are the carved wooden doors, which have been a specialty of Punjabi craftsmen for centuries.

Near the College, as a reminder of a glorious past, stands a relic of the Mughal period—the *Baradari* of Wazir Khan, a rectangular two-storey white-marble pavilion with an impeccably designed façade. It was built by the Lahore governor after the completion of the famous mosque that bears his name (described in Chapter 3). The pavilion is decorated with mosaic panels on the façade, and elegant belvederes on four sides, along with traditional *chhajja* eaves and small cupolas. According to the *Shah Jahan Namah* by Saleh Kanbuh, when Wazir Khan had finished building his mosque in the Walled City, he turned his attention to the laying of a fine garden at this spot, which he adorned with the present edifice.[17] It was called the *Nakhliya Bagh* as it contained a large number of date trees (*nakhla*).

Similar to Anarkali's Tomb, the *Baradari* of Wazir Khan has served many functions over the years: it was a Sikh military warehouse, the barracks of the British Cantonment, a post and telegraph office, a museum, and finally became part of the Punjab Public Library, which it still houses today. 'A nobler aim it could not have served. The founder of the building was himself a patron of learning and a profound scholar, and the association of his name with an institution pregnant with such significant results for the rising generation of the Punjab may be regarded as a happy coincidence.'[18]

Although the Mall was designed and built on the commission of the British government, considerable financial support for its construction came from native industrialists and businessmen, including Sir Ganga Ram, a major philanthropist and a talented engineer. He was knighted for his outstanding contributions, and a monument to him was erected on the Mall. Saadat Hasan Manto, in one of his short stories, tells us about this monument during the Hindu-Muslim riots that accompanied the Partition: An inflamed mob in Lahore, after attacking a residential area,

> 'turned to attacking the statue of Sir Ganga Ram, the Hindu philanthropist. They first pelted the statue with stones; then smothered its face with coal tar. Then a man made a garland of old shoes and climbed up to put it round the neck of the statue. The police arrived and opened fire. Among the injured was the fellow with the garland of old shoes. As he fell, the mob shouted: "Let us rush him to Sir Ganga Ram Hospital!" How ironic!'[19]

Ganga Ram's statue was not the only monument on the Mall, which made this street unique in Lahore given the Islamic ban on sculptural effigies of people; no monuments were erected to the living or dead in the old city. As traditional religious prohibitions did not apply on the Mall, a monument to Lala Lajpat Rai (1865–1928), an outstanding champion of national independence also known as the second 'Lion of the Punjab'—the first being Ranjit Singh—used to stand near Zamzama. Lala Rajpat Rai was also a Hindu; his monument did not survive the Partition; it was dismantled and erected anew in the Indian town of Simla in 1948.

Across the street from the Museum and National College of Arts, next to the gate of Punjab University, stands a monument to Professor Alfred Woolner (1878–1936), as it did fifty years ago. He was vice-chancellor of the university from 1928 until his death. Professor Woolner was an authoritative Sanskrit scholar; some of his books have been re-edited and consulted by specialists to this day. Woolner's statue is the last surviving monument from the old Mall, demonstrating that the quiet fame of scholars can outlive the loud glory of rulers, generals, and politicians.

The British architect Basil Sullivan designed the arrangement of the Mall's main squares, roads, and junctions. The Mall was a wide avenue; its different parts were connected by open squares. Streets crossed the Mall at right angles, forming intersections. In contrast, the old residential neighbourhoods of Lahore were traditionally centred on bazaars, and organized, despite their chaotic arrangement, in a series of concentric circles rather than linearly. In 1902, at the junction of the Mall with Ferozpur Road (today Fatima Jinnah Avenue), Basil Sullivan designed the junction known as Charing Cross, named after a famous crossroads in London.[20] Charing Cross, being a depository of some of the finest architectural, historical, and cultural heritages is a showpiece of Lahore. It is apt to give a brief delineation of all the built features as they play a determining role in transforming a road junction into a meaningful enclosed space.

Charing Cross started assuming its architectural character with the erection of the 'dome shaped' British Pavilion, built to mark the Golden Jubilee of Queen Victoria, the first Empress of India (from 1876 to 1901). The pristine white marble pavilion was designed by Bhai Ram Singh. A bronze statue of the Queen, wearing her royal regalia and widow's veil, was cast in London by the British sculptor Edgar Mackennal in 1900, a year before the Queen's death. The statue remained there, as a symbol of British authority for over 50 years. In 1951, it was removed and taken, on a bullock cart, to rest in the basement of the Lahore Museum. A stone replica of the Holy Qu'ran replaced it. As proposed by Sullivan, after the remodelling of Charing Cross, the Pavilion was shifted to the centre of the space, dividing it into four sections.

Even after many years of the statue's removal, the area was commonly referred to, by rickshaw and taxi drivers, as '*malika-da-but*' ('royal idol' or Queen's statue). In its place, there now stands a model of the Holy Qu'ran, placed in an east-west direction (direction of *qibla*), mainly as a symbol of the Islamic State. When the prime minister of Pakistan, Zulfikar Ali Bhutto, decided to build a monument to commemorate the Second Islamic Summit in 1974, this important urban node was renamed Faisal Chowk, in homage to King Faisal of Saudi Arabia.

The contemporary Pakistani writer Bapsi Sidhwa wrote about the attitude of Lahore's inhabitants to the Queen's statue in her novel *Ice-Candy-Man* (1988):

> '[...] Ayah takes me up Queens Road, past the YWCA, past the Freemasons' Lodge, which she calls "The Ghost Club", and across the Mall to the Queen's statue in the park opposite the Assembly Chambers [...] Queen Victoria, cast in gunmetal, is majestic, massive, overpowering, ugly. Her statue imposes the English Raj in the park.'[21]

The Charing Cross' character, of an enclosed urban open space, was completed with the construction of two flanking buildings—Shah Din Manzil in 1914 and the Masonic Lodge in 1917. These identical imposing buildings brought much order into a disorderly collection of streets and illegible urban environment. The Shah Din Manzil was named after the first Muslim Judge of the Punjab Chief Court; the Masonic Lodge has been already mentioned in Chapter 7. After the 1970s the Masonic Lodge remained desolate for many years, as nobody had ever seen the entry or exit of any person or activity at the premises. Until that time, this building was commonly known as 'Jadoo Ghar' (house of magic or witchcraft). Coincidentally, both the

Masonic Lodge and Shah Din Manzil were restored for adaptive re-use as the Punjab Chief Minister's Secretariat in 2001, and the Alfalah Bank in 2005, respectively.[22] The architects need to be appreciated for restoring both without damaging their original character.

Today, the Queen's statue, which was removed from Charing Cross, takes up a separate hall in the Lahore Museum—because of its large size and the countless bronze folds of the dress. It is surrounded by busts of the Queen's sons, Edward VII and George V. Replacement of the statue of the Queen, by the model of the Holy Qu'ran, expresses an effort to shift the stamp of colonization to one of Islamization. However, some contemporary critics have condemned this act of removing the Queen's statue, and considered it an act of 'little taste and respect for the monuments and sculpture'.[23]

Nevertheless, the most heated conflicts took place around another statue—the monument to Sir John Lawrence which stood in front of the Lahore High Court, holding a sword in one hand and a pen in the other. This statue was created by Sir Edgar Boehm, and inaugurated in 1887. The monument had a paraphrased quotation by Lawrence inscribed on its pedestal; the words sounded quite provocative: 'By which will ye be governed—the pen or the sword?'[24] During the rise of the national liberation movement in the 1920s, demonstrations calling for the removal of the monument took place in the city. However, their participants managed to break the sword in the statue's hand only, while the monument itself, with its provocative motto, was not removed until 1951.

The British did not abandon the monument to their national hero; they moved it to Derry in Northern Ireland, where it was placed in Foyle College, where Lawrence had been a student. A second, and better known, monument to Lawrence is situated in London's Waterloo Place. Lawrence's memory was perpetuated in Lahore in another way: the Mall used to be called Lawrence Road until 1876. Later, Lawrence's name was given to another street (today, Liaquat Ali Khan Road) which passes by the Lawrence Gardens (today, *Bagh-e Jinnah*). Finally, the Neoclassical building, Lawrence Hall (today, Quaid-e 'Azam library), also stands on the Mall. Thus, as historical justice would have it, everything that formerly bore the name of the

British Governor-General in colonial Lahore now bears the name of the founder of Pakistan.

Another Governor-General of the Punjab, Donald McLeod, was considerably luckier than Lawrence. His monument stands on the Lower Mall, east of the Punjab Secretariat. The monument is not a statue but a marble obelisk with a cross on top placed on a square of red sandstone and surrounded by iron railings; this apparently explains why it did not attract attention and has survived to this day.

Today, a dense stream of cars moves down the Mall round the clock, making it unsuitable for strolling. However, in the nineteenth and first half of the twentieth centuries, the street was Lahore's main promenade, as it was lined on both sides by shady trees, was clean and well-kept (it was watered twice daily), and full of amusement establishment—cinemas, cafés, and restaurants. Cars were few in the city, and people moved about in hired cabs (*tonga* and *ekka*),[25] rode bicycles, and strolled on foot.

Intizar Hussain described the life of the Mall in his essay *Thandi Sarak*:

> 'The Mall in those days, say the fifties and early sixties, was a peaceful road suitable for strolling. It was better known as "Thandi Sarak" or "Cool Street". The noisy scooter and the equally noisy rickshaw had not yet made their appearance. There were very few motor cars to be seen and, because of the slow traffic of cycles and tongas, they were not able to speed or otherwise disturb the peace on the Mall. [...] Cycles, because of their sheer abundance, appeared to rule the road. A ladies' cycle had a charm of its own—and in the early hours the Mall appeared to be flooded with girls cycling to Government College and the Punjab University. [...] The pervasive quite and sparse traffic on the Mall encouraged the gentlefolk living nearby to take advantage of the "Thandi Sarak" and come out of their houses for an evening walk. Every evening, Professor Siraj,[26] accompanied by his wife, would emerge enthusiastically from the gates of the Principal's House and walk swiftly along the footpath that accompanied the road, all the way to the Bagh-e-Jinnah Gardens. He

would be followed equally energetically by Mrs. Siraj, who somehow managed to keep up with his pace. In fact, a number of gentlemen were seen to appear on the Mall at an appointed hour with the punctuality of clocks. Maulana Salahuddin Ahmad, editor *Adabi Duniya*, left his office (situated near Regal Cinema) exactly at noon. Twirling a stick, elegantly attired in tie, suit and hat— even in the scorching heat of May and June—he could be seen walking towards Old Anarkali, where his friends […] sat waiting for him in the Nagina Bakery.'[27]

So, let us follow Professor Siraj and his wife down the Mall, eastwards from Charing Cross where the Lawrence Gardens stretch behind a red brick wall. They are adjoined by the city's zoo (*Chirya Ghar*) and a botanical garden. During the Sikh rule, the land occupied by them was a desolate wilderness. These plots of land were later bought by the Lahore municipality. When inaugurated in 1862, Lawrence Gardens covered an area of 112 acres; 600 varieties of trees and shrubs were brought there from all over the world. The head gardener of Kew Gardens in London was invited to teach the native gardeners (*mali*) how to care for British-style landscape gardens.

The Lawrence Gardens were open to both Europeans and the native elite, and offered different Western amusements: badminton, archery, tennis courts, and a unique cricket field for which turf was brought directly from England. However, the main entertainment in the Gardens was listening to music in the open air: the Lahore Police Band played there twice a week. There were two artificial mounds in the gardens; as with all elevated places in the city, they were made up of the remains of building waste and broken bricks. The mounds were turned into terrace gardens; in the evenings, people sat on platforms on top of the mounds and listened to the dashing British marches.

Among the shady trees and luxuriant shrubs stand two white two-storey buildings connected by a covered passageway: Lawrence Hall and Montgomery Hall. The former was named, as I have already mentioned, after Viceroy John Lawrence, and the latter after Sir Robert Montgomery. Both buildings were constructed in 1861–1866 in the Neoclassical style (or 'frigidly classical', to cite Kipling).[28] They are typical British countryside villas, with Doric columns and triangular pediments; one can see their likes in aristocratic suburbs of the nineteenth and early twentieth century London, such as Kenwood or Twickenham.

It was no coincidence that the British architects Stone and Gordon turned to purely English models: Lawrence Hall in the Georgian style, and Montgomery Hall in the Regency style, were built soon after the Indian Rebellion of 1857. Although the British put down the revolt, it shook their absolute certitude about the situation in India; so, it became necessary to return to a 'frigidly classical' style to regain a position of power and authority in architecture as well as in other domains. Such buildings, without any native elements, seem to have been transplanted from Great Britain to India. They were built by the East India Company in the first half of the nineteenth century in Calcutta, Simla, Lucknow, Kanpur, and other Indian cities.

Lawrence Hall was built on the donations of the European community in India, while money for the construction of Montgomery Hall was raised (most likely, in a compulsory fashion) from among the conquered chiefs of the Sikh clans. Both buildings became centres of public and cultural life in colonial Lahore. Meetings, conventions, concerts, and theatrical productions took place at Lawrence Hall. With its floors made of hard polished *deodar* wood, Montgomery Hall was used for balls and Christmas receptions. In the late nineteenth century, the Gymkhana Club (from Anglo-Indian *gymkhana* 'sports ground'), the most elite club in Lahore that was reserved exclusively for Englishmen, opened in Lawrence Hall.

Colonel Goulding wrote, about Lahore, in the second half of the nineteenth century:

> 'In those days, this was the only public building available for concerts or other entertainments […] Touring theatrical companies were unknown, but Dav. Carson and his famous troupe of Christy Minstrels were regular and welcome visitors every cold season, and never failed to draw crowded audiences to their entertainments in the Lawrence Hall. […] Anything resembling the modern "variety" entertainment was quite unknown until the end of the sixties when a touring combination known as the Star Company included Lahore in their itinerary.

They performed, of course, in the Lawrence Hall and their programme included instrumental and vocal music, songs in character, dances, etc. This company shared with Carson the credit for the earliest endeavours to make a "brighter Lahore." Other early visitors were the famous party of dwarfs [...] and a strong company of Japanese, the novelty of whose balancing and conjuring feats proved most attractive. In later years Carson was succeeded by the well-known Hudson's Surprise Party which combined Christy Minstrel items with ballad singing and music-hall turns. [...] About 45 years ago, a "strong man" who described himself as "The Great Spanish Mushroom" [he apparently wore a large hat resembling a sombrero—*A.S.*], gave a performance in the Lawrence Hall. One of his feats of strength consisted of hanging by his toes from a trapeze and firing off small cannon which was suspended from cords held in his hands. When the explosion came, every light was extinguished, numerous panes of glass were shattered, and large pieces of stucco moulding fell from the roof. The rapidity with which the audience made their way out of the only exit was astonishing and the comments of the *Civil and Military Gazette* reporter, who had been dozing comfortably in the front row, were unfit for publication.'[29]

Fifty years later, Lawrence Gardens and the villas inside it continued to attract city dwellers and excite their curiosity. 'Now I take my cousins to my favourite haunt, the beautifully laid out Lawrence Gardens with their tall majestic trees, some of them brought from England, and rows of colourful sweet-smelling flower-beds,' wrote Pran Nevile about the Lahore of the 1930s,

We take a ride round the picturesque cricket grounds, the venue of international Test matches. My cousins are delighted at the sight of a hillock full of flowers, shrubs and plants in the centre of the gardens. Next, I take them to the Open Air Theatre, built in the style of a Roman amphitheatre where amateur artists hold concerts and plays in its picturesque surroundings. From there we go around the hillock and seat ourselves on a bench from where we have a glorious view of the gardens and the Montgomery Hall housing the Gymkhana Club, a symbol of British prestige and an exclusive meeting place for the sahibs and memsahibs. No natives are permitted to enter this august building. Through the glass windows of its gaily decorated ball-room one can occasionally hear the band or catch faint reflection of the dancing couples. [...] In another part of the gardens is located the Cosmopolitan Club, a meeting place for the upcoming westernized native elite who take pride in aping the rulers and behave like brown sahibs. My country cousins are stunned to see a couple of ladies in saris playing tennis in the club's courts'[30]

On the other side of the Mall, across the Lawrence Gardens, Nedou's Hotel—the best European-class hotel in Lahore—was built on the site where the Avari Hotel is situated today. In 1876, Kipling and Thornton noted that, 'The hotels in Lahore are poor, though there is little doubt that a really good hotel would pay, owing to the large influx of travelers at certain seasons of the year.'[31] Goulding, commenting on this observation, wrote, 'The demand for such accommodation grew sufficient to ensure the success of an up-to-date hotel on a large scale, such as Mr. Nedou established some years later on the Upper Mall.'[32] Officers and civil servants visiting Lahore on business preferred to stay in traditional 'postal premises' (Dak Bungalows), one of which was located in Anarkali and the other in the Shalimar Gardens. The latter bungalow was often leased by newlyweds on honeymoon. While the Dak Bungalows were simply furnished, the service was excellent; the attendants had been schooled by military clients.

A 1940 postcard shows the imposing building of Nedou's Hotel, built in the Anglo-Indian style and marked by the influence of caravanserais: a long building with a high pediment and a multitude of arched openings. It was considered to be the best hotel in town and was highly recommended to clients by the famous Cook & Son agency. Travellers going to Lahore could buy Indian Hotel Coupons at Cook's, using them to pay for their stay at the selected hotels. In 1910, a coupon worth seven rupees covered the following services:

Bedroom, lights and service, with bath
Chota hazri, or early tea with toast
Burra hazri, or meat breakfast
Tiffin or lunch
Dinner.[33]

Curiously enough, the word *hāzrī* originally meant a ritual offering of food to a saint, or a funeral feast sent to the household of the deceased. Yet, the status of the Englishmen apparently put them somewhere between saints and the dead as their breakfast was also called *hāzrī*. In 1930, the same services cost 10–11 rupees a day, with special rebates for travelling businessmen, making it the most expensive hotel in town. The Nedou's Hotel was demolished to give way to the present Avari Hotel. For the purposes of historical comparison, a standard single room in the Avari Hotel cost seventeen thousand rupees per night in 2010.

While colonial Lahore could boast of few good hotels, and things have changed little since, its true pride was its clubs—where Englishmen traditionally spent their free time. At that time, the city had only four hotels yet nine clubs, some of which specialized in sports (Gymkhana and Commercial Gymkhana), horse races (Race Club), ballooning (Northern India Flying Club), etc. The Punjab Club, made famous by Rudyard Kipling, was located in a magnificent Neoclassical (Palladian) building across from Lawrence Gardens. There, in the course of conversation over a glass of sherry with army officers, engineers, military doctors, and army chaplains, Kipling gathered remarkable life incidents, silly anecdotes, confidential confessions, secret messages, and outright lies that formed the basis of his Indian short stories.

Today, the building of the Punjab Club is occupied by the Pakistan Administrative Staff College; the club has been moved to a smaller building, surrounded by English lawns, on Danepur Road. Its managers re-created all the interiors of the old club and maintained the atmosphere of British respect for privacy. The Punjab Club is one of the quietest places in a noisy and boisterous Lahore: visitors speak in low voices, waiters move noiselessly, and no music plays—the only sounds are the rustle of newspapers in the library and the melodious tinkling of crystal in the dining room.

When the Sikhs made Lahore their capital, they did not treat the Muslim architecture with respect, turning tombs into residences (defiling them in the process), putting guns on mosque minarets and converting them into arsenals, and stripping the buildings of their marble facing (I have spoken about 'Sikh barbarity' on numerous occasions in this book). Nevertheless, the Sikhs constructed buildings on old, and already built-up, sites that had been hallowed by the legacy of the Great Mughals. In addition, the Sikhs used Mughal building materials and imitated their architectural style, even if they vulgarized it in the process.

Although Ranjit Singh was ill-inclined towards both the Mughals and Islam in general, he considered himself to be the lawful successor to the authority that the Mughal dynasty embodied in the eyes of Indians. When he inherited power, he also inherited the space of power. He built his residence in the fort of Shahi Qila, as a continuation of the Shish Mahal, and constructed the marble pavilion of Hazuri Bagh for court receptions (*darbars*) on the site of Aurangzeb's Abdar-Khana, which lay before the entrance to the imperial mosque next to the imperial Roshnai Gate. The tombs (*samadhi*) of Ranjit Singh and Guru Arjun Dev are also located opposite the gates of the Shahi Qila, and adjoin the Badshahi Masjid.

The residences of Ranjit Singh's courtiers and successors were built exclusively within the *Anderoon Shehr*: examples are the *haweli* of Nau Nihal Singh, next to the Mori Gate, and the complex of restored buildings called the *Choona Mandi Haweli* that belonged to the Sikh court superintendent Raja Dhyan Singh and the Sikh general Khushal Singh. In other words, the chorological ideas of the Mughals and Sikhs largely coincided despite their religious and political differences: the 'accentuated points' on their 'mental maps' of Lahore are located along roughly the same lines.

The English were totally different: they distanced themselves in every possible way from the cultural and historical heritage of their colonies, and transported the British spirit and taste with them. They did not take the Indians' former glory, values, and priorities seriously, although they meticulously studied them. That is why the English always built their cities, cantonments, and civil lanes in India at new sites, that were not encumbered by historical or chorological memory or the proximity to native architecture. Although the Indians even called the East Indian Company, in accordance with traditional nomenclature, *Kumpani Bahadur*, the English, in their turn, didn't want to follow the native traditions in any respect, including city planning. So, they built their Lahore on waste ground and undeveloped land.

Moreover, an Englishman's ideal house in India was a detached bungalow in a large garden or on a lawn behind a wall, such as Colonel Creighton's house in *Kim*—it was impossible to build such residences in densely crowded urban quarters. For the English, it was not simply a matter of security and of striving to set up a 'sanitary zone': for their 'insular' mentality, the feeling of home required a territorially isolated residence, one's own 'fragment' of living nature in the form of a garden, and a lifestyle that would be hidden from the eyes of others—in a word, the same 'privacy' that is unattainable in Asian cities, where life takes place in the streets before all of society.

During the period of consolidation of Islam in the Subcontinent, i.e., during the Delhi Sultanate, Muslim architects built the first mosques out of the fragments and columns of Hindu temples—for example, the famous mosques *Quwwat ul-Islam* in Delhi and *Adhai-din-ka-jhonpra* in Ajmer. The Sikhs, who came to power after the Muslims in the Punjab, turned mosques into *gurdwaras* and used Muslim building materials, technologies, and 'architectural glossary'— arches, cupolas, and entrances porticos. In contrast, the English built their living space anew outside the walls of the densely settled cities, using European models and technologies; the functional conversion of old buildings (such as the transformation of Anarkali's Tomb into a parish church) was more an exception to the rule.

Another 'exception to the rule' is situated on the same stretch of the Upper Mall that I have been describing all this time: the Governor's House, which stands behind a high brick wall across from Lawrence Hall. This official residence of all Governor-Generals of the Punjab, from Robert Montgomery on, was built around a tomb dating from Shah Jahan's time. The engineer and Lahore historian Kanhaya Lal considered it to be the tomb of Saint Sayyid Badruddin Jilani. Yet, according to Latif's more generally accepted view, it contained the remains of Muhammad Qasim Khan, Emperor Akbar's maternal cousin.

Muhammad Qasim Khan died at a very advanced age, greatly outliving his cousin Akbar and nephew Jahangir. During the reign of Shah Jahan, he was considered the oldest representative of the ruling dynasty. Qasim Khan's longevity may have stemmed from his love of sports: he was said to be an invincible wrestler (*kushtibaz*) and a generous patron of the sport. He inhabited an entire *mohalla* in the Mozang quarter (to the west of the present-day Mall) with wrestlers. Before the arrival of the British, Qasim Khan's tomb was called the Wrestler's Dome (*Gumbaz-e kushtiwala*).

The Sikhs, as was their custom, used the tomb to their own ends. It was converted into the residence of *jamadar* Khushal Singh, and barracks for his soldiers were built in the vast garden around the tomb. The English bought the building and surrounding territory from Khushal Singh's descendants and began to reconstruct or, more precisely, enlarge the tomb with countless new annexes until it turned into Government House. Latif, who always approved of British experiments with native architecture, wrote, 'The interior of the dome is now used as the dining-room, and a very admirable dining-room it makes. The arches around it serve as recesses for side-boards, the room being lighted through slits in the dome. The walls are decorated with enamelled pottery-work, and the alcoves of the central hall are embellished with fresco designs.'[34]

Up to the late nineteenth century, the site of Government House was isolated and disconnected from the city's infrastructure, possibly for the sake of security. In the 1880s, the American painter Edwin Lord Weeks visited Lahore and was struck by the howling jackals in the garden of Government House: 'Government House, the seat of the Lieutenant Governor of the Punjab, stands in attractive grounds near the fine park known as Lawrence Gardens, on the outskirts of the civil station. The flower-beds and the parterres which adorn the public and private grounds in this neighbourhood are more luxuriant and varied than the winter gardens of the Riviera. In the early morning, as well as at night, they are much frequented by jackals, which show their appreciation of them by trotting about in couples through the shrubbery. An open-air fete has been held in one of these gardens in the afternoon, and when the last guests had departed, many of them in furs and ulsters, and while we were standing before the chimney fire within, the conversation was interrupted by the howls of a band of these nocturnal ramblers just outside the doors.'[35]

In 1905, Government House was restored and expanded on the occasion of the visit of the Prince and Princess of Wales (the future King George V and Queen Mary). Craftsmen from the Mayo School of Arts replaced the marble floors with teak parquet, refurbished the frescoes with oil paints, and replaced the woodcarving with plaster moulding. All in all, not a trace remained of the Mughal interior. Nevertheless, even in its new form, the building continued to be uncomfortable to live in, as if it retained the memory of its original funerary function. Select British travellers to Lahore, who paid a visit to the Governor, complained about the dark and stuffy residence, the small rooms, the steep stairs, the poor acoustics in the ballroom, etc.

A northern wing, with a big reception room (Durbar Hall), was adjoined to the building by Basil Sullivan in 1915. He also designed the building's exterior decorations, with numerous moulded corbels in the Neoclassical style. At the same time, the wall surrounding Government House was adorned with two carved iron gates made by native blacksmiths.

Today, the Mall continues to be a centre of power and authority in the city's chorology; most of the public buildings have the same functions as they did 150 years ago: the hospital is still a hospital, the court is still a court, and educational institutions have become even more numerous. Of course, new buildings have also appeared on the Mall; they were built by new generations of architects, who were influenced by Bauhaus,[36] Le Corbusier, and Frank Lloyd Wright.[37]

One of the best-known buildings is WAPDA House (an abbreviation of Water and Power Development Authority), built by the American architect Edward Durell Stone.[38] It has been described as 'A parody on a Victorian imitation of a Mughal imitation of a Gujrati pavilion. Buildings like the WAPDA House in Lahore are responsible for the notion that architecture is a luxury we can best do without.'[39] Another contemporary building on the Mall is the Alhamra Arts Council, built by the Pakistani architect Nayyar 'Ali Dada.[40] Winner of the Aga Khan Award for Architecture, the Alhamra Arts Council resembles a truncated pyramid of red planes or slabs coming together at obtuse angles.

The *topophilia* of the Mall is more contradictory than the chorological parameters of the Walled City. On the one hand, the 'Cool Street' is a living reminder of the city's colonial past, associated with the debasement of the national dignity of its inhabitants. On the other, it is an object for national pride, of these same inhabitants, an architectural symbol of the development of the institutes of democracy, a ceremonial façade, and evidence of metropolitan status. Historical cataclysms and geopolitical transformations, which made Lahore a Pakistani city from being an Indian one, and a predominantly Muslim city instead of a multi-religious centre, have had little impact on the overall atmosphere of the Mall. The concentration of 'key' buildings is still very high, and the 'gesture' of power and authority, as expressed through architecture, is still extremely expressive. The Mall today is an intermediary, or transitory, zone that spatially and historically connects the medieval feudal city with the modern megalopolis.

Naulakha pavilion, Lahore fort.

EPILOGUE

Lahore vs. Lucknow

Topophilia is a cognitive category and a phenomenon of consciousness; yet, its sources lie in the emotional sphere. The intuitive feeling of our identity, and of our belonging to a given place, becomes a fact of our consciousness that we acquire through certain cognitive efforts, yet the feeling remains a feeling. It is the locus where the 'eidetic reduction' of the intuitive and subjective, and the transition to the sphere of 'refined consciousness', take place, constituting the essence of the phenomenological mechanism. *Topophilia* is, simultaneously, an object of consciousness and a phenomenon of the *Lebenswelt*, i.e., a product of the emotional sphere that is intrinsically connected to all the senses.

The cultural and geographic image of Lahore is, above all, a visual image: our vision focuses on city landscapes, architectural forms and volumes, the dynamic rhythm of domes, minarets, and arcades, and the bright light and vivid colours of the natural surroundings. Our hearing perceives the calls of the *azan*, the monotonous sounds of prayer, the typical noises of bazaars, the cries of hawkers, the roulade of street singers and, finally, the melody of languages (Urdu and Punjabi) characteristic of this city.

Smell, the most reliable witness, instantly recognizes the aromas of seasonings, the spicy smell of foods, and the fragrance of rose oil that mingles with fresh fruit scents or the 'Asian stench'. The role played by taste, in creating the cultural and geographic image of a city,

was described in detail in the chapter on the Lahoris' eating habits;
one cannot get a true idea of Lahore without the taste sensations—
the Rabelaisian abundance of fried meat, thick sauces, freshly baked
bread, and sugary sweets.

Finally, touch provides evidence of prickly Lahore dust that covers
the skin during the dry winter season; the sticky humidity of the
barsat; garden freshness that caresses the face; and burning heat or
icy cold (depending on the season) under one's feet, as the floors are
made of stone everywhere (in mosques, tombs, and private homes)
and it is the custom to take off one's shoes.

Still, one may ask: does the *topophilia* of Lahore differ from
the *topophilia* of other Muslim cities in South Asia, where one
sees the same domes, minarets, and arcades; where similar sounds
and noises are heard; and where the nose senses the same eternal
contrasts between aroma and stench? In this respect, one should
compare Lahore with Delhi or Agra, yet such studies have already
been published. Let us turn to a comparison between Lahore and
Lucknow. Such a comparison is apt: Lahore and Lucknow are major
cities that lie in the same geopolitical space, i.e., in the northern part
of the Indian Subcontinent—Lahore in the north-west and Lucknow
in the north-east. Up until 1947, they were part of a single state:
undivided India.

There are similarities, too, between the legendary origins of these
cities and the etiology of their names. Lahore was founded, according
to tradition, by Lava, son of the god Rama; the legendary founder of
Lucknow was Rama's brother Lakshman. These mythical and epical
heroes are their respective cities' eponyms. Ancient Lahore began
with the Fort of Lava—*Lav-kot*; Lucknow originated around Hill of
Lakshman—*Lachman Tila*. Lahore subsequently developed, according
to the principles of the compact settlement of different trade and
vocational groups, around specialized bazaars (*mandi*). Lucknow was
similarly settled by caste groups that clustered around the market
squares (*ganj*).

During the historical period up to the ninth-tenth centuries,
both cities were ruled by Hindu dynasties: Lahore was subordinated
to the Rajput clan of the Chauhans, and Lucknow was part of the
Hindu principality of Kannauj. In the eleventh century, Lahore and

Kannauj, with Lucknow, were conquered by Mahmud Ghaznavi, which led to the rise of Lahore and the decline of Lucknow. In the late twelfth century, both cities were conquered by Sultan Qutub-ud-Din Aibak and became part of the Delhi Sultanate. Finally, both cities became part of the emerging Mughal Empire in the sixteenth century: Lahore in 1526 under Babur, and Lucknow soon afterwards (in 1555) under Humayun.

Nevertheless, the external similarity of historical development says little about the true role of these cities during the medieval period. Lahore was a capital city for many centuries (first of the Ghaznavids, then of the Mughals, and finally of the Sikhs), a major geopolitical and cultural centre, a crossroads for migratory flows, the first 'trophy' of foreign conquerors, and an outpost on the road to the rest of the Subcontinent. It is described, at length, in Muslim historical works; the sixteenth and seventeenth centuries were its heyday.

In contrast, Lucknow was virtually unknown until the early eighteenth century: it was medieval backcountry, and a small provincial town, that was occasionally mentioned in Mughal chronicles as a centre for one of the five territorial districts of the province (*suba*) of Awadh.

In the first half of the eighteenth century, the situation changed completely: the power of the Great Mughals began to decline and, in this context, the *Nawab-Wazirs* who ruled Awadh declared it to be an independent principality with its capital first in Faizabad and then in Lucknow. Lucknow rose politically, and developed economically, turning into a rich and flourishing city with magnificent architecture. In the context of the decline and destruction of imperial Delhi, it became the main haven for the intelligentsia from the capital, and a centre for Muslim culture and Urdu poetry, up until the British annexation of 1856. Thus, the heyday of Lucknow was the eighteenth and the first half of the nineteenth century.

During this time, Lahore underwent difficult tribulations: Sikhs and Afghans fought over the city, turning it into ruins, until Ranjit Singh came to power in 1798 and created an independent Sikh state. In 1849, Sikh rule ended, and Lahore and all of the Punjab became British. In other words, the periods of the rise and fall of Lahore and Lucknow were not synchronous: when the former flourished, the latter lay in obscurity; when the latter expanded, the former was in ruins.

Lahore was the capital of different, predominantly Muslim, states for a long time. It is still the cultural capital of Pakistan today. Thus, Lahore does not suffer from the inferiority complex of a 'former capital'. As for Lucknow, it was the capital of a Muslim principality for a short time—a little over a century. Today, it is the capital of a large state with a predominantly Hindu population, which most likely explains why its old city is marked by a deep feeling of provincialism and nostalgia for bygone (i.e., 'Muslim') glory. When I wrote my book about Lucknow, I did not yet know anything about 'humanistic geography', *psychogeography*, and *topophilia*. Nevertheless, the very notion of 'nostalgia', which was a cornerstone of my understanding and study of Lucknow, is a phenomenological concept as it lies at the intersection of the emotional and cognitive spheres.

The *Nawab-Wazirs* who ruled Lucknow were Shias, and the city was Shia in architecture, culture, and ritual during its golden age. Lahore was ruled by Sunni dynasties, and Sunnis always predominated there. This difference had an impact on the architecture of the two cities: while the chorology of Lahore stretches, as I mentioned above, between mosque and tomb, the cultural space of Lucknow is dominated by the *imambara*, a Shia religious building for the commemoration of the martyrs, and the royal palace (the *Nawabs* of Awadh proclaimed themselves kings from 1819 on). This does not mean that Lucknow lacks saints' tombs and rulers' mausoleums; simply that they play a less important role in the city's chorological system than in Lahore.

Lahore is a Mughal imperial city that was part of the Great Mughal Empire for three centuries. Like Delhi and Agra, it is marked by the elegant and refined style of the Mughal architecture, landscape design, and Persian-language literature. The characteristic features of the Lahore style are classicism, continuation of the general Timurid heritage, monumentality, and universality. It also accounts for the city's metropolitan and, to a large extent, cosmopolitan lifestyle.

As the capital of Awadh, Lucknow developed in constant opposition to Mughal Delhi, and its cultural values took shape as a stubborn rejection of Delhi authority and superiority. Rejecting the Mughal heritage, Lucknow created its own 'Grand Style'—the *Lakhnawiyat*—that may be called the Indian version of the Baroque style. All spheres of culture and human life were subordinated to it and, in particular, Lucknow's pretentiousness and mannerism (*takalluf*) that sometimes verges on the grotesque. Nevertheless, despite all its aesthetic novelty and high artistic merit, the *Lakhnawiyat* has always been a regional and provincial style (*desi*) in the dimensions of the Indian Subcontinent.

Nevertheless, as the reader will recall, Mughal Lahore also had its own *desi* component (the famous 'Lahore school' of architecture, painting, and decorative and applied arts). What is the difference? As a style, the *Lakhawiyat* drew its ideas, images, and means of expression from three sources: the Hindu-Muslim, the early Indian, and the Western European traditions, of which the latter got evident priority. The resulting eclecticism resembled the European Baroque style, with its grandiose spirituality and purely material excessiveness of form and decoration.

The Lahore regional style had totally different origins. In it, an ethnic Punjabi substrate shines through the Mughal aesthetic canons, artistic models, and building techniques. This is a totally different process than the *Lakhnawiyat* method of assimilating and transforming European elements. Generally speaking, it is this ethnic Punjabi component that makes Lahore's *topophilia* stand out and differentiates it from the chorological models of Lucknow, Hyderabad (Deccan), Peshawar, or Hyderabad (Sind), i.e., the old Muslim cities of the Subcontinent with their own ethnic substrates.

Nevertheless, all the aforementioned historical and cultural differences notwithstanding, Lahore and Lucknow have something in common: the nature of emotional ties between the inhabitants and their city. Residents of Lahore and Lucknow have always treated their cities as exceptionally valuable places without compare and objects of personal affinity and pride, of which a lot of evidence has come down to us in language and literature. For example, in our day, the inhabitants of Lahore have invented the homonym 'city of Love' that is a wordplay on the English 'city of Luv (epic Lava)'. Personifying the city, giving it many flattering epithets, according it lofty individual qualities, and creating city legends at every occasion and with respect to every cultural and geographic object—in a word, constantly mythologizing the urban image—is typical of both Lahoris and Lucknawis.

This also explains the evident similarities between the Lahore and Lucknow lifestyles: the combination of religiousness that can verge on fanaticism with hedonism that borders on dissoluteness; the unbridled passion for spectacles, celebrations, fairs, and strolling; the love of poetry and poetic contests; and the ideology of the *homo ludens*, and the attitude towards the city as a zone of amusement. Lucknawis may well have outdone Lahoris in the latter.

Lucknow is the birthplace of Urdu-language theatre, which appeared there in the early nineteenth century. An apotheosis of spectacle and entertainment, it is a non-traditional art form in Muslim society. Cock and animal fights, and other lowbrow amusements, flourished in Lucknow. Moreover, Lucknow's residents were proud of their famous *tawaif* courtesans and considered the Chowk red-light area to be one of the city's main attractions. In contrast, Lahoris had a more reserved and critical attitude towards their Shahi Mohalla. At the same time, kite flying became a favourite pastime and a real art form both in Lahore and Lucknow, which Lahoris turned into a national celebration.

The cultural and geographic image of Lahore and its *topophilia* arose as a palimpsest, as shown by numerous written and oral sources cited in this book, including accounts by court chroniclers and European travellers, poetic chronograms of the dates of construction of architectural monuments, sayings and proverbs, city legends, memoirs, works of fiction, studies by modern scholars, and official documents. Many of these sources contradict each other: what thrilled Indians and Pakistanis often evoked the irritation and censure of their Western contemporaries, whose views were also not homogeneous.

One could say that every new generation of authors writing about Lahore partially 'effaced' the accounts of their predecessors and created an image of the city 'over' the existing one. Nevertheless, the contours of the old depiction continued to stand out in the new image. In this way, one can hear, in Iqbal's laconic image of Lahore, the accounts of Mughal chroniclers, while Faiz' romantic metaphor of the 'City of Lights' contains echoes of the Punjab poetic tradition derived from Shah Hussain. The goal of my book was to restore, and bring to the surface, all the faded and effaced lines and colours that the people of the different periods and cultures have used to depict Lahore, i.e., to re-create the *topophilia* of the city in a historic retrospective.

My personal 'relations' with Lucknow and Lahore formed in different ways. For many years, my professional work—literary and theatre studies, translation, etc.—were connected in one or another way with Lucknow. When I first visited the city in 1984, I already had a 'mental map' of it; my living first-hand impressions drew upon my 'cultural experience', i.e., upon the recognition of the familiar. Here, I followed in the steps of Proust, who had read John Ruskin's *The Stones of Venice* and passionately fallen in love with the city long before he saw it with his own eyes.

In contrast, my notions of Lahore were very vague and based on associations with the Mughal capitals of Delhi and Agra. For this reason, my first encounter with this city in 1997 was a strong and direct experience that stirred up my fantasy and kindled the desire, not only to know Lahore better, but also to fall in love with it. This is precisely what happened when my thirst for new impressions was backed up by my professional interests, which were centred on the National College of Arts.

Generally speaking, the love for 'other' cities, in which we were not born and where we do not have friends and relatives, ultimately depends on our ability to imagine ourselves as residents of these cities, i.e., on the power of our imagination. If our imagination suggests to us that we could be happy in this foreign city, the latter, together with all its streets, squares, mosques or churches, colours, and sounds, immediately sails into the harbour of our consciousness.

In *psychogeography*, the term 'dreamland city' refers to a city which is not ours yet but with which we connect our individual and professional self-realization for one reason or other. Thus, no matter what the 'dreamland city' is like in reality, we experience it as an ideal and as an object of constant reflection. For Western people, such spaces of desire include Jerusalem, Rome, Paris, Venice, London, and New York.

I have already mentioned that *topophilia* is a given and an element of the *Lebenswelt*. In this aspect, as a feeling of home and a sensation of belonging to one's native city and one's own identity, it is experienced by all people. *Topophilia* has always been expressed in the language of art, and artistic images, by writers and artists. Yet, there is another category of people for whom *topophilia* is connected to their professional or, more precisely, scholarly activity—Asian scholars.

No matter what Asian scholars study—Persian Sufism, Japanese theatre, Malay classical literature, or Cantonese dialect—the subject of their research is geographically localized in certain cities. In the process of the laborious study of languages, the decryption of cultural codes, field and office research, and the emergence of professional and friendly ties, these cities become closely familiar to our consciousness. In these territories, domesticated by knowledge and converted from magical far-away lands into imaginary homelands, we often experience the fullness and vigour of real life that we lack in our everyday routine at home. Herein, the true triumph of *topophilia* is manifested.

NOTES

Chapter 1: On *Topophilia*

1. Yi-Fu Tuan, *Topophilia: A Study of Environmental Perception, Attitudes, and Values*, Englewood Cliffs, NJ: Prentice-Hall, 1974.
2. Ibid., p. 4.
3. http://docs4.chomikuj.pl/62336211,0,0,Husserl,-Edmund.
4. The *horizon* is a phenomenological term or metaphor that refers to an essential aspect of every intentional experience. The horizon assures the connectedness of the stream of consciousness. The meaning constituted by consciousness is only apparent through the interpretation of horizons.
5. Bachelard, Gaston, *La Poétique de l'espace* (1957), English tr.: *The Poetics of Space*, Boston: Beacon Press, 1994.
6. Ibid., p. 3.
7. Ibid., p. 6.
8. Ibid., p. 7.
9. Chorology (from Greek *khōros*, 'place, space') means the study of the causal relationship between geographical phenomena occurring within a particular region.
10. 'Then I saw a new heaven and a new earth; for the first heaven and the first earth had passed away, and the sea was no more. And I saw the holy city, the new Jerusalem, coming down out of heaven from God, prepared as a bride adorned for her husband.' (Revelation 21:1–2), Holy Bible, The New Revised Standard Version, Cambridge: Cambridge University Press, 2007.
11. 'And the Lord said, "If I find at Sodom fifty righteous in the city, I will forgive the whole place for their sake."' (Genesis 18:26). Holy Bible, The New Revised Standard Version.
12. Babylon (Babel) also has a negative connotation in the Muslim tradition. In Babylon, the angels Harut and Marut teach people forbidden magic. At-Tabari's ninth-century chronicle *History of the Prophets and Kings* (*Tarikh al-Rusul wa al-Muluk*) recounts how King Nimrod had built a tower in Babel that Allah destroyed, as a result of which people began to speak different languages and ceased to understand each other.
13. (Matthew 5:14). Holy Bible, The New Revised Standard Version.

14. Ash, Amin and Nigel Thrift, *Cities: Reimagining the Urban*, Cambridge: Blackwell, 2002: 9.
15. Debord, Guy, *Introduction to a Critique of Urban Geography*, http://www.bopsecrets.org/SI/urbgeog.htm.
16. http://www.3ammagazine.com/3am/psychogeography-merlin-coverley/.
17. Debord, Guy, *Psychogeographical Guide of Paris*, http://imaginarymuseum.org/LPG/Mapsitu1.htm.
18. Ackroyd, Peter, *London: The Biography*, London: Chatto &Windus, 2000.
19. Pamuk, Orhan, *Istanbul: Memories and the City*, New York: Vintage Books, 2006.
20. Suvorova, Anna, *Nostalgia po Lakhnau* (Nostalgia for Lucknow), Moscow: 'Tadem', 1995.
21. Latif, Syad Muhammad, *Lahore: History, Architectural Remains and Antiquities*, Lahore: New Imperial Press, 1892; rpt. Lahore: Sang-e-Meel Publications, 1994.
22. Sidhwa, Bapsi, (ed.), *Beloved City: Writings on Lahore*, Karachi: Oxford University Press, 2005.
23. A cultural artefact is a 'term used in the social sciences [...] for anything created by humans which gives information about the culture of its creator and users. [...] For example, in an anthropological context, a 17th Century lathe or piece of faience, and a television all provide a wealth of information about the time in which they were manufactured and used. Cultural artifacts can provide knowledge about technological processes, economy and social makeup, and a host of other subjects.' http://en.wikipedia.org/wiki/Cultural_artifact.

Chapter 2: 'Lahore is Lahore'

1. Patras Bukhari, 'Lahaur ka jughrafia', in *Patras ke Mazamin*, Karachi: Fazli Sanz, 2003, p. 140.
2. Mumtaz, Kamil Khan, 'The Walled City of Lahore: Directions for Rehabilitation', in Renata Holod (ed.), *Conservation as Cultural Survival*, Philadelphia: The Aga Khan Award for Architecture, 1980, p. 43.
3. Aijazuddin, F.S., *Lahore Recollected: An Album*, Lahore: Sang-e-Meel, 2004, p. 9.
4. Qadeer, Muhammad, *Lahore: Urban Development in the Third World*, Lahore: Ferozsons, 1983, p. 72.
5. Patras Bukhari, *Lahaur ka Jughrafia*, p. 141.
6. Ibid., p. 142.
7. Latif, Syad Muhammad, *Lahore: Its History, Architectural Remains and Antiquities*, Lahore, 1892; reprint Lahore: Sang-e-Meel Publications, 1994, p. 24.
8. Herbert, Thomas Sir, *A Relation of Some Yeares Travaile into Afrique, Asia, Indies*, New York: Da Capo Press, 1971, reprint, p. 69.
9. Tavernier, J.B., *Travels in India*, 2 vols., Trans. V. Ball and ed. W. Crooke, 1925; reprint Delhi: Oriental Books Reprint Corporation, 1977, vol. I, p. 187.
10. Patras Bukhari, *Lahaur ka Jughrafia*, p. 142.

11. *Hudud al-Alam, The Regions of the World: A Persian Geography*, A.H. *372–A.D. 982*, translated and explained by V. Minorsky; with the preface by V.V. Barthold, London 1937, p. 134.

12. Mahmud's love affair with his young slave, Malik Ayaz, became a legendary example of love and devotion, and was a celebrated symbol of the kind of relationship in which a love-struck powerful man can become 'a slave to his slave'.

13. Temple, Richard, *The Legends of the Punjab*, 2 vols., Islamabad: Institute of Folk Heritage, 1981, reprint, vol. II, p. 189.

14. Kipling J.L., Thornton T.N., *Lahore As It Was: A Travelogue*, 1860, Lahore: NCA Publications, 2002, reprint, p. 118.

15. Burnes, Alexander, *Travels into Bokhara: Together With a Narrative of a Voyage on the Indus*, 3 vols., Lahore: Sang-e-Meel, 2003, reprint, vol. III, 124.

16. al-Hujwiri, Abul Hasan Ali ibn Osman ibn Abi Ali al-Jullabi al-Ghaznavi, *Kashf al-mahjub*, Persian text, index and introduction by V.A. Zhukovsky. Leningrad: Academia, 1926.

17. Quote from Goulding, H.R., *Old Lahore: Reminiscences of a Resident*, Lahore: Universal Books, 1924, reprint, p. 37.

18. Kipling, Rudyard, *Kim*, Chapter 3, http://www.gutenberg.org/etext/2226.

19. *Manrique, Fray Sebastien*. Travels of Fray Sebastien Manrique: 1629–1643. 2 vols. Trans. by C.E. Luard. Oxford: Hakluyt Society, 1927: 199

20. Milton, John, *Paradise Lost*, Penguin Books, 2000, p. 257.

21. Quote from Latif, Syad Muhammad, *Lahore: Its History, Architectural Remains and Antiquities*, p. 14.

22. Ibid., p. 16.

23. The gate, for the removal of refuse and waste materials from the city (Mori Darwaza), was not always considered to be a full-fledged city gate. This led to the popular joke that Lahore has 'twelve-and-a-half gates'.

24. Quote from Kerr, Robert, *A General History and Collection of Voyages and Travels*, vol. 8, Project Gutenberg, http://www.gutenberg.org/etext/13366.

25. Quote from Aijazuddin, F.S., *Lahore: Illustrated Views of the 19th Century Lahore*, Lahore: Vanguard Books, 1991, p. 15.

26. 'And I say also to you, that you are Peter, and on this rock I will build my church; and the gates of hell shall not prevail against it' (Matthew, 16:18).

27. *Pishtaq*—Iranian term for a portal projecting from the facade of a building. This device is common in Anatolian and Iranian architecture although it also occurs in India. In its most characteristic form, it consists of a high arch set within a rectangular frame which may be decorated with bands of calligraphy, glazed tilework, and geometric and vegetal designs [Andrew Petersen, *Dictionary of Islamic Architecture*, London: Routledge, 1996].

28. Kipling, Rudyard, *Kim*, Chapter 1, http://www.gutenberg.org/etext/2226.

29. Latif, Malik, *Awlia-e Lahaur*, Lahaur: Sang-e-Meel, 199, p. 294.

30. Patras Bukhari, *Lahaur ka Jughrafia*, p. 143.

31. Lal, Rai Bahadur Kanhaya, *Tarikh-e Lahaur*, reprint, Lahaur: Majlis-e taraqqi-e adab, 1987, p. 134.

32. Ibid., p. 89.
33. Nevile, Pran, *Lahore: A Sentimental Journey*, New Delhi: Penguin Books, 2006, p. xxviii.
34. Latif, Syad Muhammad, *Lahore: Its History, Architectural Remains and Antiquities*, p. 71.
35. Aijazuddin, F.S., *Lahore: Illustrated Views of the 19th Century Lahore*, p. 85.

Chapter 3: Between Mosque and Tomb

1. Mumtaz, Kamil Khan, *Architecture in Pakistan*, Singapore: Mimar, 1989, p. 51.
2. Pietre dure (Italian 'hard stones'): technique of using exquisitely cut and fitted, highly polished coloured stones to create what amounts to a painting in stone.
3. Mumtaz, Kamil Khan, *Architecture in Pakistan*, pp. 59–60.
4. Since 2001, Lahore has acquired the status of a city district that includes 9 administrative towns, 22 localities, and 19 neighbourhoods. Among the latter are the Walled City and the old Mughal suburbs of Shahdara, Baghbanpura, and Mughalpura.
5. Latif, Syad Muhammad, *Lahore: Its History, Architectural Remains and Antiquities*, Lahore, 1892; reprint, Lahore: Sang-e-Meel Publications, 1994, p. 113.
6. Malika az-Zamani (also known as Badshah Begum, died 1778) was the daughter of Emperor Farrukh Siyar (1713–1719) and the Hindu princess Maharajkumari Indra Kunwar. Her only son, Ahmad Shah, from her marriage to Muhammad Shah ruled for several years until he was blinded and deposed in 1754 by 'Alamgir II. After this, Malika az-Zamani was forced to leave Delhi.
7. Lal, Rai Bahadur Kanhaya, *Tarikh-e Lahaur*, Lahore: Majlis-e taraqqi-e adab, 1987, p. 123.
8. Projecting eaves (*chhajja*) are a widespread element in Mughal and Rajput architecture. They are used both for decorative purposes (kiosks and tower tops) and for utilitarian aims (attached to supports around the entire perimeter of the façade, for example in Salim Chishti's tomb at Fatehpur-Sikri, they protect from the sun and create shade).
9. *Islimi* is a type of Muslim ornament that combines vines and spirals, and is found in an endless variety of forms. It derives from the Hellenistic ornamental motif of the flowing grape vine.
10. In 1839, Ranjit Singh was succeeded by his feeble-minded elder son, Kharak Singh, who died a year later. His son, Nau Nihal Singh, died on his coronation day as a result of an accident (cf. Chapter 2). This led to a battle for the Sikh throne between Ranjit Singh's youngest son, Sher Singh, and Kharak Singh's widow, Maharani Chand Kaur. Sher Singh became king but was killed two years later by his rivals; the fort was captured by Hira Singh, who became a powerful vizier under the new ruler, Dalip Singh.
11. Shahzad, Ghafir, *Lahaur ke Manar*, Lahore: Idraq Publications, 2001, p. 122.
12. Mumtaz, Kamil Khan, *Architecture in Pakistan*, p. 78.

13. Lal, Rai Bahadur Kanhaya, *Tarikh-e Lahaur*, p. 236.

14. The Mughal Empire was a military state, and the system of *mansabdari* (ranks of imperial officials) was patterned after the military system. Imperial officials were divided into 33 ranks. The ranks corresponded to the number of cavalrymen (men and horses) that the *mansabdar* had to supply. The *mansabdari* ranks ranged from a commander of ten soldiers to a commander of ten thousand soldiers. The ranks of 'Commander of 10,000', 'Commander of 8,000', and 'Commander of 7,000' were reserved for Akbar's sons. Wazir Khan was a 'Commander of 5,000', i.e., of 5,000 men and 5,000 horses.

15. *Nazr* was an element of court etiquette in which a lower-ranking official made a gift to a higher-ranking official.

16. Saleh Kanbuh, Muhammad, *Shah Jahan Namah*, Mutarjim Mumtaz Liaqat, Lahore: Sang-e-Meel, 2004, p. 54.

17. Kipling, J.L., Thornton, T.H. *Lahore As It Was. Travelogue, 1860*. Reprint. Lahore: NCA Publications, 2002: 63.

18. *Band-i rumi* is an ornament made of a continuous inclined or straight grid of oval or multilateral cells that may include different decorative motifs. *Girih* is a complex geometric ornament consisting of religious legends that are inscribed in rectangular figures.

19. The chronogram of the date of construction is contained in the last words of another inscription—'The founder of this mosque is Wazir Khan' (*bānī-yi masjid wazīr khān*) which gives the date: year 1044 AH.

20. Latif, Syad Muhammad, *Lahore: Its History, Architectural Remains and Antiquities*, p. 221.

21. Chughtai, 'Abdullah, *Tarikhi masajid-e Lahaur*, Lahaur: Kitab-khanah-e nauras, 1974, p. 221.

22. Latif, Syad Muhammad, *Lahore: Its History, Architectural Remains and Antiquities*, pp. 222–23.

23. Ibid., p. 207.

24. Saleh Kanbuh, Muhammad, *Shah Jahan Namah*, p. 107.

25. Kipling, J.L., Thornton, T.H., *Lahore As It Was*, p. 96.

26. Mumtaz, Kamil Khan, *Architecture in Pakistan*, pp. 67–68.

27. Thompson, J.P., 'The Tomb of Jahangir', *Journal of the Punjab Historical Society*, 1911, No. 1, pp. 31–49.

28. http://www.server786.com/150buzurg/indexLahore150buzurg.htm.

29. Suvorova, Anna, *Muslim Saints of South Asia: The Eleventh to Fifteenth Centuries*, London-New York: RoutledgeCurzon, 2004, pp. 35–58.

30. Dara Shikoh, Muhammad, *Safinat al-awliya*, Urdu main tarjuma Muhammad 'Ali Lutfi, Karachi: Nafis Akademi, 1965, p. 58.

31. Hasan, Masoodul, *Data Ganj Bakhsh*, Lahore: Ferozsons, 1972, p. 106.

32. Goulding, H.R., *Old Lahore: Reminiscences of a Resident*, Lahore: Civil and Military Gazette Printing, 1924, p. 2.

33. Iqbal, Muhammad, *The Secrets of the Self*. Trans. by R.A. Nicholson, Lahore: Farhan Publishers, 1977, p. 118.

34. Other examples of such double veneration were the saints Fariduddin Masud (Baba Farid), whose poems (*shlokas*) became part of the Sikh canon *Guru Granth*, and Nasiruddin Chiragh-i Dehli, to whom Hindu mystics (*nath yogis*) dedicated hymns.

35. Jahangir, Nur al-Din Muhammad. *Tuzuk-i-jahangiri*. Trans. A. Rogers, ed. H. Beveridge, 1909–14; reprint, Delhi: Munshiram Manoharlal, 1968, p. 147.

36. Quote from: Latif, Malik. *Awliya-e Lahaur*, p. 217.

37. Dara Shikoh has narrated that his grandfather, Emperor Jahangir, once invited Mian Mir to the court, received him with great respect, and promised to fulfil any of his desires. 'On this said the holy Sheikh, "My only want is that Your Majesty would not give me the trouble of coming to you again." With the assurance from the Emperor that he would be no more troubled to visit him, the Sheikh withdrew.' [Dara Shikoh. *Sakinat al-awliya*, p. 98]

38. According to one anecdote, Jahangir came to Mian Mir's monastery (*khanaqa*) asking the saint to pray for the success of his military campaign against the independent principalities in the Deccan. At the same time, a poor man came to the *khanaqa* with a rupee. The saint told him to give it to the neediest person there. No one wanted to accept the gift. Then the saint pointed to the emperor, and told the poor man, 'Give this rupee to His Majesty. He is the neediest of us all. His large empire is not enough for him, and he needs the Deccan, too.' [Cited from Dara Shikoh, *Sakinat al-awliya*, p. 126] Another anecdote relates that the saint's disciples put a gatekeeper before the *khanaqa*'s gate, in order to reduce the number of visitors. Jahangir, once while calling on Mian Mir was stopped by the gatekeeper. He flew into a rage and told the saint, 'There shouldn't be any gatekeepers at a dervish's doorstep' (*ba dar-i darwish darban nabayad*). The saint replied, 'They should be to prevent the dog of this world from entering' (*bibayad ki sag-i dunya na-ayad*) (Ibid., p. 132).

39. Cunningham, J.D., *History of the Sikhs*, New Delhi: D.K. Publishers Distributors, 1996, p. 131.

40. Jahangir himself explained the causes of Guru Arjun's arrest and execution as follows: 'In Govind Wal, on the banks of the Beas, there lived a Hindu, named Arjan, who had assumed the garb of a spiritual guide, or *Sheikh*. He made numbers of stupid Hindus, nay, even foolish and ignorant Muslims, captives to his wiles and had the drum of his sanctity loudly beaten. They called him Guru. Disciples flocked around him from all sides and evinced the greatest respect for him. [...] The idea struck me several times to put a stop to this trickery, or to make the Guru a convert to Islam, till, at last, at this time Khusrow crossed the river in that direction. The Guru wanted to see him, and he happened to encamp at the place where the Guru lived. He had an interview with the Prince and supplied him with much information. He applied to the Prince's forehead the mark of saffron, called in the dialect of the Hindus *Kashka*; they do it by way of good omen. No sooner did I hear this, then, convinced as I was of the absurdity of the notion, I ordered the Guru to be brought into my presence. I ordered his sons and his habitations and dwellings to be made over to Murtaza

Khan [Sheikh Farid Bukhari, the governor of the Punjab—*A.S.*]. All his property was confiscated to the State, and he himself placed in rigorous confinement.' [Jahangir, Nur al-Din Muhammad, *Tuzuk-i Jahangiri*, pp. 178–79]. Most scholars believe that the real cause of Guru Arjun's arrest was the rapid spread of Sikhism, which alarmed the Mughals, rather than his symbolic support for the rebellious prince.

41. Dara Shikoh, *Sakinat al-awliya*, pp. 211–12.
42. Ibid., p. 213.
43. Chopra, R.M., *Great Sufi Poets of the Punjab*, Calcutta: Iran Society, 1999, p. 90.

Chapter 4: The Name of the Garden: Shalimar and Others

1. 'Allami, Abu'l-Fazl, *Akbarnama*, 3 vols., Persian text edited by H. Blochmann, Calcutta: Royal Asiatic Society of Bengal, 1877–86, translation by H. Beveridge, 1902–39; rpt. Delhi: Ess Ess Publications, 1973, vol. I, pp. 355–56.
2. Naeem, Mir, M. Hussain, and James L. Wescoat Jr., *Mughal Gardens in Lahore: History and Documentation*, Lahore: Department of Architecture, Lahore University of Engineering and Technology, 1996, p. 64.
3. Jairazbhoy, R.A. 'Early Garden-Palaces of the Great Mughals', *Oriental Art* IV, 2 (1958), pp. 68–75.
4. Wescoat, James L., Jr., 'Gardens of Conquest and Transformation: Lessons from the Earliest Mughal Gardens in India', *Landscape Journal* 10:2 (1991), pp. 105–14.
5. Gulbadan Bano, *Humayun Nama*, translation by Annette S. Beveridge, New Delhi: Goodword Books, 2001, p. 108.
6. Nevile, Pran, *Lahore: A Sentimental Journey*, New Delhi: Penguin Books, 2006, pp. 12–20.
7. *The Gulistan of Sa'di*, Introduction, http://classics.mit.edu/Sadi/gulistan.1.introductory.html.
8. The Holy Bible. New King James Version, http://www.biblegateway.com/passage/?search=SongOfSongs%204&version=NKJV.
9. For examples: Richard of Saint-Laurent's treatise *Mariale* (thirteenth century), the anonymous treatise *Der lustliche Wurtzgarten* (fifteenth century), Stefan Lochner's painting *Madonna in the Rose Bower* (*ca.* 1440), Martin Schongauer's *Madonna in an Enclosed Garden* (second half of the fifteenth century), and even Raphael's *Madonna of the Meadow* (1505) and *La belle jardinière* (1507).
10. The Qu'ran is cited in the translation by M.H. Shakir, http://al-quran.info.
11. Quotation from: Dickie, James (Yacub Zaki), 'The Mughal Garden: Gateway to Paradise', *Muqarnas* 3 (1986), pp. 128–37, 129.
12. Koch, Ebba, 'The Mughal Waterfront Garden', in *Gardens in the Time of the Great Muslim Empires*, edited by A. Petruccioli, Leiden, New York: E.J. Brill, 1997, pp. 140–60.

13. Koch, Ebba, 'Mughal Palace Gardens from Babur to Shah Jahan', *Muqarnas* 14 (1997), pp. 143–65.
14. Dar, Saifur Rahman, *Historical Gardens of Lahore*, Lahore: Aziz Publishers, 1982, p. 6.
15. Foster, William (ed.), *Early Travels in India, 1583–1619*, 1921; rpt. Delhi: Oriental Books Reprint Corporation, 1985, pp. 165–66.
16. Bada'uni, 'Abd al-Qadir, *Muntakhab at-Tavarikh*, 3 vols., Persian text edited by M.A. Ali, Calcutta: Royal Asiatic Society of Bengal, 1869, translations by G.S.A. Ranking (Vol. 1), W.H. Lowe (Vol. 2), and T.W. Haig (Vol. 3), 1898–99; rpt. Delhi: Idarah-i Adabiyat-i Delli, 1973, vol. 2, p. 197.
17. Pierre Du Jarric, *Akbar and the Jesuits: An Account of the Jesuit Missions to the Court of Akbar*, New York: Harper & Brothers, 1926, p. 72.
18. Here and below where no sources are cited, facts and dates are taken from the chronological table—Brand, Michael, *Garden, City and Empire: The Historical Geography of Mughal Lahore*, website 'Gardens of the Mughal Empire', http://mughalgardens.org/html/resources.html.
19. Sikander, Sattar, 'The Shalamar: A Typical Muslim Garden', in *Environmental Design* 2 (1986), pp. 24–29.
20. Moore, Thomas, *Lalla Rookh: an Oriental Romance*, London: Darf, 1986, p. 102.
21. Eden, Emily, *Up the Country: Letters written to her Sister from the Upper Provinces of India*, 1830; rpt. London: Virago, 2003, p. 223.
22. Singh, Bhagwan, 'Shalamar, not Shalimar', in *The Tribune*, Chandigarh, 09.12.2001.
23. Rehman, Abdul, 'Garden Types in Mughal Lahore according to Early-Seventeenth Century Written and Visual Sources', in *Gardens in the Great Muslim Empires*, edited by Petruccioli, pp. 161–72.
24. Dar, Saifur Rahman, 'Shalimar Garden', in *Cultural Heritage of Pakistan*, Karachi: Pakistan Department of Archaeology, 1967, pp. 35–47.
25. Kausar, Sajjad, Michael Brand, and James L. Wescoat, Jr., *Shalamar Garden: Landscape, Form and Meaning*, Karachi: Pakistan Department of Archaeology, 1990, p. 1.
26. Chopra R.M., *Great Sufi Poets of the Punjab*, Calcutta: Iran Society, 1999, p. 135.
27. Sikander, Sattar, 'The Shalamar: A Typical Muslim Garden', pp. 24, 27.
28. Latif, Syad Muhammmad, *Lahore: History, Architectural Remains and Antiquities*, Lahore: New Imperial Press, 1892; rpt. Lahore: Sang-e-Meel Publications, 1994, p. 141.
29. Shafi, Maulvi Muhammad, 'The Shalimar Gardens of Lahore', in *Islamic Culture* 1: 1927, p. 59ff.
30. Garrett, H.L.O., *The Punjab a Hundred Years Ago as Described by V. Jacquemont and A. Soltykoff*, Lahore: Sang-e-Meel, 1997, p. 104.
31. http://mughalgardens.org/html/home.html.
32. Khokar, Massood ul-Hassan, 'Tomb of Sharaf un-Nisa Begum Known as the Sarvwala Maqbara at Lahore', *Pakistan Journal of History and Culture* III (1982), pp. 111–16.

33. Brand, Michael, 'The Shahdara Gardens of Lahore', in *Mughal Gardens*, edited by Wescoat and Wolschke-Bulmahn, pp. 189–212.

34. Wescoat, James L. Jr., Michael Brand, and Naeem Mir, 'The Shahdara Gardens of Lahore: Site Documentation and Spatial Analysis', *Pakistan Archaeology* 25 (1993), pp. 33–42.

35. Khan, Ahmad Nabi, 'The Hiran Minar', *Pakistan Archaeology*, VI (1969), pp. 67–75.

36. Sultana, Salma, 'Architecture of Sheikhupura Fort in Historic Perspective', *South Asian Studies*, vol. 5 (1989), pp. 103–17.

37. Villiers-Stuart, C.M., *Gardens of the Great Mughals*, London: A. & C. Black, 1913, reprint, Asian Educational Service, 2005.

Chapter 5: The 'Immured Bride': A City Legend

1. In early Welsh sources, Merlin is called Emrys. He declares the origin of the collapsing walls: a pool in which two dragons lie. After much digging, this proves to be true and a white and a red dragon are found. These dragons fight a fierce battle, with the red being victorious in the end—which is how the Red Dragon supposedly found its way onto the Welsh flag. 'Vortingern Studies', http://www.vortigernstudies.org.uk/artcit/dinas.htm.

2. Dundes, Alan (ed.), *The Walled-up Wife: A Casebook*, Madison: The University of Wisconsin Press, 1996, pp. 157–160.

3. Ibid., p. 95.

4. Ibid., pp. 4–10.

5. Ibid., pp. 56–60.

6. Khokar, Massood ul-Hassan, 'Tomb of Sharaf un-Nisa Begum Known as the Sarvwala Maqbara at Lahore', *Pakistan Journal of History and Culture* III (1982), pp. 111–16.

7. This legend has nothing to do with the real history of the tower, because Sumbeka was forcibly detained by Moscovite forces in 1551 and moved to the city of Kasimov where she died years later.

8. Syad Muhammad Latif wrote that the practice of foundation sacrifice, while laying the corner-stone of public buildings, existed in India until the seventeenth century and had Hindu origins, although it was not limited to the sacrifice of girls. He wrote, 'Shah Jahan revived the Hindu custom of laying the foundation of public buildings in human blood.... A stair-case in the Shalimar gardens of Lahore is pointed out where a boy had been sacrificed by order of the Emperor on the occasion of the laying of the foundations' [Latif, Syad Muhammad, *Lahore: History, Architectural Remains and Antiquities*, Lahore: New Imperial Press, 1892; rpt. Lahore: Sang-e-Meel Publications, 1994, p. 121].

9. Chaudhry, Nazir Ahmed, *Anarkali: Archives and Tomb of Sahib Jamal*, Lahore: Ferozsons, 1956, p. 35.

10. The current building of the Shish Mahal cannot be considered the authentic 'natural setting' of the Anarkali legend as it was totally rebuilt during the reign of Shah Jahan.

11. Latif, Syad Muhammad, op. cit., p. 187.

12. Quotation from: Kureshi, Shahnaz, 'The Legend of Anarkali', in Bapsi Sidhwa (ed.), *Beloved City: Writings on Lahore*, Karachi: Oxford University Press, 2005, pp. 86–87.

13. Quotation from: Kerr, Robert, *A General History and Collection of Voyages and Travels*, Vol. 8, Project Gutenberg, http://www.gutenberg.org/etext/13366.

14. Eraly, Abraham, *The Last Spring: The Lives and Times of the Great Mughals*, Delhi: Viking, 1977, p. 185.

15. Foster, William (ed.), *Early Travels in India, 1583–1619*, 1921; rpt. Delhi: Oriental Books Reprint Corporation, 1985, p. 213.

16. Garrett, H.L.O., *The Punjab a Hundred Years Ago as Described by V. Jacquemont and A. Soltykoff*, Lahore: Sang-e-Meel, 1997, p. 182.

17. Baqir, Muhammad, *Lahore, Past and Present: Being an Account of Lahore Compiled From Original Sources*, Lahore: Punjab University Press, 1952, p. 164.

18. Parihar, Subhash, 'Riddle of Anarkali and her Tomb', in *The Tribune*, 8 April 2000.

19. Goulding, H.R., *Old Lahore: Reminiscences of a Resident*, Lahore: Civil and Military Gazette Printing, 1924, p. 79.

20. Sir Henry Montgomery Lawrence was a British officer and statesman. He was the elder brother of John Lawrence, viceroy of India (see Chapter 8), and took part in the First Anglo-Burmese and First Anglo-Afghan Wars. He founded boarding schools for the sons of military men serving in India—the so-called 'Henry Lawrence boys' and died during the siege of the British Residency in Lucknow.

21. Eastwick, E.B., *Handbook of the Punjab, Western Rajputana, Kashmir, and Upper Sindh*, London, 1883.

22. Aijazuddin, F.S., *Lahore: Illustrated Views of the 19th Century*, Lahore: Vanguard Books, Ltd., 1991, pl. 89–91.

23. Taj, Imtiaz 'Ali, *Anarkali*, Bhopal: Bhopal Buk haus, 1977, p. 5.

24. Jodha Bai may be a historical figure (although this is disputed by Salman Rushdie in his novel *The Enchantress of Florence*) and one of ten Rajput princesses who were married to Akbar. However, the mother of Salim (Jahangir) and of two of Akbar's daughters was a different Rajput princess—Rajah Amber's daughter Hira Kumari, better known as Mariam Zamani. She is buried in Lahore, and a famous city mosque bears her name.

25. For a further discussion on the influence of Taj's play on subsequent screenplays of the story, see: Desoulieres, Alain, 'Historical Fiction and Style: The Case of *Anarkali*', in *The Annual of Urdu Studies*, 2007, vol. 22.

26. In 1958, Madhubala and Dilip Kumar were scheduled to perform together in the film *The New Era* (*Naya Daur*). However, Madhubala's father opposed this on grounds of decency and forced his daughter to break the contract. The

film's producer, B.R. Chopra, filed a suit, demanding that Madhubala pay a forfeit. During the trial, Dilip Kumar testified against Madhubala, spoiling their relations for ever.

Chapter 6: 'Bread and Games!'

1. Kipling, J.L. & Thornton, T.H., *Lahore as It Was: Travelogue*, 1860, reprint. Lahore: NCA Publications, 2002.
2. Nevile, Pran, *Lahore: A Sentimental Journey*, New Delhi: Penguin Books, 2006, pp. xix–xx.
3. Chughtai's short story was accused of portraying lesbian relations between a married middle-class woman and her servant. Another outstanding Urdu prose writer, Saadat Hasan Manto, was also tried in this 'indecency affair' for his short story 'Smell' ('Bu'). The accusations against the writers were ultimately dropped, largely thanks to the defence by Chughtai's sharp-witted lawyer who convinced the court that only someone with experience of lesbian love could possibly see a lesbian subtext in this story about the life of women behind the purdah. Thus, making such an accusation against the writer was tantamount to admitting that her readers, who were mostly respectable Muslim women, had engaged in lesbian relations.
4. Chughtai, Ismat, *My Friends, My Enemy: Essays, Reminiscences, Portraits*, translated by Tahira Naqvi, New Delhi: Kali for Women, 2001, pp. 174–182.
5. Otis Skinner, Cornelia, *Elegant Wits and Grand Horizontals*, New York: Houghton Mifflin, 1962, p. 55.
6. Quraishi, Samina, *Lahore, the City Within*, Singapore: Concept Media, 1988, pp. 70–71.
7. Hussain, Intizar, 'Pak Tea House: chai ki mez se footpath tak', in *The Annual of Urdu Studies*, 2001, vol. 16.
8. Memon, Muhammad 'Umar, 'Editorial', in *The Annual of Urdu Studies*, 2001, vol. 16, p. 1.
9. A sociological term that denotes the average person.
10. Dara Shikoh, Muhammad, *Sakinat al-awliya: ahwal wa faza'il-i Hazrat Mian Mir*, Urdu men tarjuma az Maqbul Beg Badahshani, Lahore: Pikijeez, 1971, p. 132.
11. Chopra, R.M., *Great Sufi Poets of the Punjab*, Calcutta: Iran Society, 1999, p. 92.
12. Anas, Syed Muhammad, *The Kites of Blasphemy*, http://www.albalagh.net/food_for_thought/basant.shtml.
13. Le Tourneur d'Ison, Claudine, *Hira Mandi*, Paris: Albin Michel, 2005.
14. Brown, Loise, T*he Dancing Girls of Lahore: Selling Love and Hoarding Dreams in Pakistan's Ancient Pleasure District*, New York: Fourth Estate, 2005, p. 75.
15. Kapur, Promilla, *The Life and World of Call-girls in India*, Delhi: Vikas, 1978, p. 51.

16. Joardar, B., *Prostitution in Nineteenth and Early Twentieth Century Calcutta*, Delhi: Inter-India Publications, 1985, p. 65.

17. Suroor, Mirza Rajab 'Ali Baig, *Fasana-e Ajaib*, Lahore: Sang-e-Meel, 2009, p. 28.

18. Nevile, Pran, *Lahore: A Sentimental Journey*, p. 75.

19. A reference to Muhammad bin Qasim, the Arabian general who led the first military expedition against the Sindh and Punjab in 711.

20. Sidhwa, Bapsi (ed.), *Beloved City: Writings on Lahore*, Karachi: Oxford University Press, 2005, p. xi.

21. The Hudood (Arabic 'limits, restricting laws') includes not only articles on blasphemy, consumption of alcohol, theft, etc., but also a Law on Adultery (Zina Ordinance) that declares that all extramarital relations between people that have attained puberty are criminal offences. A married man or woman who has sexual relations with a third party is punished by stoning to death. If the sexual partners are unmarried, they are whipped a hundred times each. Women who have been raped are also punished for zina, if they are unable to present the testimony of four male witnesses in their defence, i.e., prove that they have been raped. Although a dozen death sentences were promulgated for zina in Pakistan over the last twenty years, none have been executed, and the condemned (mostly women) have spent time in prison. The Zina Ordinance evoked strong protests from the world community as a violation of international law and human rights. Yielding to these protests, President Musharraf abrogated the Zina Ordinance in 2006.

22. Brown, Loise, *The Dancing Girls of Lahore: Selling Love and Hoarding Dreams in Pakistan's Ancient Pleasure District*, p. 189.

23. Saeed, Fouzia, *Taboo! The Hidden Culture of a Red Light Area*, Karachi: Oxford University Press, 2002, p. 67.

24. Ibid., pp. 34–41.

25. The many tombs of Punjabi saints in Lahore and on its outskirts notwithstanding, the inhabitants of the Hira Mandi consider Lal Shahbaz Qalandar to be their patron saint. His tomb is in the city of Sehwan in Sindh. On his feast day ('urs), the *kanjari* and their families fill the trains going from Lahore to Sehwan.

26. Nevile, Pran, *Lahore: A Sentimental Journey*, p. 80.

27. Saeed, Fouzia, *Taboo! The Hidden Culture of a Red Light Area*, p. 213.

Chapter 7: The City of Dreadful Night

1. Aurangzeb became a hero of English literature long before Thomas Moore. He is the subject of the tragedy *Aureng-Zebe* (1675) by the famous English playwright John Dryden (1631–1700).

2. Their names are Zebunnisa, Zinatunnisa, and Mihrunnisa from Aurangzeb's marriage with Dilras Bano; Badrunnisa from his wife Nawab Rai Bai; and Zubdatunnisa from his relationship with Aurangabadi Mahal.

3. Moore, Thomas, *Lalla Rookh: An Oriental Romance*, London: Darf, 1986, p. 128.

4. Scott, Jonathan Captain, *Firishta's History of the Dekkan*, London: J.V. Eddowes, 1794.
5. Moore, Thomas, *Lalla Rookh: An Oriental Romance*, p. 232.
6. Hoppner, John, Oriental Tales, London: J. Hatchard, 1805.
7. Moore, Thomas, *Lalla Rookh: An Oriental Romance*, p. 129.
8. Bernier, Francois, *Travels in the Mogul Empire: A.D. 1656–1668*, translated by A. Constable, 1914; rpt. Delhi: S. Chand & Co., 1979.
9. Moore, Thomas, *Lalla Rookh: An Oriental Romance*, p. 233.
10. Garrett, H.L.O., *The Punjab a Hundred Years Ago as Described by V. Jacquemont and A. Soltykoff*, Lahore: Sang-e-Meel, 1997, p. 138.
11. http://www.classic-music.ru/massenet.html.
12. Ewen, David, *Encyclopedia of the Opera*, New Enlarged Edition, New York; Hill and Wang, 1963, p. 297.
13. The first performer of the role of Sita was the French singer of Polish descent Josephine de Reszke (1855–1891), a lyric-dramatic soprano and a prima donna at the Grand Opéra. The best performer of the role of Sita in the twentieth century was considered to be Joan Sutherland—in a 1977 production at the Vancouver Opera (Canada) on the occasion of the hundredth anniversary of Massenet's opera. The most recent production of *The King of Lahore* took place at the Teatro La Fenice (Venice) in 2003, with Annalise Raspagliosi in the role of Sita.
14. Tolstoy, Leo, *What is art?*, http://www.archive.org/stream/whatisart00tolsuoft/whatisart00tolsuoft_djvu.txt.
15. Ibid.
16. Blavatsky, H.P., *The Durbar in Lahore*, http://www.scribd.com/doc/21184316/The-Durbar-in-Lahore-Blavatsky.
17. Ibid.
18. Kipling, R., *Something of Myself and Other Autobiographical Writings*, Cambridge University Press, 1990, p. 4.
19. In his poem 'To the City of Bombay', Kipling wrote:
(Neither by service nor fee
Come I to mine estate–
Mother of Cities to me,
For I was born in her gate,
Between the palms and the sea,
Where the world-end steamers wait.)-http://www.daypoems.net/poems/1825.html
20. http://www.readbookonline.net/readOnLine/2450/
21. http://www.readbookonline.net/readOnLine/2421/
22. http://www.readbookonline.net/readOnLine/8181/
23. Government College (founded in 1864) is Pakistan's oldest university, and one of the most prestigious in the country. Among its alumni are the poet and thinker Muhammad Iqbal, the poets and writers Faiz Ahmed Faiz, Patras Bukhari, Sufi Ghulam Mustafa Tabassum, Khushwant Singh, the actor Balraj Sahni, the

premier ministers Inder Kumar Gujral, Nawaz Sharif, Mir Zafarullah Khan Jamali, and the. Nobel laureates in physics and medicine Abdul Salam and Har Gobind Khorana.

24. http://www.readbookonline.net/readOnLine/8181/

25. Ibid.

26. Thomson, James, *The City of Dreadful Night*, London: Watts & Co., 1932, p. 71.

27. http://www.readbookonline.net/readOnLine/2429/

28. Ibid.

29. Here Kipling cites the chronogram of the cannon's manufacturing date that is written on its pedestal: 'A weapon like a fire-raining dragon' (*tup paikari azhdaha-i atishbaz*).

30. Kipling, Rudyard, *Kim*, Chapter 1, http://www.gutenberg.org/files/2226/2226-h/2226-h.htm.

31. Latif, Syad Muhammmad, *Lahore: History, Architectural Remains and Antiquities*, Lahore: New Imperial Press, 1892; rpt. Lahore: Sang-e-Meel Publications, 1994, p. 383.

32. Op. cit., p. 384.

33. Kipling, Rudyard, *Kim*, Chapter 1.

34. Kipling, J.L. & Thornton, T.H., *Lahore As It Was, Travelogue, 1860*, reprint, Lahore: NCA Publications, 2002, pp. 76–78.

35. Kipling, Rudyard, *Kim*, Chapter 1.

36. Kipling, J.L. & Thornton, T.H., *Lahore As It Was, Travelogue*, p. 102.

37. Kipling, Rudyard, *Kim*, Chapter 2, http://www.gutenberg.org/etext/2226.

38. Nevile, Pran, *Lahore: A Sentimental Journey*, New Delhi: Penguin Books, 2006, p. 91.

39. In a number of short stories, such as 'The Approach to Al-Mu'tasim', Borges cited Indian toponyms as a rhythmic technique: 'The story begun in Bombay moves on into the lowlands of Palanpur, lingers for an evening and a night before the stone gates of Bikaner, tells of the death of a blind astrologer in a Benares sewer; the hero [...] prays and fornicates in the pestilential stench of the Machua Bazaar in Calcutta, sees the day born [...] in Madras, sees evenings die [...] in the state of Travancore, falters and kills in Indapur. The adventure closes its orbit of miles and years back in Bombay itself [...]', http://www.digiovanni.co.uk/borges_papers.php?section=the+garden+of+branching+paths&article=the+approach+to+al-mu'tasim. In the same story, Borges cited Kipling's short story 'On the City Wall' in connection with Muharram.

40. Borges, a man of encyclopaedic learning, in addition to Kipling used other sources of information about Lahore including Thomas Moore's poem: Borges' short story 'The Masked Dyer Hakim of Merv' was a paraphrase of Moore's interpolated poem *The Veiled Prophet of Khorassan*.

41. Borges, Jorge Luis, *Collected Fictions*, Tr. Andrew Hurley, New York: Penguin, 1999, p. 494.

42. Op. cit., p. 501.

43. Op. cit., p. 503.

44. Borges, Jorge Luis, *Collected Fictions*, p. 509.

45. Op. cit., p. 497.

46. Azad, Muhammad Husain, *Darbar-e akbari*, Lahore: Kapur art printing works, 1910.

47. Iqbal, Muhammad, *Kalam-e Urdu-e 'Allama Iqbal, Bang-e dara, Mukamal aur salis farhang ke sath*, Hyderabad: Khusami buk depo, n.d.

48. Translation by M.A.K. Khalil, http://www.allamaiqbal.com/works/poetry/urdu/bang/translation/index.htm.

49. Faiz Ahmed Faiz, *Zindan-namah*, Karachi: Maktab-e karawan, 1977.

50. Translation by Agha Shahid Ali, http://jannah.org/madina/index.php?topic=454.0;wap2.

Chapter 8: Down the Cool Street

1. The Mall Road is named after the central street of London, which leads from Buckingham Palace to Trafalgar Square. Ceremonial royal processions pass down the Mall.

2. For more information about Henry Lawrence, who tragically died during the siege of the Residency in Lucknow, see the note to Chapter 5. His younger brother John Lawrence (1811–1879) was the first British Governor-General of the Punjab and, subsequently, the Viceroy of India (1864–1869).

3. Charles Mansel (1806–1886) worked as a civil servant in India, holding different administrative positions in Agra, Calcutta, Lahore, and Nagpur.

4. Charles James Napier (1782–1853) was Commander-in-Chief of British forces in India and a hero of the British Empire. He won a victory at the Battle of Miani (1843), which led to the annexation of Sind. His statue has been erected on Pall Mall street in London. Napier came to Lahore in 1846 to subdue the Sikhs and returned to England by 1851. Thus he had no direct connection with the construction of the Mall Road.

5. Helen Blavatsky described the Cantonment as follows: 'On the other hand, the so-called Cantonments in towns like Allahabad, Cawnpore, Amritsar, Lahore and others are not like towns at all…. They are merely suburban divisions of Indian towns, built, for the most part, after the Mutiny. Some 30 years ago there was a jungle or forest around almost every town, where fakirs and saintly people found salvation after renouncing the world. After growing alarmed during the suppression of the mutiny, the English chased them away, cleaned out the thickets, and through them laid out broad, interminable avenues, selecting the intermediate groves for their residences. One can drive for hours on end along wonderful smooth avenues shaded with centuries-old trees, and not see a single house. At some distance, here and there, you glimpse double white posts with the names of those who live several hundred yards beyond them. To reach any one of these you have to pass through the gateless entrances, and only then a white bungalow surrounded with verandas will emerge from the shelter of the

shady, moss-covered trees.'—Blavatsky, H.P., *The Durbar in Lahore*, http://www. scribd.com/doc/21184316/The-Durbar-in-Lahore-Blavatsky.

6. Sir Robert Montgomery (1809–1887) was Governor-General of the Punjab in 1859–1865. The city of Montgomery (today, Sahiwal) in the Punjab was named after him.

7. Cited from: Aijazuddin, F.S., *Lahore: Illustrated Views of the 19th Century*, Lahore: Vanguard Books, Ltd., 1991, p. 17.

8. The Lower Mall was originally called Donald Town, in honour of Donald McLeod (1810–1872), Governor-General of the Punjab.

9. Cited from: Aijazuddin, F.S., *Lahore Recollected: An Album*, Lahore: Sang-e-Meel, 2004, p. 87.

10. Cited from: Mumtaz, Kamil Khan, *Architecture in Pakistan*, Singapore: Mimar, 1985, p. 110.

11. Kerr, Robert, *A General History and Collection of Voyages and Travels*, Vol. 8, Project Gutenberg: http://www.gutenberg.org/ebooks/html.

12. Sir Ganga Ram (1851–1927) was a civil engineer and philanthropist. He took part in the design and construction of the following buildings: General Post Office, Lahore Museum, Aitcheson College, Mayo School of Arts, Ganga Ram Hospital, Lady Mclagan Girls High School, and other major public buildings on the Mall. He also built Model Town, the first contemporary residential neighbourhood in Lahore.

13. Dayal Singh Majithia (1848–1898) was a banker and philanthropist who founded the Punjab National Bank, the newspaper *The Tribune*, and many educational institutions in India and Pakistan, including the college and library that bear his name in Lahore. He also founded the Lahore branch of the Brahmo Samaj Society.

14. Samina Choonara (ed.), *'Official' Chronicle of Mayo School of Art*, Lahore: NCA Publications, 2003, p. 78.

15. For further information on Bhai Ram Singh, see: Vandal, Pervez and Sajida, *The Raj, Lahore and Bhai Ram Singh*, Lahore: NCA, 2006.

16. http://www.nca.edu.pk/intro.htm.

17. Saleh Kanbuh, Muhammad, *Shah Jahan Namah*, Mutarjim Mumtaz Liaqat, Lahore: Sang-e-Meel, 2004, p. 198.

18. Latif, Syad Muhammmad, *Lahore: History, Architectural Remains and Antiquities*, Lahore: New Imperial Press, 1892; rpt. Lahore: Sang-e-Meel Publications, 1994, p. 188.

19. The public sculptures of historic Lahore, http://pakistaniat.com/2007/04/17/ pakistan-lahore-statue-sculpture-lajpat-rai-woolner-victoria-lawrence-ganga-ram.

20. Charing Cross (today Faisal Chowk) was named after the crossroads of the Strand, Whitehall, and Cockspur Street in London. The name stems from the cross that King Edward I erected, in the thirteenth century, in memory of his wife Eleanor of Castile in the village of Charing (which subsequently became the centre of London).

21. Bapsi Sidhwa, *Ice-Candy-Man*, London: Heinemann, 1988, p. 91.

22. Lari, Yasmin, *Lahore—Illustrated City Guide*, Karachi: Heritage Foundation Pakistan, 2003, p. 22.

23. Chaudhry N.A., *Lahore: Glimpses of a Glorious Heritage*, Lahore: Sang-e-Meel Publication, 1998, p. 199.

24. Aijazuddin, F.S., *Lahore Recollected: An Album*, p. 133.

25. *Tonga* and *ekka* were both two-wheel carts drawn by a single horse. Passengers sat facing the coachman in the *ekka*, and with their backs to him in the *tonga*.

26. Professor Sirajuddin was Dean of the Department of English, and then Rector of Government College for a long time. He was subsequently appointed Rector of Punjab University.

27. Hussain, Intizar, 'The Cool Street', in Bapsi Sidhwa (ed.), *Beloved City: Writings on Lahore*, Karachi: Oxford University Press, 2005, pp. 294–95.

28. Kipling J.L. & Thornton T.H., *Lahore As It Was, Travelogue*, 1860, reprint, Lahore: NCA Publications, 2002, p. 92.

29. Goulding, H.R., *Old Lahore: Reminiscences of a Resident*, Lahore: Civil and Military Gazette Printing, 1924, pp. 25–27.

30. Nevile, Pran, *Lahore: A Sentimental Journey*, New Delhi: Penguin Books, 2006, pp. 17–18.

31. Kipling J.L. & Thornton T.H., *Lahore As It Was*, p. 99.

32. Goulding, H.R., *Old Lahore: Reminiscences of a Resident*, p. 51.

33. Aijazuddin, F.S., *Lahore Recollected: An Album*, p. 158.

34. Latif, Syad Muhammmad, *Lahore: History, Architectural Remains and Antiquities*, p. 297.

35. Cited from: Aijazuddin, F.S., *Lahore Recollected: An Album*, p. 158.

36. Bauhaus (German 'House of Building'), or the Higher School of Construction and Artistic Design, was an artistic educational institution and artistic association in Germany (1919–1933) that gave rise to many wonderful ideas and outstanding artists in the twentieth century. The Bauhaus motto was 'art and technology—a new unity'.

37. Frank Lloyd Wright (1867–1959) was an innovative American architect who had a major impact on the development of Western architecture in the first half of the twentieth century. He was the creator of 'organic architecture' and a proponent of the open layout.

38. Edward Durell Stone (1902–1976) was an American architect who worked in the Art Deco style. His realized projects include the Museum of Modern Art in New York and the US Embassy in New Delhi.

39. Mumtaz, Kamil Khan, *Architecture in Pakistan*, p. 179.

40. Nayyar 'Ali Dada (born 1945) is a leading Pakistani architect; he has been responsible for the majority of the building and restoration projects in contemporary Lahore, including the Expo Centre, the Qaddafi Stadium, and the Shakir 'Ali Museum.

BIBLIOGRAPHY

Ackroyd, Peter. *London: The Biography*. London: Chatto & Windus, 2000.

Ahmad, Zulfiqar, ed. *Notes on Punjab and Mughal India: Selections from Journal of the Punjab Historical Society*. Lahore: Sang-e-Meel Publications, 1988.

Aijazuddin, F.S. *Lahore Recollected: An Album*. Lahore: Sang-e-Meel, 2004.

Aijazuddin, F.S. *Lahore: Illustrated Views of the 19th Century*. Lahore: Vanguard Books, Ltd., 1991.

Akbar, Muhammad. *Punjab under the Mughal Raj*. 1948; rpt. Lahore: Vanguard, 1985.

Akbar, Sadiq, Abdul Rehman and M. Ali Tirmizi. 'Sultanate Period Architecture'. *Architectural Heritage of Pakistan* II. Lahore: Anjuman Mimaran, 1990.

al-Hujwiri, Abul Hasan Ali ibn Osman ibn Abi Ali al-Jullabi al-Ghaznavi. *Kashf al-mahjub*. Persian text, index and introduction by V.A. Zhukovsky. Leningrad: Academia, 1926.

Ali, Reza H. 'Urban Conservation in Pakistan: A Case Study of the Walled City of Lahore'. In *Architectural and Urban Conservation in the Muslim World*. Geneva: The Aga Khan Trust for Culture, 1990.

'Allami, Abu'l-Fazl. *A'in-i Akbari*, 2 vols. Persian text ed. H. Blochmann. Calcutta: Royal Asiatic Society of Bengal, 1867–77. Trans. in 3 vols. by H. Blochmann (Vol. 1; 2nd ed. revised by D.C. Phillot), 1927, and H.S. Jarrett (Vols. 2 and 3; revised by J.N. Sarkar), 1948–49; rpt. Delhi: Munshiram Manoharlal, 1977.

'Allami, Abu'l-Fazl. *Akbarnama*, 3 vols. Persian text ed. H. Blochmann. Calcutta: Royal Asiatic Society of Bengal, 1877–86. Trans. H. Beveridge. 1902–39; rpt. Delhi: Ess Ess Publications, 1973.

Amin, Ash and Nigel Thrift. *Cities: Reimagining the Urban*. Cambridge: Blackwell, 2002.

Andrews, P.A. 'Lahawr'. *Encyclopedia of Islam*. Rev. Ed. Vol. 5. Leiden: E.J. Brill, 1982, pp. 597–601.

Ansari, M.A. 'Palaces and Gardens of the Mughals'. *Islamic Culture* XXXIII (1959): 50–70.

Azad, Muhammad Husain. *Darbar-e akbari* (Court of Akbar). Lahore: Kapur art printing works, 1910.

Bachelard, Gaston. *La Poétique de l'espace* (1957), English tr.: *The Poetics of Space.* Boston: Beacon Press, 1994.

Bada'uni, 'Abd al-Qadir. *Muntakhab at-Tavarikh,* 3 vols. Persian text ed. M.A. Ali. Calcutta: Royal Asiatic Society of Bengal, 1869. Trans. G.S.A. Ranking (Vol. 1), W.H. Lowe (Vol. 2), and T.W. Haig (Vol. 3). 1898–99; rpt. Delhi: Idarah-i Adabiyat-i Delli, 1973.

Bapsi Sidhwa, ed. *Beloved City: Writings on Lahore.* Karachi: Oxford University Press, 2005.

Bapsi Sidhwa. *Ice-Candy-Man.* London: Heinemann, 1988.

Baqir, Muhammad. *Lahore, Past and Present: Being an Account of Lahore Compiled From Original Sources.* Lahore: Punjab University Press, 1952.

Bernier, Francois. *Travels in the Mogul Empire: A.D. 1656–1668.* Trans. A. Constable. 1914; rpt. Delhi: S. Chand & Co., 1979.

Blavatsky, H.P. *The Durbar in Lahore*-http://www.scribd.com/doc/21184316/The-Durbar-in-Lahore-Blavatsky.

Borges, Jorge Luis. *Collected Fictions.* Translated by Andrew Hurley. NY: Penguin Books, 1999.

Brand, Michael. 'Surveying Shahdara'. In *The Mughal Garden.* Edited by Hussain et al., pp. 123–8.

Brand, Michael. 'The Shahdara Gardens of Lahore'. In *Mughal Gardens.* Ed. Wescoat and Wolschke-Bulmahn, pp. 189–212.

Brand, Michael. Garden, City and Empire: The Historical Geography of Mughal Lahore. Website 'Gardens of the Mughal Empire': http://mughalgardens.org/html/resources.html.

Brookes, John. *Gardens of Paradise: The History and Design of the Great Islamic Gardens.* London: Weidenfeld and Nicolson, 1987.

Brown, Loise. *The Dancing Girls of Lahore: Selling Love and Hoarding Dreams in Pakistan's Ancient Pleasure District.* New York: Fourth Estate, 2005.

Burnes, Lt. Alexander. *Travels into Bokhara: Together with a Narrative of a Voyage on the Indus.* 3 vols. Reprint. Lahore: Sang-e-Meel Publications, 2003.

Chandra, Satish. *Medieval India: from Sultanate to the Mughals.* New Delhi: Har-Anand Publications, 2000.

Chaudhry, Nazir Ahmed. *A Short History of Lahore and Some of Its Monuments.* Lahore: Sang-e-Meel Publications, 2000.

Chaudhry, Nazir Ahmed. *Anarkali: Archives and Tomb of Sahib Jamal.* Lahore: Ferozsons, 1956.

Chaudhry, Nazir Ahmed. *Lahore Fort: A Witness to History.* Lahore: Sang-e-Meel, 1999.

Chaudhry, Nazir Ahmed. *Lahore: Glimpses of a Glorious Heritage.* Lahore: Sang-e-Meel Publication, 1998.

Choonara, Samina (ed.). *'Official' Chronicle of Mayo School of Art.* Lahore: NCA Publications, 2003.

Chopra, Gulshan Lal. *A Short History of Lahore and its Monuments.* Lahore: Vanguard, 1937.

Chopra, R.M. *Great Sufi Poets of the Punjab.* Calcutta: Iran Society, 1999.

Chughtai, 'Abdullah. *Tarikhi masajid-e Lahore* (Historical Mosques of Lahore). Lahore: Kitab-khanah-e nauras, 1974.

Chughtai, Ismat. *My Friends, My Enemy. Essays, Reminiscences, Portraits.* Trans. Tahira Naqvi. New Delhi: Kali for Women, 2001.

Chughtai, Maqsood Ahmad. *Pakistan Travel Book.* Lahore: Jahangir Book Depot, 2000.

Coverley, Merlin. *Psychogeography.* London: Pocket Essentials, 2006.

Crooke, William. *The Popular Religion and Folklore of Northern India.* 2 vols. Delhi: Munshiram Manoharlal, 1968.

Cunningham, J.D. *History of the Sikhs.* New Delhi: D.K. Publishers Distributors, 1996 (reprint).

Dar, Saifur Rahman. 'Shalimar Garden'. In *Cultural Heritage of Pakistan.* Karachi: Pakistan Department of Archaeology, 1967: 35–47.

Dar, Saifur Rahman. *Historical Gardens of Lahore.* Lahore: Aziz Publishers, 1982.

Dar, Saifur Rahman. *Survey of Historical Monuments in Punjab: District Sheikhupura.* Lahore, 1987.

Dara Shikoh, Muhammad. *Safinat al-awliya* (Note-book of the saints). Urdu men tarjuma Muhammad 'Ali Lutfi. Karachi: Nafis Akademi, 1965 (1986): 128–37.

Dara Shikoh, Muhammad. *Sakinat al-awliya: ahwal wa faza'il-i Hazrat Mian Mir* (Dwellings of the saints: life and virtues of Saint Mian Mir). Urdu men tarjuma az Maqbul Beg Badahshani. Lahore: Pikijeez, 1971.

Debord, Guy. *Introduction to a Critique of Urban Geography*-http://www.bopsecrets. org/SI/urbgeog.htm.

Debord, Guy. *Psychogeographical Guide of Paris*-http://imaginarymuseum.org/LPG/ Mapsitu1.htm.

Desoulieres, Alain. 'Historical Fiction and Style: The Case of Anarkali'. In *The Annual of Urdu Studies,* 2007, vol. 22.

Dickie, James (Yacub Zaki). 'The Mughal Garden: Gateway to Paradise'. *Muqarnas* 3.

Du Jarric, Pierre. *Akbar and the Jesuits: An Account of the Jesuit Missions to the Court of Akbar.* New York: Harper & Brothers, 1926.

Dundes, Alan (ed.). *The Walled-up Wife: A Casebook.* Madison: The University of Wisconsin Press, 1996.

Eastwick, E.B. *Handbook of the Punjab, Western Rajputana, Kashmir, and Upper Sindh.* London, 1883.

Eaton, Richard. *India's Islamic Tradition: 711–1750.* New York: Oxford University Press, 2003.

Eden, Emily. *Up the Country: Letters written to her Sister from the Upper Provinces of India.* 1830; rpt. London: Virago, 2003.

Elliot, H.M. *The History of India, as Told by Its Own Historians. The Muhammadan Period.* London: Trubner Company, 1867–1877.

Eraly, Abraham. *The Last Spring: The Lives and Times of the Great Mughals.* Delhi: Viking, 1977.

Eraly, Abraham. *The Mughal Throne: The Saga of India's Great Emperors*. London: Weidenfeld & Nicolson, 2003.

Ewen, David. *Encyclopedia of the Opera: New Enlarged Edition*. New York: Hill and Wang, 1963.

Faiz Ahmed Faiz. *Zindan-namah* (Book of jail). Karachi: Maktab-e karawan, 1977.

Felix, Rev. Father. 'Jesuit Missions in Lahore'. In selections from the *Journal of the Punjab Historical Society*, I, pp. 83–127, ed. by Zulfiqar Ahmad. Lahore: Sang-e-Meel Publications, 1982.

Ferishta, Mahomed Kasim. *History of the Rise of the Mahomedan Power in India*. Trans. John Briggs. 4 vols. Lahore: Sang-e-Meel, 1977.

Fisher, Michael Herbert. *Visions of Mughal India: An Anthology of European Travel Writings*. London: I.B. Tauris, 2007.

Foltz, Richard. *Mughal India and Central Asia*. Karachi: Oxford University Press, 1998.

Forster, G. *Journey from Bengal to England*. New Delhi: Munshiram Manoharlal Publishers, 1997.

Foster, William (ed.). *Early Travels in India, 1583–1619*. 1921; rpt. Delhi: Oriental Books Reprint Corporation, 1985.

Garrett, H.L.O. *The Punjab a Hundred Years Ago as Described by V. Jacquemont and A. Soltykoff*. Lahore: Sang-e-Meel, 1997.

Gilmore Hankey Kirke, Ltd. *The Walled City of Lahore, Endemic Failure in Traditional Buildings*. Lahore: for the Lahore Development Authority, 1986.

Glover, William. *Making Lahore Modern: Constructing and Imagining a Colonial City*. Minneapolis: University of Minneapolis Press, 2008.

Golombek, Lisa. 'From Tamerlane to the Taj Mahal'. In *Essays in Islamic Art and Architecture*. Ed. Abbas Daneshvari. Malibu: Undena Publications, 1981.

Goulding, H.R. *Old Lahore: Reminiscences of a Resident*. Lahore: Civil and Military Gazette Printing, 1924.

Grewal, J.S. & Banga, Indu (eds.). *Early Nineteenth Century Panjab: From Ganesh Das's Char Bagh-i-Panjab*. Amritsar: Department of History, Guru Nanak University, 1975.

Grey, C. 'The Story of Anarkali'. *Journal of the Punjab Historical Society* III (1934), pp. 76–80.

Gulbadan Bano. *Humayun Nama*. Trans. Annette S. Beveridge. New Delhi: Goodword Books, 2001.

Gulzar, G.N. and S. Chatterjee (eds.). *Encyclopedia of Hindi Cinema*. Delhi-Mumbai, 2003.

Gupta, S.N. *Catalogue of Paintings in the Central Museum, Lahore*. Calcutta: Baptist mission press, 1922.

Hardy, Peter. *Historians of Medieval India: Studies in Indo-Muslim Historical Writing*. 1962; rpt. Westport, Connecticut: Greenwood Press, 1982.

Hasan, Masoodul. *Data Ganj Bakhsh*. Lahore: Ferozsons, 1972

Herbert, Thomas Sir. *A Relation of Some Yeares Travaile into Afrique Asia, Indies*. New York: Da Capo Press, 1971, rpt.

Hudud al-'alam. 'The Regions of the World,' a Persian Geography A.H. *372–*A.D. *982.* Translated and explained by V. Minorsky. London: GMS, 1937.

Husain, Intizar. 'Pak teahouse: chai ki mez se footpath tak'. In *The Annual of Urdu Studies*, 2001, vol. 16.

Hussain, M., A. Rehman and J.L. Wescoat Jr. (eds.). *The Mughal Garden: Interpretation, Conservation, and Implications.* Lahore: Ferozsons, 1996.

Innes, Arthur D. and Gough, Charles. *Annexation of Punjab.* 1897; rpt. Delhi: National Book Shop, 1984.

Iqbal, Muhammad. *Kalam-e Urdu-e 'Allama Iqbal. Bang-e dara.* (Iqbal's Urdu Poetry. 'The Sound of Caravan Bell'). Mukamal aur salis farhang ke sath. Hydarabad: Khusami buk depo, n.d.

Iqbal, Muhammad. *The Secrets of the Self.* Trans. by R.A. Nicholson. Lahore: Farhan Publishers, 1977.

Ishtiaq Khan, Muhammad. *World Heritage Sites in Pakistan.* Islamabad: UNESCO, 2000.

Jahangir, Nur ad-Din Muhammad. *Jahangirnama.* Trans. Wheeler M. Thackston. Seattle and Washington, DC: University of Washington Press and Arthur M. Sackler Gallery, 2000.

Jahangir, Nur ad-Din Muhammad. *Tuzuk-i Jahangiri.* Trans. A. Rogers, ed. H. Beveridge. 1909–14; rpt. Delhi: Munshiram Manoharlal, 1968.

Jairazbhoy, R.A. 'Early Garden-Palaces of the Great Mughals'. *Oriental Art* IV, 2 (1958): 68–75.

Joardar, B. *Prostitution in Nineteenth and Early Twentieth Century Calcutta.* Delhi: Inter-India Publications, 1985.

Kapur, Promilla. *The Life and World of Call-girls in India.* Delhi: Vikas, 1978.

Kausar, Sajjad, Michael Brand and James L. Wescoat, Jr. *Shalamar Garden: Landscape, Form and Meaning.* Karachi: Pakistan Department of Archaeology, 1990.

Kausar, Sajjad. 'Shalamar Garden, Lahore'. In *The Mughal Garden.* Ed. Hussain et al., pp. 133–42.

Kerr, Robert. *A General History and Collection of Voyages and Travels.* Vol. 8. Project Gutenberg: http://www.gutenberg.org/ebooks/html.

Khan, Ahmad Nabi. 'Lahore under the Rule of Babur and Humayun: A Reappraisal'. *Pakistan Journal of History and Culture* III (1982): 74–91.

Khan, Ahmad Nabi. 'Lahore: the Darus Saltanat of the Moghul Empire under Akbar (1556–1605)'. *Journal of the Research Society of Pakistan* XXI, no. 3 (1984), pp. 1–22.

Khan, Ahmad Nabi. 'The Hiran Minar'. *Pakistan Archaeology*, VI (1969).

Khan, Khalil Ahmad. *Union Catalogue of Books on Architecture Available in the Libraries of Lahore.* Lahore: National College of Art, 1981.

Khan, Muhammad Walliullah. *Lahore and its Important Monuments.* Lahore: Pakistan Department of Archaeology, 1959.

Khokar, Massood ul-Hassan. 'Tomb of Sharaf un-Nisa Begum Known as the Sarvwala Maqbara at Lahore'. *Pakistan Journal of History and Culture* III (1982): 111–16.

Khosla, B.P. *The City Guide Lahore*. Lahore: Ferozsons, 1932.

Kipling, J.L. & Thornton, T.H. *Lahore As It Was*. Travelogue, 1860, reprint. Lahore: NCA Publications, 2002.

Kipling, R. Kim.-http://www.gutenberg.org/etext/2226.

Kipling, R. *Something of myself and other autobiographical writings*. Cambridge University Press, 1990.

Koch, Ebba. 'Mughal Palace Gardens from Babur to Shah Jahan'. *Muqarnas* 14 (1997): 143–65.

Koch, Ebba. 'The Char Bagh Conquers the Citadel: An Outline of the Development of the Mughal Palace Garden'. In *The Mughal Garden*. Ed. Hussain et al., pp. 55–60.

Koch, Ebba. 'The Mughal Waterfront Garden'. In *Gardens in the Time of the Great Muslim Empires*. Ed. A. Petruccioli, Leiden, New York: E.J.Brill. 1997, pp. 140–60.

Lal, Rai Bahadur Kanhaya. *Tarikh-e Lahaur* (A History of Lahore). Lahore: Majlis-e taraqqi-e adab, 1987, rpt.

Lal, Rai Bahadur Kanhaya. *Tarikh-e Punjab* (A History of the Punjab). Lahore: Majlis-e taraqqi-e adab, 1981, rpt.

Lari, Y. *Lahore—Illustrated City Guide*. Karachi: Heritage Foundation Pakistan 2003.

Latif, Malik. *Awliya-e Lahaur* (Saints of Lahore). Lahore: Sang-e-Meel, 1999.

Latif, Syad Muhammmad. *History of the Punjab (from 1792 to 1849)*. Lahore: 1916.

Latif, Syad Muhammmad. *Lahore: History, Architectural Remains and Antiquities*. Lahore: New Imperial Press, 1892; rpt. Lahore: Sang-e-Meel Publications, 1994.

Macdougall, Elizabeth B. and Ettinghausen, Richard (eds.). *The Islamic Garden*. Washington, DC: Dumbarton Oaks, 1976.

Maclagan, E.D. 'The Earliest English Visitors to the Punjab 1585–1627'. In selections from *Journal of the Punjab Historical Society*, II, 9–34. Zulfiqar Ahmad (ed.) Lahore: Sang-e-Meel Publications, 1982.

Mahmud, Muhammad Khalid. 'The Mausoleum of Emperor Jahangir'. *Arts of Asia*. Jan–Feb (1983), pp. 57–66.

Manrique, Fray Sebastien. *Travels of Fray Sebastian Manrique: 1629–1643*. 2 vols. Trans. C.E. Luard. Oxford: Hakluyt Society, 1927.

Moore, Thomas. *Lalla Rookh: an Oriental Romance*. London: Darf, 1986

Mumtaz, Kamil Khan. 'The Walled City of Lahore: Directions for Rehabilitation'. In *Conservation as Cultural Survival*. Ed. Renata Holod. Philadelphia: The Aga Khan Award for Architecture, 1980.

Mumtaz, Kamil Khan. *Architecture in Pakistan*. Singapore: Mimar, 1985.

Mumtaz, Kamil Khan. *Modernity and Tradition: Contemporary Architecture in Pakistan*. Karachi: Oxford University Press, 2000.

Nadiem, Ihsan H. *Gardens of Mughal Lahore*. Lahore: Sang-e-Meel, 2005.

Naeem Mir, M. Hussain, and James L. Wescoat Jr. *Mughal Gardens in Lahore: History and Documentation*. Lahore: Department of Architecture, Lahore University of Engineering and Technology, 1996.

Nevile, Pran. *Lahore: A Sentimental Journey*. New Delhi: Penguin Books, 2006.

Newell, H.A. *Lahore—Capital of the Punjab*. Lahore: Guide Books, 1917.

Nijjar, Bakhshish Singh. *Punjab under the Great Mughals*. Bombay: Thacker & Co., 1968.

Noe, Samuel V. 'Old Lahore and Old Delhi: Variations on a Mughal Theme'. *Ekistics* XLIX (1982), pp. 306–19.

Orlich, Capt. Leopold von. *Travels in India including Sindh and the Punjab*. 2 vols. Trans. H. Evans Lloyd. London: 1845.

Osborne, W.G. *The Court and Camp of Runjeet Singh*. 1840; rpt. Karachi: Oxford University Press, 1973.

Otis Skinner, Cornelia. *Elegant Wits and Grand Horizontals*. New York: Houghton Miffin, 1962.

Pamuk, Orhan. *Istanbul: Memories and the City*. New York: Vintage Books, 2006.

Patras Bukhari. *Lahaur ka jughrafia* (Geography of Lahore). In *Patras ke Mazamin*. Karachi: Fazli Sanz, 2003.

Petersen, Andrew. *Dictionary of Islamic Architecture*. London: Routledge, 1996.

Petruccioli, Attilio (ed.). *Gardens in the Time of the Great Muslim Empires: Theory and Design*. Special issue of *Muqarnas*. Leiden, New York: E.J. Brill, 1997.

Punekar, S.D. and Rao, Kamala. *A Study of Prostitutes in Bombay*. Bombay: Lalvani Publishing House, 1967.

Qadir, Muhammad. *Lahore: Urban Development in the Third World*. Lahore: Ferozsons, 1983

Quraishi, Samina. *Lahore, the City Within*. Singapore: Concept Media, 1988.

Rajput A.B. *Architecture in Pakistan*. Karachi: Pakistan Publications, 1963.

Ramakrishna, Lajwanti. *Panjabi Sufi Poets*, A.D. *1460–1900*. Calcutta: Oxford University Press, 1978.

Rehman, Abdul. 'Garden Types in Mughal Lahore according to Early-Seventeenth Century Written and Visual Sources'. In *Gardens in the Great Muslim Empires*. Ed. Petruccioli, pp. 161–72.

Rehman, Abdul. *Historic Towns of Punjab: Ancient and Medieval Period*. Lahore: Ferozsons, 1997.

Saeed, Fouzia. *Taboo! The Hidden Culture of a Red Light Area*. Karachi: Oxford University Press, 2002.

Saleh Kanbuh, Muhammad. *Shah Jahan Namah*. Mutarjim Mumtaz Liaqat. Lahore: Sang-e-Meel, 2004.

Sarkar, K.M. *The Grand Trunk Road in the Punjab*. Lahore: Punjab Government Record Office Publications, 1926.

Schimmel, Annemarie. *The Empire of the Great Mughals: History, Art, and Culture*. Lahore: Sang-e-Meel, 2005.

Shafi, Maulvi Muhammad. 'The Shalimar Gardens of Lahore'. *Islamic Culture* 1: 1927: 59ff.

Shahzad, Ghafir. *Lahaur ke manar* (Minarets of Lahore). Lahore: Idraq Publications, 2001.

Sikander, Sattar. 'The Shalamar: A Typical Muslim Garden'. In *Environmental Design* 2 (1986): pp. 24–29.

Singh, Bhagwan. 'Shalamar, not Shalimar'. *The Tribune*, Chandigarh, 09.12.2001.

Singh, Chetan. 'Centre and Periphery in the Mughal State: The Case of Seventeenth Century Panjab'. *Modern Asian Studies* 22, 2 (1988): 299–318.

Stierstorfer, Klaus (ed.). *Women Writing Home, 1700–1920: Female Correspondence across the British Empire.* 6 vols. London: Pickering & Chatto Publishers, 2000.

Sultana, Salma. 'Architecture of Sheikhupura Fort in Historic Perspective'. *South Asian Studies*, vol. 5 (1989): 103–17.

Suroor, Mirza Rajab 'Ali Baig. *Fasana-e ajaib* (The Enchanting Story). Lahore: Sang-e-Meel, 2009.

Suvorova, Anna. *Masnavi: A Study of Urdu Romance.* Karachi: Oxford University Press, 2000.

Suvorova, Anna. *Muslim Saints of South Asia: The Eleventh to Fifteenth Centuries.* London, New York: RoutledgeCurzon, 2004.

Taj, Imtiaz 'Ali. *Anarkali.* Bhopal: Bhopal Buk haus, 1977.

Tavernier, J.B. *Travels in India.* 2 vols. Trans. V. Ball and ed. W. Crooke. 1925; rpt. Delhi: Oriental Books Reprint Corporation, 1977.

Taylor, Brian. 'The Walled City'. In *MIMAR 24: Architecture in Development.* Singapore: Concept Media Ltd., 1987.

Temple, Richard. *The Legends of the Punjab.* 2 vols. Islamabad: Institute of Folk Heritage, 1981 reprint.

Thompson, J.P. 'The Tomb of Jahangir'. *Journal of the Punjab Historical Society*, no. 1 (1911): 31–49.

Thomson, James. *The City of Dreadful Night.* London: Watts & Co., 1932.

Vandal, Pervez and Sajida. *The Raj, Lahore and Bhai Ram Singh.* Lahore: NCA, 2006.

Villiers-Stuart, C.M. *Gardens of the Great Mughals.* London: A. & C. Black, 1913, reprint, Asian Educational Service, 2005.

Vogel, J. Ph. 'The Shalamar Bagh of Lahore in 1712'. In extracts from *Journal of the Punjab Historical Society*, Vol. I, p. 217. Zulfiqar Ahmad (ed.) Lahore: Sang-e-Meel Publications, 1982.

Vogel, J. Ph. *Tile Mosaics of the Lahore Fort.* 1920, rpt. Karachi: Pakistan Publications, n.d.

Wescoat, James L. Jr. 'From the Gardens of the Qur'an to the Gardens of Lahore'. *Landscape Research* 20 (1995): 19–29.

Wescoat, James L. Jr. 'Gardens of Conquest and Transformation: Lessons from the Earliest Mughal Gardens in India'. *Landscape Journal* 10:2 (1991): 105–14.

Wescoat, James L. Jr. 'Gardens of Invention and Exile: The Precarious Context of Mughal Garden Design during the Reign of Humayun (1530–1556)'. *Journal of Garden History* 10: 106–116, 1990.

Wescoat, James L. Jr. 'Gardens vs. Citadels: The Territorial Context of Early Mughal Gardens'. In *Garden History: Issues, Approaches, Methods,* pp. 331–58. Ed. J.D. Hunt. Washington, D.C.: Dumbarton Oaks, 1992.

Wescoat, James L. Jr. 'Introduction: The Mughal Gardens Project in Lahore'. In *The Mughal Garden*. Ed. Hussain et al., pp. 9–22.

Wescoat, James L. Jr. 'Lahore'. *The Dictionary of Art*. Macmillan Publishers, 1995.

Wescoat, James L. Jr. 'Ritual Movement and Territoriality during the Reign of Humayun'. *Environmental Design: Journal of the Islamic Environmental Design Center*. 1–2 (1991): 56–63, p. 59.

Wescoat, James L. Jr. and Joachim Wolschke-Bulmahn (eds.). *Mughal Gardens: Sources, Places, Representations, and Prospects*. Washington: Dumbarton Oaks, 1996.

Wescoat, James L. Jr. and Joachim Wolschke-Bulmahn. 'The Mughal Gardens of Lahore: History, Geography and Conservation Issues'. *Die Gartenkunst* 6 (1994): 19–33.

Wescoat, James L. Jr., Michael Brand, and Naeem Mir. 'The Shahdara Gardens of Lahore: Site Documentation and Spatial Analysis'. *Pakistan Archaeology* 25 (1993): 33–42.

Yi-Fu Tuan. *Topophilia: A Study of Environmental Perception, Attitudes, and Values*. Englewood Cliffs, NJ: Prentice-Hall, 1974.

Zaman, Fakhar (ed.). *Pakistan ke Sufi sho'ara* (Sufi Poets of Pakistan). Islamabad: Akadami-e adabiyat-e Pakistan, 1995.

INDEX

A

'Abdul Hamid Lahori, 70, 71, 88, 91
'Abdul Qadir Jilani, 54, 70
Ackroyd, Peter, 13, 14
Ahmad, Bashir, 201
Ahmad, Salahuddin, 207
Aibak, Qutub-ud-Din, 33, 34, 40, 65, 221
Akbar, Jalaluddin Muhammad, 32, 34,
    35, 39, 41, 42, 43, 51, 77, 81, 86, 87,
    101, 113, 114, 115, 116, 118, 119,
    120, 125, 127, 128, 129, 165, 214
'Ala ul-Mulk, Mullah, 97
'Alamgir II, 54
Albert Victor, Duke of Clarence, 183
al-Biruni, Abu Rayhan, 30
Alexander the Great, 30
al-Hujwiri, Abul Hasan 'Ali (*see* Data
    Ganj Bakhsh), 30, 42, 68, 69, 73
'Ali, Caliph, 54
'Ali, Shakir, 201
Allami, Abul Fazl, 119, 120
Amir Khusrau, 31, 83, 140
Amrohi, Kamal, 155
Anarkali, Sharafunnisa Nadira, 113, 114,
    115, 116, 117, 118, 119, 120, 121,
    122, 123, 124, 125, 126, 128, 129,
    130, 131, 202, 213
Anjali Devi, 124
Arjun Dev, Guru, 33, 63, 71, 72, 212
Asif, Akbar, 130
Asif, Karim, 124, 125, 128, 130
Auckland, George Eden, 173

Aurangzeb 'Alamgir, Muhyuddin, 25, 28,
    38, 41, 53, 54, 73, 81, 85, 87, 88,
    92, 102, 118, 163, 164
Azad, Muhammad Husain, 188
Azmi, Kaifi, 155

B

Bab (Sayyid 'Ali Muhammad Shirazi), 36
Baba Farid (Fariduddin Masud), 68
Baba Shah Jamal, 73
Babur, Zahiruddin, 26, 52, 66, 78, 101,
    221
Bachelard, Gaston, 6, 7
Badayuni, Shakeel, 126
Bahadur Shah I (*see* Shah 'Alam), 41,
    43, 92
Bahauddin Zakariya Multani, 68
Bahu, Sultan, 68, 141
Baig, Rizwan, 130
Bakhtin, Mikhail, 143
Balban, Ghiyasuddin, 34
Balzac, Honoré, 13
Baqir, Muhammad, 120
Barani, Ziauddin, 34
Barr, William, 101
Barthold, Vassily, 28
Baudelaire, Charles, 13, 137
Beg, Mirza Sultan, 58
Benjamin, Walter, 14, 16
Bernier, Francois, 54, 165
Bhangi, Hari Singh, 181
Bhutto, Zulfikar 'Ali, 65, 204

Bibi Pakdaman, 73
Bilawal, Sheikh, 71
Bizet, Georges, 167
Blake, William, 13
Blavatsky, Helena, 172
Boehm, Edgar, 205
Borges, Jorge Luis, 186, 187, 188, 189
Bourke, Richard (Earl of Mayo), 199
Brand, Michael, 92
Brangwyn, Frank, 180
Brunton, William, 185
Buddhu (potter), 65
Bukhari, Patras, 21, 25, 26, 28, 40
Bulleh Shah, 68, 94, 141
Burnes, Alexander, 30
Byron, George Gordon, 167

C

Callot, Jacques, 14
Carné, Marcel, 124
Chaghatai, Muhammad Sultan, 185
Chand Kaur, Maharani, 56
Chaudhri, R.S., 124
Chhajju Bhagat, 74
Chishti, Ghulam Ahmed, 151
Chishti, Khwaja Mu'inuddin, 68
Choudhri, Mohkam Din, 40
Chughtai, 'Abdur Rahman, 122, 123, 201
Chughtai, Ismat, 135, 136
Cimarosa, Domenico, 167
Coverley, Merlin, 12
Curzon, Lord George, 84
Cyrus the Great, 81

D

Dada, Nayyar 'Ali, 215
Dadu Dayal, 74
Dai Anga (Sharafunnisa), 58, 65, 100
Danial (prince), 117, 119
Data Ganj Bakhsh (see al-Hujwiri, Abul Hasan 'Ali), 30, 42

Daumier, Honoré, 14
David, Félicien, 167
Debord, Guy, 11, 12
Delibes, Léo, 167
Devika Rani, 129
Dhoni Chand, 198
Dickens, Charles, 9, 13, 175
Dietrich, Marlene, 157
Doré, Gustav, 179, 180
Dostoyevsky, Fyodor, 9
Durrani, Ahmad Shah, 26, 63, 181

E

Eastwick, E.B., 122
Eden, Emily, 90, 173
Edward VII, 205
Emis (general), 121
Eraly, Abraham, 119

F

Faisal, king of Saudi Arabia, 204
Faiz, Faiz Ahmed, 16, 139, 189, 190, 191, 192, 224
Faraz, Ahmad, 139
Fathulla Shah, Mullah, 73
Fatimah, the daughter of the Prophet [PBUH], 54, 141
Finch, William, 34, 118, 119, 120, 198
Firishta, Muhammad Qasim Hindu Shah, 79
Flaubert, Gustav, 15

G

Gallet, Louis, 168
Ganga Ram, 198, 200, 202
Gautier, Théophile, 15
Geddes, Patrick, 10
George V., 205, 215
Ghalib, Mirza, 103
Ghani, Shah 'Abdul, 73, 101
Ghaus, Muhammad, 38, 73

Ghaznavi, Mahmud, 26, 29, 31, 168, 221
Ghore Shah, 74
Ghulam Rasul, 198
Ghuri, Shahabuddin, 26
Gilyarovsky, Vladimir, 13
Glinka, Mikhail, 170
Goulding, H.R., Colonel, 208, 210
Gounod, Charles, 167
Guerlain, Jean-Paul, 90
Gul Begum, 157
Gulbadan Begum, 78

H

Hakim (prince), 117
Hamsun, Knut, 18
Haqiqat Rai Puri, 141
Har Gobind, Guru, 72
Herbert, Thomas, 27, 28
Hogarth, William, 14
Hoppner, John, 165
Humayun, Nasiruddin, 51, 77, 78, 85, 88, 221
Hunter, Alexander, 199
Husain, Imam, 54, 178
Hussain, Intizar, 16, 137, 139, 206
Hussain, Iqbal, 147, 148, 154, 160
Husserl, Edmund, 3, 4, 6

I

I'timad-ud-Daula, 51, 67
Iltutmish (sultan), 33
'Imadulmulk (vizier), 63
Iqbal Bano, 151
Iqbal, Muhammad, 16, 41, 69, 70, 99, 189, 190, 192, 224

J

Jahanara (Begum Sahib), 95
Jahangir, Nuruddin (see Salim), 32, 34, 38, 51, 52, 59, 66, 67, 70, 71, 72, 81, 85, 86, 87, 88, 89, 92, 99, 101, 102, 113, 114, 115, 116, 117, 118, 119, 120, 121, 123, 124, 125, 127, 128, 129, 165, 190, 196, 214
Jan Muhammad, 198
Jaswantlal, Nandalal, 124
Jaypala (king), 32
Jeejebhoy, Jamshetji, 199
Jilani, Sayyid Badruddin, 213
Jindan, Maharani, 64
Jinnah, Muhammad 'Ali, 195
Jodha Bai, Rani, 123, 125
Joyce, James, 4

K

Kaki, Qutub-ud-Din Bakhtiyar, 140
Kalu Ram, 141
Kamal Pasha, Anwar, 124
Kamran, Mirza, 101
Kanbuh, 'Inayatullah, 65
Kanbuh, Muhammad Saleh, 58, 65, 66, 70, 91, 202
Kanhaya Lal, Rai Bahadur, 200, 213
Kapoor, Prithviraj, 125, 127
Khah-i-Khanan (Zafar Jung Kokaltash), 65
Khan, 'Ali Mardan, 65, 92, 100, 165
Khan, 'Inayat, 94
Khan, Adham, 117
Khan, Asaf, 66, 85, 101
Khan, Ayub, 93, 140
Khan, Genghis, 26, 39
Khan, Hakim 'Ilmuddin Ansari Wazir, 58, 201, 202
Khan, Khafi, 92
Khan, Khalilullah, 92
Khan, Muhammad Qasim, 213, 214
Khan, Nawab Bhikari, 63
Khan, Nawab Khan Bahadur, 112
Khan, Shah Wali, 181, 182
Khan, Ustad Bade Ghulam 'Ali, 126, 151, 160
Khan, Zakariya, 141

Khizr, Khwaja, 38, 39
Khosrow (prince), 72, 88, 118
Khurram (prince; *see* Shah Jahan), 28, 32, 51, 52, 53, 55, 65, 66, 71, 87, 92, 93, 95, 100, 102, 118, 213, 214
Khwaja Dost Munshi, 77
Khwaja Ubaid, 181
Kipling, John Lockwood, 60, 135, 174, 183, 199, 200, 201, 207, 210
Kipling, Rudyard, 1, 9, 16, 18, 31, 37, 38, 66, 173, 174, 175, 176, 178, 179, 180, 182, 184, 185, 186, 188, 189, 190, 192
Koka, Fidai Khan, 54, 102
Koka, Zain Khan, 120
Kumar, Ashok, 155
Kumar, Dilip, 125, 127, 128, 129
Kumar, Kishore, 129
Kumar, Pradeep, 124
Kumar, Raj, 155, 156
Kumari, Meena, 124, 155
Kurbsky, Andrei, 112

L

Ladli Begum, 66, 101
Latif, Syad Muhammad, 17, 213, 214
Lawrence, Henry, 121, 195, 196
Lawrence, John, 195, 196, 205, 206, 207
Le Corbusier, Charles-Édouard Jeanneret, 215
Lean, David, 127
Lefebvre, Henri, 10
Lutyens, Edwin, 102

M

Macgregor, George, 62
Mackennal, Edgar, 203
Madho Lal Husain (*see* Shah Husain), 50, 68, 69, 73, 87, 101, 141, 191, 224
Madhubala (Mumtaz Jahan), 125, 128, 129
Madini, Muhammad Hayat, 92

Maham Anga, 117
Majithia, Dayal Singh, 198
Malik Ayaz, 29, 33, 40, 42
Malika az-Zamani (Badshah Begum), 54
Malika Pukhraj, 151
Man Bai, 120
Mangeshkar, Lata, 126, 125
Manrique, Fray Sebastian, 32
Mansel, Charles, 195
Mansoor, Shoaib, 130
Manto, Saadat Hasan, 16, 137, 139, 189, 202
Mariam Zamani (Hira Kumari), 38, 43, 59
Mary (queen), 215
Massenet, Jules, 167, 168, 170, 172
McLeod, Donald, 206
Memon, Muhammad Umar, 139
Meyerbeer, Giacomo, 167
Mian Mir, 50, 54, 65, 68, 69, 70, 71, 72, 73, 74, 87, 99, 120, 141
Milton, John, 32, 163
Minorsky, Vladimir, 28
Mir Amman, 79
Mir Hasan Ali, Mrs, 173
Mir Mannu, 63
Miraji, 139
Miran Badshah (Sayyid Ishaq Gazeruni), 62
Montgomery, Robert, 195, 207, 213
Moorcroft, William, 35
Moore, Thomas, 16, 89, 90, 163, 164, 165, 166, 167, 170, 171, 188
Moti Ram, 46
Mozart, Wolfgang Amadeus, 167
Mu'min 'Ishaqbaz, 88
Muhammad [PBUH], the Prophet of Islam, 54, 70, 141
Muhammad Shah, 54
Mullah Shah, 99
Mumford, Lewis, 10
Mumtaz Mahal, 58, 95
Mumtaz, Kamil Khan, 24, 50, 57, 58, 67
Murad Bakhsh (prince), 118

Murad Begum, 63
Musa (prophet), 38

N

Nadir Shah, 26
Nadira Begum, 65, 99
Naheed, Kishwar, 192
Napier, Charles James, 195, 196
Nasim, Dayashankar, 79
Naushad, 'Ali, 126, 155
Nazar, Qayum, 139
Nedou, Michael Adam, 210
Nerval, Gerard de, 15
Nevile, Pran, 135, 192
Niyazi, Munir, 139, 192
Nizami, Hasan, 33, 35
Nizamuddin Awlia, 140
Nur Jahan (empress), 27, 66, 67, 89,
    101, 115, 124, 130
Nur Jahan (singer), 124, 151

P

Pamuk, Orhan, 14, 15
Parks, Fanny, 173
Parvez (prince), 120
Phalke, Dadasaheb, 123
Pir Makki, 73
Poe, Edgar Allan, 13
Proust, Marcel, 3, 7, 18, 225
Ptolemy, Claudius, 17, 30, 32

Q

Qadeer, Muhammad, 23
Qalandar, Lal Shahbaz, 68
Qasim, Muhammad bin, 32, 92
Quincey, Thomas de, 13, 175
Quraishi, Samina, 138

R

Rafi, Mohammed, 126

Rai, Lala Lajpat, 203
Rashid al-Din (historian), 31
Roberts, Julia, 157
Roy, Bimal, 128
Roy, Bina, 124
Roy, Prafulla, 124
Rubinstein, Anton, 170, 171
Ruskin, John, 225
Ruswa, Mirza Muhammad Hadi, 155

S

Sa'di, Abu Muhammad Muslih al-Din
    bin Abdallah Shirazi, 80
Sabuktigin, 29, 33
Salim, prince (*see* Jahangir), 32, 34, 38,
    51, 52, 59, 66, 67, 70, 71, 72, 81,
    85, 86, 87, 88, 89, 92, 99, 101, 102,
    113, 114, 115, 116, 117, 118, 119,
    120, 121, 123, 124, 125, 127, 128,
    129, 165, 190, 196, 214
Scott, Jonathan, 165
Selznick, David, 124
Shabistari, Mahmud, 79
Shah 'Alam (*see* Bahadur Shah I), 41,
    43, 92
Shah Husain (*see* Madho Lal Husain),
    50, 68, 69, 73, 87, 101, 141, 191,
    224
Shah Jahan, Shahabuddin (*see* Khurram),
    28, 32, 51, 52, 53, 55, 65, 66, 71,
    87, 92, 93, 95, 100, 102, 118, 213,
    214
Shah Murad, 117
Shakespeare, William, 188
Shamshad Begum, 126
Sharafunnisa Begum, 65, 100, 112
Sharif, Hajji Muhammad, 122, 201
Sharif, Nawaz, 69
Sharif, Omar, 127
Shattari, Muhammad Ghausi, 79
Shikoh, Dara, 39, 54, 65, 68, 69, 72, 73,
    87, 88, 99, 118, 120, 140
Shuja, Sultan, 118

Shujaullah, Sheikh, 201
Sidhwa, Bapsi, 17, 137, 150, 204
Simpson, William, 42
Sinclair, Iain, 13
Singh, Bhai Ram, 183, 200, 201, 203
Singh, Gujjar, 97
Singh, Hira (nazim), 148
Singh, Hira (vizier), 56
Singh, Kharak, 38, 121
Singh, Khushal, 212, 214
Singh, Lahna, 97
Singh, Nau Nihal, 38, 212
Singh, Raja Dhyan, 212
Singh, Raja Man, 114, 123
Singh, Ranjit, 33, 35, 38, 39, 40, 43, 54,
  56, 63, 64, 74, 97, 98, 99, 121, 157,
  178, 181, 203, 212, 221
Singh, Sardar Maha, 54
Singh, Sher, 56, 120
Singh, Sobha, 97
Sirajuddin, Professor, 206, 207
Smith, Bosworth, 195
Soltykoff, Alexy, 98, 120, 165, 166
Spontini, Gaspare, 167, 168, 172
Stone, Edward Durell, 215
Sue, Eugene, 9
Sullivan, Basil, 203, 204, 215
Sulochana (Ruby Myers), 124
Sultan, Sheikh, 62
Sultanpuri, Majrooh, 155
Sumbeka (Söyembikä), 112
Suri, Sher Shah, 26, 77
Suroor, Rajab Ali Beg, 150
Syad Suf, 62

T

Taj, Imtiaz 'Ali, 123
Tavernier, Jean Baptista, 27, 28
Tchaikovsky, Pyotr, 167
Terry, Edward, 119, 120
Thomson, James, 178, 179
Thornton, Thomas, 66, 135, 196, 210
Timur, 26, 54, 77

Tolstoy, Leo, 170, 171, 172
Toulouse-Lautrec, Henri, 147
Tumansky, A., 28

U

'Umar, Caliph, 70

V

Ventura (general), 121
Verdi, Giuseppe, 167
Victoria (queen), 183, 203
Villiers-Stuart, Constance Mary, 102
Vortigern (king of England), 107

W

Wade, Colonel, 101
Weeks, Edwin Lord, 214
Wescoat, James, 78
Wilber, Donald, 82
Wilde, Oscar, 105
Woolner, Alfred, 203
Wright, Frank Lloyd, 215

X

Xavier, Father, 88
Xuanzang, 30

Y

Yi-Fu Tuan, 1, 2, 6, 36
Yusuf, Mian Muhammad, 93

Z

Zaki (martyr), 39, 43
Zanjani, Miran Husain, 73
Zebunnisa (Makhfi), 65, 85, 96
Zia-ul-Haq, 140, 152, 153
Zinatunnisa (princess), 58